eli's
story

Eli's Story

A Twentieth-Century Jewish Life

Meri-Jane Rochelson

Interviews with Eli G. Rochelson
by Burton L. Rochelson

Wayne State University Press
Detroit

Library of Congress Cataloging Number: 2018933409

ISBN 978-0-8143-4021-9 (paperback)
ISBN 978-0-8143-4494-1 (case)
ISBN 978-0-8143-4022-6 (ebook)

Wayne State University Press
Leonard N. Simons Building
4809 Woodward Avenue
Detroit, Michigan 48201-1309

Visit us online at wsupress.wayne.edu

For David, Danny, Ellis, Serafima, Jordan,
Sam, Karl, and Jack
and all who are yet to be

And in memory of
Borya

Contents

Preface and Acknowledgments

THIS BOOK, THE life story of Eli G. Rochelson (1907–1984), takes as its starting point the story as he told it himself in interviews forty years ago with his son, my brother, Burton L. Rochelson. Since then, a great many interviews have been done by Holocaust survivors, and a great many books have been written. Each narrative adds something to the historical record and keeps the details of experience alive. *Eli's Story* begins long before the Holocaust and ends long after, telling of a life that was more than suffering and survival. In the Introduction that follows, I describe the reasons for some of the choices I have made. Here, I wish to thank all those who made the book itself possible. This was a very large group, and I hope that anyone I may have omitted will forgive me.

This book was many years in the making, beginning with the interviews done by Burt. Indeed, Burt has been a partner in this enterprise from the start, and it is not only because of the interviews that I could not have done the book without him. My work on the manuscript began in earnest in 2010, after our mother died and Burt and I went through the many papers that she, our father, and other relatives had amassed. Thus, I owe a deep debt of gratitude to Pearl and Eli Rochelson themselves, and to Ida and David Robinson, Eli's sister-in-law and brother in the United States, who recognized that photographs and documents needed to be preserved. In the seven years I have been at work on *Eli's Story*, Burt and I have gone through and shared many of those items together; he has reviewed drafts;

and we have discussed and occasionally argued. Most importantly, Burt has encouraged me throughout this lengthy and complex task. The book belongs to us both.

Of course, the book would not have appeared without valued support from institutions and other individuals. I am grateful to Targum Shlishi, a Raquel and Aryeh Rubin Foundation, for a grant that enabled me to travel to do research at libraries and archives. I am also indebted to the extraordinary librarians, archivists, and other staff at those institutions. These include Gunnar Berg, archivist at the YIVO Institute for Jewish Research; Megan Lewis, Vincent Slatt, Elliott Wrenn, and Ron Coleman, librarians at the United States Holocaust Memorial Museum (USHMM); Anne-Marie Belinfante, specialist in the Dorot Division of the New York Public Library; the staff of the United Nations Relief and Rehabilitation Administration (UNRRA) Archives in New York; the librarians and staff in the research division of Yad Vashem; and Galina Baranova, director of the Lithuanian State Archives. Sara-joelle Clark of the Survivors Registry at the USHMM long ago sent me copies of documents from the International Tracing Service held at the museum. Robert Ehrenreich had suggested not only that I get those but also that I visit and search the archives myself. He was right on both counts. I am also grateful to the staff at the International Tracing Service in Bad Arolsen, Germany, who replied to my very earliest requests for information in 1989. My warmest thanks, as well, to Robin Harp of the USHMM Photo Archives, to Emanuel Saunders of the Yad Vashem Photo Archive, to Charlotte Bonelli of the American Jewish Committee, and to Yedida Kanfer of the Jewish Family and Children's Services Holocaust Center in San Francisco for permission to reproduce or quote from materials in their collections.

I owe enormous thanks to a number of Holocaust survivors who gave of their time to talk with me personally and to give me information about their own experiences, as well as their connections to my father. These include Masha Zulzberg Lidor, Shalom Eilati, and Moshe Kravetz in Israel, and Josef Griliches, Nissan Krakinowski, Sol Lurie, Tonia Rotkopf

Blair, and Rabbi Laszlo Berkowits in the United States. I also learned a great deal in conversation with family members: Nissan Krakinowski's daughters Pessie and the late Shayndee Krakinowski Altman, and Sharon Caspi and Meirav Furth, daughter and granddaughter of Masha Lidor. I have learned, too, from the families of people that my father knew in Kovno: Lily Perry, Thelma Silber, and Janina Pace, widows of three of Eli's doctor friends, and Bella and Benny Pace; Sharon Silber, Joanne Silber Ronay, and Bobbie Silber Lamont; Cindy, Ken, and Jeff Perry; Paulina Rosenstein; and Dan A. Nabriski, children of several of the Kovno doctors.

Family genealogists, in particular Eric M. Bloch and the late George Rockson, both building upon the work of the late Francis R. (Bob) Wilson, as well as Deana Sanditen Maloney, have helped me enormously in this project. Bette Stoop Mas, a member of the LitvakSIG listserv, was exceptionally helpful in enabling me to discover a previously unknown branch of my paternal grandmother's family, and in the process she introduced me to the outstanding assistance provided by the Family History Library of Salt Lake City, operated by the Church of the Latter Day Saints. LitvakSIG, itself, has been a treasure, and I have learned an enormous amount through discussion posts and connections made through them, as well as through the Kaunas and Suwalki District Research Groups. The tireless researchers in these groups, headed by Dorothy Lievers, Eden Joachim, and Ralph Salinger, post a wealth of data to contributors before it is available on JewishGen.org, another outstanding resource of which I made extensive use. My cousin Greta Minsky expanded my knowledge of Tulsa family history and explained important connections I had not been aware of between my Rochelson family and the Fenster branch. Cousin Debi Sanditen helped me with Sanditen connections, while Nathan Bloch, grandson of Ben Bloch, helped me understand the history of the Midwestern branch of the family. On the Lubovsky side, Pierre Pizzochero provided a wealth of information on European cousins, and Bill and Sandy Esner introduced me—in a few cases, literally—to American cousins I had not known existed before. Gerald Stern, an Englishman who replied to my e-mailed request about a name in his online family tree, set in motion my reconnecting with Masha Lidor and her family.

I have gained extremely valuable scholarly advice and support from Marsha Rozenblit, as well as from Natalia Aleksiun, Oren Stier, Kenneth Waltzer, Deborah Lipstadt, Ellen Cassedy, Margaret Stetz, and a number of other scholars whose papers I have heard or whose work I have read; comments from the anonymous readers for Wayne State University Press helped me to make this a better book than it might have been. Ralph Berger, a dear friend and the coauthor of his own parents' memoir, *With Courage We Shall Fight*, inspired and encouraged me throughout this project. Renée Kaufman generously shared with me her family's story, in conversation and in the published history written by Rebecca Boehling and Uta Larkey.

Many of my colleagues at Florida International University read and commented on early versions of the narrative or assisted me in other important ways: my thanks go to Lynne Barrett, Heather Blatt, Nathaniel Cadle, Peter Craumer, Yesim Darici, Debra Dean, Vernon Dickson, Bruce Harvey, Marilyn Hoder-Salmon, Kathleen McCormack, Carmela McIntire, Asher Milbauer, Joyce Peterson, Heather Russell, Heidi Scott, Richard Sugg, James Sutton, and Donna Aza Weir-Soley. Kai Weir-Soley, to whom I told the story as he worked on a school project, reminded me of how valuable such a story can be to young people, especially to one as kind and sensitive as he. Térèse Campbell and Marta Lee, as always, provided outstanding staff support along with the care and interest that comes from years of friendship and working together. I am grateful to the English department and the university for awarding me emerita status, and to the College of Arts, Sciences, and Education for giving me a well-equipped office after my retirement, all of which enabled me to complete this book without distractions and with maximum access to university library resources.

Translators were essential to this project. I am grateful to Roland Pabst for translations from German, and to Olga Skarlat—my former student, now an attorney—for translations from Russian. Nissan Krakinowski helped translate the article in *Der Tog*, and Pearl Tucker assisted with Yiddish, as well, in early stages of the project. For the most part, my Yiddish translator was Rivka Schiller, an outstanding professional translator and researcher, whose expertise extended from published documents and handwritten letters to an important postcard, the scrawled Yiddish of which was nearly indecipherable. My dear friend Nurit Nahmani produced the simultaneous English translation of Moshe Kravetz's in-person Hebrew interview. All of them helped me hear my lost family speak.

Almost finally, I extend enormous gratitude to my editors at Wayne State University Press—Kristin Harpster, Rachel Ross, Ceylan Akturk, Kristina Stonehill, Emily Nowak, and Jamie Jones—for giving me outstanding guidance and support at every stage and in every dimension of this project. Sandra Judd was a thorough, intelligent, and understanding copyeditor, helping to make my writing and documentation in this book the best they can be. Kathryn Peterson Wildfong was my initial editor on *Eli's Story* and is now, deservedly, the director of the press. She was the editor on my last book, and she encouraged me to submit the proposal for this one. I am grateful to have been able to work with Kathy for so many years, and to have had the benefit of her wisdom for so long and in so many ways.

My nephew Ellis Rochelson keyed in an early draft of part of the transcript, and my son, Daniel Mintz, digitized the audiotapes so that I could transcribe them all as easily as possible. But, of course, beyond technical assistance, all of my family, as well as my friends, have brought joy to my life while I worked on a story that was often less than joyful. Robyn Armon Rochelson and Burt's family—Dave, Ebonie, and Jack; Ellis and Emily; Jordan and Julianne; Jesse; Jenna and Jared, Lily and Brody—have kept me and Burt going with encouragement and inspiration. My mother-in-law, Eleanor Mintz, exemplifies all that is good in a very long life, and I am grateful to her as well as to my late father-in-law, Samuel I. Mintz. Joel Mintz shares my life and has shared this story, and, in this project as always, has buoyed me with his love and support. My son and daughter, Daniel and Serafima Mintz; my daughter-in-law, Sarah Allison; and my grandchildren,

Sam and Karl, are my greatest blessings. With them, I know I can achieve anything.

I dedicate this book to the youngest descendants of Eli G. Rochelson and to those who will follow.

So I end where I began, with Pearl and Eli, whose love and whose own determination created and nurtured a new family, and who gave me the strength and the skills to complete this book.

And with Burt, who has been by my side throughout, and who shares Eli's story.

Chronology of Eli G. Rochelson, MD

Life and History

INFORMATION ABOUT THE Holocaust and the Kovno ghetto, in particular, is indebted to the chronology in *Hidden History of the Kovno Ghetto* (United States Holocaust Memorial Museum 241–49). Vital records information comes from the All Lithuania Database of JewishGen.com, the lists originally compiled by the Kaunas District Research group of LitvakSIG, records in the International Tracing Service files of the United States Holocaust Memorial Museum (USHMM), interviews, and family records.

c. 1830

Ilija Gershon Rochelson, grandfather of Eli G. Rochelson, is born.

1864

Bere-Mikhel (or Mikhel Ber; Hebrew name Dov Mikhael) Rochelson is born on July 17 (old style)/July 30 (new style); parents Ilija Gershon (Eliyahu Gershon or Eli'Gershon) and Devorah (Dvera) Rochelson.

1869 (possibly 1865)

Henye Lubovsky is born on October 5? (old style)/October 18? (new style); parents David and possibly Sora Mendelzon Lubovsky.

1907

August 19 (old style)/September 1 (new style)/22 Elul (Hebrew calendar): Ilija Gershon (Eli Gershon) Rochelson is born in Kovno, Russian Empire; parents Bere-Mikhel and Henye Lubovsky Rochelson.

1908

June 25? (old style)/July 12? (new style): Serafima Meerovich is born in St. Petersburg, Russia; parents Saveli and Mariya Meerovich.

1915

May 2–5 (old style)/May 15–18 (new style): Jews are expelled from the western Russian empire. The Rochelson family eventually settles in the area of Rostov-na-Donu (Rostov-on-Don), where Eli attends a Russian Jewish gymnasium.

June 5: Pearl Friedman is born in Brooklyn, New York; parents Max and Masha Rubin Friedman.

1918 or 1919

Eli is infected with Spanish flu during the epidemic, as well as other serious illnesses, and survives.

1921

After famine during the postrevolution Russian Civil War, the family returns to Kovno.

1927

Eli Rochelson and Serafima Meerovich graduate from the Russian Gymnasium of the Teachers' Association, in Kaunas.

1931

July 1–15: David and Ida Robinson (Eli's brother and sister-in-law from Brooklyn) visit the family in Kovno.

1932

Eli Rochelson begins studies at the medical faculty of the University of Vytautas the Great, Kaunas.

April 5: Bere-Mikhel Rochelson dies of pulmonary disease, in Kaunas.

1934

January 22: Eli Rochelson marries Serafima Meerovich, in Kaunas.

April 19: Chaye/Anna Rochelson Arendt, Eli's sister, dies in Berlin of rheumatic heart disease. Eli and his mother travel to the funeral.

October 19: Boris (Borya) Rochelson is born in Kaunas; parents Eli and Serafima Meerovich Rochelson.

1935

Eli begins military service in the Lithuanian Army.

1939

Eli is admitted to candidacy in medicine, University of Vytautas the Great; he completes his military service.

1940

June 15: Eli Rochelson is awarded an MD degree, University of Vytautas the Great (Kaunas Medical College); he goes to work as a medical intern at the university and in a health facility for government workers.

June 15: Soviets invade and occupy Lithuania.

1941

June 22: Nazis invade and occupy Lithuania, including Kaunas. June–September: Mottel (Eli's brother) and Henye Rochelson are murdered in or near the town of Plokščiai, where they have been living.

August 15: All Jews left in Kovno, nearly thirty thousand in all, are now in the Kovno ghetto. Eli, his wife and child, and other relatives are among them.

August 18: Intellectuals Action. Five hundred Jews from the Kovno ghetto are taken away and killed. Avraham Rochelson is taken but sent back. Cousin David Lubovsky is murdered.

October 4: Nazis destroy the hospital in the Kovno ghetto by setting it on fire. All staff and patients inside are killed.

October 28: The Great Action in the Kovno ghetto. All assemble in Demokratu Square early in the morning. Selections last until nearly evening, and more than 30 percent are selected to be killed.

December 7: Japanese bomb Pearl Harbor, and the United States declares was on Japan.

December 11: Germany declares war on the United States.

1943

September 15: Nazis begin work to turn the Kovno ghetto into a concentration camp.

November 1: Kovno ghetto is officially reclassified as KL Kauen, a concentration camp.

November 30: Eli, Serafima, and Boris Rochelson are among one thousand Jews taken to a work camp in Aleksotas, outside the Kovno ghetto.

1944

Early March: Serafima develops diphtheria, and the family returns to the ghetto. Boris (Borya) develops meningitis.

March 27–28: "Children's Action" in all the Baltic ghettos. In Kovno, "up to 1,300" children and people over fifty-five years of age are rounded up and killed. Eli is able to save Borya.

July 8–14: Nazis liquidate the Kovno ghetto, deporting the population to Stutthof and Dachau. On the last day, they burn the ghetto buildings to the ground, killing most of those who hid beneath them.

July 12–13: Serafima, Rose, and Sarah Rochelson (Eli's wife, sister-in-law, and niece) are processed into KL Stutthof.

July 15: Eli and Boris Rochelson are processed into KL Dachau.

July 26: Boris Rochelson, in a group of 131 boys from Kovno, is sent on a train to Auschwitz.

July 29: Avraham Rochelson, Eli's brother, is processed into KL Dachau.

August 1: The Soviet Army enters the Kovno ghetto, liberating those who remain.

August 1: The boys from Kovno (minus two who jumped off the train) enter Auschwitz-Birkenau. Boris Rochelson is among them.

September 18 and 19: On Rosh Hashanah, many of the Kovno boys are selected and murdered in the gas chambers. Borya may have been among them. On Yom Kippur, more of the Kovno boys are selected and killed.

1945

January 7: Avraham Rochelson is transported from Dachau to Flossenbürg.

January 25: The liberation of Stutthof begins, with forced marches by land and sea; it will not be completed until April, when the remaining inmates are liberated by Soviet troops. Serafima Rochelson dies of starvation, exhaustion, and disease around the time of liberation. Rose Rochelson dies of dysentery; Sarah Rochelson dies at the same time as her mother. Exact dates of these deaths are unknown.

January 27: Auschwitz is liberated by Soviet troops.

February 19 or (more likely) March 28: Avraham Rochelson dies in Flossenbürg. Late April: Eli is among a large group of prisoners evacuated from Dachau by train. When the station is bombed along the route, he and others escape, hiding out in the forest for two or three days.

April 29: US troops liberate Dachau. Eli and those he is hiding with are liberated in the forest by US soldiers.

Early May: Dr. Eli Rochelson assists Dr. Solomon Nabriski in establishing the hospital at the Landsberg-am-Lech displaced persons camp and administers its outpatient clinic. This is Hospital #2014 in the American Zone.

May 27: Liberation Concert by the St. Ottilien orchestra, made up of Holocaust survivors at St. Ottilien displaced persons camp, close to Landsberg. October: Landsberg becomes an all-Jewish camp, as other displaced persons are transferred to different locations.

1946

February 9–11: Eli Rochelson participates in a conference of liberated Jewish doctors in the American Zone, held at Landsberg.

March 27: Eli gives a lecture at Landsberg as part of the culminating events of "Sanitary Month."

March 27: Eli registers with the American Joint Distribution Committee to emigrate to the United States.

April 18: Eli is living at an emigration center in Munich.

June 6: Eli leaves for the United States on the repurposed US troopship *Marine Flasher*.

June 18: Eli arrives in New York. His brother David meets him at the dock and he goes to live with Dave and his wife, Ida, in Brooklyn.

August 1: Eli begins a year's internship at Israel Zion Hospital in Brooklyn (later Maimonides Medical Center). He lives on the hospital campus.

October 28: Eli publishes an article commemorating the fifth anniversary of the Kovno ghetto Great Action in *Der Tog*, a Yiddish newspaper published in New York.

December 27: An article is published in *Aufbau/Reconstruction*, a German-Jewish newspaper published in New York, summarizing testimony by Eli and others regarding medical atrocities during the Holocaust. Eli begins to gather materials to establish that he received a medical degree in Kaunas, Lithuania.

1947

August: Eli takes on a residency at the Casualty Hospital in Washington, DC. He stays for a few months and then leaves to work at the Swedish Hospital of Brooklyn.

September 13: Eli takes and passes the English exam of the University of the State of New York, State Education Department, Professional Division.

1948

July 1: Eli receives his initial license to practice medicine in New York State.

September 13: Eli is notified that he has passed the subject exams for his full medical license.

October 12: On Kol Nidrei night, Masha Friedman is injured outside a synagogue near her home in Crown Heights, Brooklyn. She goes with her daughter Pearl by ambulance to the Swedish Hospital of Brooklyn, where Dr. Eli Rochelson treats her.

1949

April 29: Eli Rochelson marries Pearl Friedman in Brooklyn. Eli establishes his first medical practice at 542 Parkside Avenue.

1950

October 12: Meri-Jane Rochelson is born in Brooklyn. She is named after her maternal grandfather, Max (Mota), and her paternal grandmother (Henye).

October 15: The Landsberg displaced persons camp is closed.

1953

September 14: Burton Lee Rochelson is born. He is named after Borya and a maternal relative, Lazar (Lazer), who had lived a very long life.

1955

Summer: Pearl and Eli Rochelson buy a house at 817 East 17th Street in Brooklyn and move there with their children. Eli purchases the building at 493 Marcy Avenue, Brooklyn, and moves his office to the ground floor.

1983

Spring: Eli's and Pearl's first grandchildren are born, in March and May. There will eventually be more.

1984

January: Eli sells his medical building and practice to a doctor who had immigrated to the United States from Africa.
February 15: Eli Gershon Rochelson dies, in Brooklyn.

1994

Pearl Rochelson sells the house in Brooklyn and moves to an apartment in Manhattan.

2010

January 9: Pearl moves to Hollywood, Florida.
February 3: Pearl Friedman Rochelson dies. She is buried next to Eli at Beth David Cemetery in Elmont, New York.

Introduction

THIS BOOK TELLS the story of my father, Eli G. Rochelson, MD, whose life and memory spanned two world wars, several migrations, an educational odyssey, the massive disruption of the Holocaust, and, finally, a frustrating yet ultimately successful effort to restore his professional credentials and identity, as well as reestablish family life. Only recently, listening to a now-digitized recording, did I learn that Dad, decades ago, once suggested to my brother that he, our mother, and I might all work on a book together—his story. I am quite sure, however, that when he talked about it, our father used the word *book* and not *story*. Especially in the days before the internet, only a published book had for him the gravitas as well as the breadth for the story he had to tell. He was approximately the age that I am now when, in the middle 1970s, he took the first steps toward the book's production and recorded his life's story in several different audiotapes. The most comprehensive was recorded by my brother, Burt Rochelson, at the time a student, now also a physician.

Burt interviewed our father for a recording of over six hours, beginning with his earliest memory and ending with reflections on his life, current issues, and hopes and concerns for the future. The narrative of this book is largely based on that interview, so much so that when I quote from it I do not include specific citations to the interview; in this book it is the default story of my father's life in his own words. At an earlier time, however, in a short taped interview with Burt that I refer to as Tape 1, our father set out his desire for a book about his life and spoke in detail about certain episodes, in particular his experience in the Kovno ghetto. I refer to that tape, with citation, when its narrative especially illuminates the story.

At around the same time that my brother was recording his long interview, Marsha Rozenblit, now Harvey M. Meyerhoff Professor of Jewish History at the University of Maryland but then a graduate student as well as a friend of mine, was working part-time as an interviewer for a study sponsored by the American Jewish Committee (AJC). The study intended to assess the adaptation of Holocaust survivors to life in America, and when Marsha asked my father if she could interview him, he readily agreed. As she explained to me later, however, when the interviewers began questioning the survivors about life in America, all of them found the same thing: while the survivors answered the questions politely, what they really wanted to talk about was their Holocaust experience. The AJC allowed for this shift in focus, and the audiotapes and transcripts they collected are now housed in the Dorot Jewish Division of the New York Public Library (NYPL). I suspect that the two long interviews, the one now in the NYPL collection and the one conducted by Burt, both done in the middle 1970s, influenced each other in terms of subjects discussed or omitted. As with Tape 1, at points I bring in details from the NYPL interview that are significant to the narrative as a whole. The audiotapes of the NYPL interview are available to researchers in the Dorot Collection, and I am grateful to the American Jewish Committee, which holds the copyright, for permission to quote from its transcript. For readers who would like to see in its entirety the long family interview on which this book is based, I include a transcript as appendix F in this volume.

Writing this book—*Eli's Story*—keeps a promise that I made to my father many decades ago when it became clear that, somehow, I would become a writer. Years before Holocaust memoirs were as popular and frequent as they are today, my father knew that his life experience could not simply vanish with him, and he wanted his book to be written. Had I known sooner that he had made the request of all our nuclear family, I might have avoided a good deal of worry and guilt. For many years I felt that my father had placed upon me a solemn burden, a task that I hoped and wanted to fulfill but that I also feared I never would. As I embarked on the life of a scholar, I frequently asked myself how I could write about other people, literary figures, when this important task was left undone. Finally, it was achievement in the academic realm that allowed me to realize I could do this, too. After publishing a book about another determined (and, as my father might have put it, stubborn) Jewish man, the British writer and activist Israel Zangwill, I knew that I indeed had the skills and ability, as well as the desire, to publish my father's story, and I realized, too, that it was time.

Burt felt the burden as well. Years after he interviewed our father, he wrote a play describing the experience of hearing his stories for the first time. In it he described three types of survivors: those who spoke about the Holocaust all the time, those who never would, and those, like our father, who would speak of their experience when asked, and to whom world history and personal history meant much more when described together. His protagonists were three different children of survivors, whose approaches to life had been affected by their parents' experiences in diverse and sometimes problematic ways. In a later, published short story, "An Old Fashioned Doctor," Burt describes the compassion and hope that Eli shared with the patients, the "surviving remnant,"[1] whom he cared for as a doctor in a displaced persons camp after the war. When Burt and I many years later met Nissan Krakinowski,[2] who had been one of Dad's first patients at the Landsberg displaced persons (DP) camp hospital, he said that Dad had saved his life when he was a teenager, not only by treating his illness but by sitting next to him and telling him, "you'll be all right," by reminding

---

1. "Surviving remnant" is an English translation of a Hebrew term, *Shearit ha-Pleitah*, that has been used to describe Holocaust survivors since the time of the liberation. Lists of survivors appeared in books with that title, often compiled in the displaced persons camps.

2. The story of how we met Nissan appears later in this book. Among other things, Nissan helped us translate an article our father had written for an American Yiddish newspaper in 1946 (see chapter 5 and appendix D).

him of hope. Burt recalls that, when he was a medical student, Dad would say to him, "where there's life, there's hope," a thought that would guide him throughout his own career. He thought of it once more when he met Nissan, for whom our father had given such meaning to the phrase. It is not surprising that, having lived in a house where story and history were always just a question away, Burt and I each felt compelled to write about it, difficult though its content often was.

None of the interviews my father did with Burt followed currently accepted practices for recording testimony—guidelines developed in various ways by the United States Holocaust Memorial Museum, Yad Vashem, the Fortunoff Video Archive at Yale, Stephen Spielberg's Shoah Foundation, and other repositories of Holocaust testimony—because most of those guidelines and repositories did not yet exist, and today's practices were a long way from being codified and known. But by asking questions to which he wanted the answers, Burt obtained a detailed and fascinating account of our father's life, reminiscent, in some ways, of David Boder's early interviews. Boder, an American professor emeritus of psychology, conducted some of the first interviews of survivors in displaced persons camps and translated many of those interviews into English. I read some of them in the research library of Yad Vashem, including two interviews of survivors from Kovno. Boder prefaces his interview of Jacob Oleiski, the ORT director whom my father knew and worked with at the Landsberg DP camp, with the statement that this interview, like some others, must be considered as a "background" recording, since the speakers "were so absorbed in their community responsibilities that they could not be induced to keep the interview predominantly on topics of a strictly personal nature" (Oleiski 1), and, indeed, one senses in Oleiski's words the understanding that he is always speaking as a public figure.[3] The

---

3. ORT is a Jewish organization founded in the Russian Empire in 1880, when the acronym stood for the Russian words for the organization's title, which in English is the Society for Trades and Agricultural Labor. It is now a worldwide organization using only the acronym, although in English ORT initially stood for Organization

interview with Ephraim Gutman, however, is more personal in nature and, like my father's, mixes first-person recollections with accounts of what he must have learned after the fact. Boder's interviews have the great value of having been conducted soon after the Shoah ended, while his subjects were close in time to their Holocaust experiences and still among the displaced survivors in Europe. The Yad Vashem web page, introducing its own collections of written survivor testimonies, adds that testimony "provides a retrospective account distanced in time (as opposed to accounts written during the Holocaust)." In this sense even the stories that Boder recorded were "distanced in time." Yet all victim and survivor accounts, however and whenever obtained, testify to Nazi atrocities. Even where they might differ in small details, as occurs throughout the many testimonies I have read and listened to, they confirm the most essential narratives of what took place in Europe during the war years and immediately after.

This biography is more than a Holocaust narrative, however, although there is one at its center. In beginning Eli's story with his earliest recorded memories and ending it with what I remember of his death, I reveal a life that was violently interrupted and then, with difficulty and perseverance, recovered in both new and continued directions. Although the Holocaust shaped my father's subsequent life, it was not his whole life. It was to honor the meaningfulness of his entire life that my brother started his recordings by asking about our father's earliest memory, and then continuing into the present. In this he anticipated the practices of later, more formal, interview projects, such as those of the Fortunoff Archive at Yale, the US Holocaust Memorial Museum, Yad Vashem, and the Shoah Foundation. In her study of interviews of the same Holocaust survivors done fifty years apart—soon after the Holocaust by Boder and by social service agencies in Europe,

---

for Rehabilitation and Training. Jacob Oleiski led the organization in Lithuania from 1927 to 1941; he then established ORT schools in the Kovno ghetto and the Landsberg DP camp. He eventually became the director of ORT in Israel, and an ORT school in Jerusalem is named in his honor ("The History of ORT").

and in the 1990s by projects such as those mentioned—Sharon Kangisser Cohen reports that the early interviews focused solely on Holocaust experiences, while later interviews, using different protocols, included whole life stories (20–21).[4] Moreover, Cohen found, while in earlier interviews survivors tended to focus on personal actions and physical trauma, in interviews fifty years later they tended additionally to emphasize the ways in which others tried to help (48–54, 73). My father, interviewed by his son not even thirty years after the war ended, presents both kinds of testimony, and often emphasizes the acts of those who at various times saved his life and the lives of his family.

I have structured this biography as a full-life account for the same reason Burt asked our father about his entire life in the interview. The Holocaust was central to Eli Rochelson's experience, and I believe it shadowed everything in his life from 1945 on. But he was close to thirty-four years old when the Nazis invaded Kovno. He had a wife, a child, and a medical degree. Starting the story long before the Holocaust helps explain who this person was whose life was interrupted and, indeed, devastated; recounting his experiences after liberation reveals how he worked and fought to reconstruct a meaningful career and family life. More broadly, this far-reaching account of one life in its entirety serves to enrich understanding of the interwar era for European Jews, and of the lives of survivors after leaving Europe. Eva Hoffman has pointed out that the very real "hardships [of emigration] . . . have gone relatively unnoticed, or at least unremarked, in literature about post-Holocaust lives" (79). Just as the account of his experiences in Landsberg-am-Lech adds to a growing and important body of scholarship on displaced person camps and the postwar years in Europe, my father's struggles with relief organizations in the United States, his determined and undaunted efforts to restore his medical credentials, and

---

4. One of the most fascinating parts of Cohen's study is when she demonstrates how Boder's interviews reveal him learning and absorbing, for the first time, details that have come to be familiar to students of the Holocaust, such as conditions in barracks and in transport cattle cars (58–63).

the various indignities he suffered as a "refugee" form an important part of his narrative and of the history of emigrants' adaptation.

Still, there remains the question of my own place in this story. Marianne Hirsch, in her introductory essay to *The Generation of Postmemory*, accurately and poignantly expresses such questions as they relate specifically to children of Holocaust survivors, now increasingly active in conveying their families' experiences: "What do we owe the victims? How can we best carry their stories forward, without appropriating them, without unduly calling attention to ourselves, and without, in turn, having our own stories displaced by them?" (Hirsch 2). As I began work on this book, I did not much consider my own story, or even think that I had a story to be displaced. This was about my father, and it was his story he had asked me to tell. Indeed, I still have trouble with the word *postmemory*, since it can imply a memory that the child of a survivor possesses or creates, beyond and to an extent superseding the survivor's own memory of trauma. For me, that first-person memory is what matters above all, and I at first considered that whatever I added in research and commentary must necessarily remain fluid, contestable, and incomplete. Yet, as I pursued my research, I came to see that the interview my father gave some forty years ago told a story that he himself revised and modified in other retellings, as is true of most such testimonies. His recollections and my reflections are equally yet differently truthful, and equally yet differently subjective.

A great deal of this book is based on research: in documents and letters that my father saved; in family letters, photographs, and other papers saved by his brother David, who immigrated to the United States in 1912 and thus received many mailings from Kovno; in scholarly as well as personal archives; in published books, articles, and recorded testimonies; and in interviews I personally conducted with other Holocaust survivors, particularly from Kovno. As I have suggested, the testimonies and interviews I have listened to themselves contain gaps, incoherencies, and incompleteness. However, for as much of this story as I am able to tell, I rely significantly, for context, on those testimonies and on all of these sources. But I have done all this research for another reason, too, and not only to convey the most accurate account that I can. I have done it because I am a scholar, and research is what I do. Research and writing are how I learn, and how I tell stories that are important to me. I wanted to present my father's life in the context of its history, to fill in, as well as I could, details he omitted as well as larger historical currents that he may have taken for granted in his personal account. My research findings are not part of my father's testimony, but they are part of his story.

James Young's concept of "received history" perhaps most directly describes my project: "a double-stranded narrative that tells a survivor-historian's story and my own relationship to it" (21, 23). But that still does not remove the unease that comes from being even a strand in this webwork. In *Maus*, Art Spiegelman foregrounds his role as his father's interviewer and biographer, as well as his son. Frames showing the two at a kitchen table and elsewhere in Vladek's house in Rego Park, tape recorder between them, remind readers insistently of the process by which Art obtained the story. This seeming transparency should allay anyone's doubts about Art as a reliable interpreter. But, of course, it is never so clear-cut. Early in volume two, we see Art consumed with doubt: "Depressed again?" asks his wife, Françoise. "Just thinking about my book," answers Art; ". . . it's so presumptuous of me. I mean, I can't even make any sense out of my relationship with my father . . . How am I supposed to make any sense out of Auschwitz? . . . Of the Holocaust?" (2:14; ellipses as in original). Expressing this feeling of inadequacy, as at so many points elsewhere, Art Spiegelman becomes part of the story he has to tell, and one cannot read *Maus* without seeing it as Art's story as well as Vladek's. It becomes the story of the child as well as the survivor, and as such it has become a key document of Holocaust memory and the second generation. I empathize with the dilemma that Art Spiegelman enunciates and explores, particularly the sense of presumptuousness. Yet while I did not set out to become a part of my father's story, I find I cannot avoid it.

Growing up in Brooklyn, New York, in the 1950s and '60s, in a largely Jewish neighborhood, attending public schools but with mostly Jewish friends, I didn't think of myself, specifically, as a "child of a survivor." That term did not yet exist, and thus I felt no particular connection to the few other children I knew whose parents had also come from Europe. I knew that, unlike my closest friends' parents, my father was European, spoke with an accent, and was a little older; I knew, too, that, because he was a doctor, we lived in a private home while most of my friends lived in apartments. As I will describe, I knew there had been a "persecution," as my father called it, but none of this seemed relevant to my life as an outgoing young girl and teenager. I was active in student government and musical shows in high school and popular in the slightly more intellectual crowd. When I entered Smith College as a first-year student, however, I felt for the first time that I was in an alien milieu. I had never aspired to the preppy style of dress of some of my classmates at Midwood High School, but they had always seemed a small group; at Smith the style and the ethos it embodied appeared to be genuine, not borrowed, and it seemed to be the norm. So did a level of self-confidence that I felt I never could achieve, with standards of speech and behavior that I didn't understand. The wealthier girls in high school were children of clothing manufacturers and the like; at Smith, they were daughters of Wall Street. Their lives seemed perfect to me and, although I might not have expressed it so at the time, not shadowed by sadness or self-doubt. I loved the academics of Smith, as well as the Jewish student activities, and I developed some close and lasting friendships with young women who were also "different" in some way. But none of this was enough to sustain me. After two years I transferred to Barnard, where being a Jew from Brooklyn did not make me an anomaly. Even there, however, I still was not focused on my father's Holocaust experience.

Sometime after my college graduation Burt recorded the interview that became the heart of this narrative. I listened to it, learned a lot, but clearly did not take in everything. I remember feeling sad, but not shocked. I had always seen my father as being open about his past, telling his children stories of the Holocaust, as well as of his early life, although wisely emphasizing stories of courage and even adventure, such as his escape from a train just before liberation, rather than incidents of pain or humiliation. Still, I knew what persecution, in my father's stories, meant; as a young child riding the New York City subways—confusing the words *persecute* and *prosecute*—I thought that people could be killed for spitting on the platform or in the train cars. But, really, I knew very little, and for most of my young life I had the sense that it was not a good idea to ask questions. When I was about ten years old I contracted measles, a common occurrence for children in 1960, before the advent of the vaccine. I had an especially severe case, however, and I lost a day to high fever. I remember, after I recovered from my delirium, overhearing my mother on the telephone explaining to someone how nearly hysterical my father had become, and I heard something about his child being the same age. Later I would learn that my father heard his son had been killed after contracting measles in Auschwitz. At that time, however, I asked no questions. I didn't tell my mother I had overheard her conversation, and I didn't let on, to her or my father, that I knew there had been another child. That was the first big secret I felt I had to keep, until eventually, to my great relief, I was allowed to know.[5]

When I was a teenager I learned more about my father's first wife and son. We were celebrating my parents' anniversary with lunch at the café in Rockefeller Center. It was late April, and we were probably eating outdoors. I remember that the four of us were all in a good mood, and when it came time to order dessert Dad ordered a Napoleon—a layered

---

5. I nearly left that incident out of this account, thinking that the event I record next was my first awareness of my father's earlier family. And, indeed, I must have suppressed it, if I had no awareness of my father's first wife at the time of the next incident that I record. I was reminded of this earlier event when I read the article by Trachtenberg and Davis, who report a support group member's reaction to such knowledge as, "It knocked the wind out of me; I could hardly breathe" (299). I was in their support group, as I will explain, one of the first for children of survivors in the United States, and I knew that what they reported was my reaction. I had often had memories of myself leaning over the staircase banister, listening to my mother's conversation. Was I only ten years old, or did she tell someone the story later? Memory is slippery.

pastry of rich crumbly sheets of dough filled with custard. He reminisced that his mother-in-law made the most delicious Napoleons. "Your mother-in-law?" I remember asking with a smile; "you mean your mother." (My mother's mother, the grandmother I knew and loved, did not make anything like Napoleons.) "No, my mother-in-law," he said, with certainty, and then my mother gave him a look and he said, "Oh, yes, that's right, my mother." I knew there was more to this story, but I did not dare ask. After all, this was my parents' anniversary, and any mother-in-law who used to make Napoleons was in the category of knowledge I was not supposed to have. We ate our desserts, and I have no recollection of what mine was. That was during my healthy, normal, American high school days. I suppose I compartmentalized that secret, too, but it remained with me.

Sometime later, I went to talk with my father in his study, as I often did. The large front room on our second floor was divided into my parents' bedroom and Dad's study by a wall unit that my parents had designed. A kind of wood and fiberglass panel formed a barrier above a credenza of drawers in the study; my mother's dresser filled the space on the other side. The study was warm and inviting, with a dark mahogany desk in front of dark wood bookcases and a nonworking fireplace, the opening of which was surrounded by small, old-looking ceramic tiles. A painting over the hearth showed a kind, wise man with a white beard, talking with someone at his desk.[6] The mantelpiece held various objects dear to my father, including a heavy metal object on a marble base, which I long thought was an inactive grenade but which may instead be the head of a projectile

---

6. This was *The Discussion*, a painting by an artist named Piczelya that our parents had purchased from the collection of Gershon Fenster, one of Eli's relatives who had immigrated to Tulsa, Oklahoma. Gershon, married to Dad's first cousin Rivka, worked with his Sanditen cousins in Otasco, the auto supply business they had founded, and collected modern art with an emphasis on works by Jewish artists. While Burt and I were growing up, our mother sold paintings from the collection for the Fensters from our attic in Brooklyn. Each of us now owns a few of those they bought; *The Discussion* is in Burt's study.

weapon. I never found out exactly how or when during the war that missile part had come into Dad's possession, but there was something reassuring to me in the fact that he had found and saved it, a kind of protection, or a sign of strength and victory.

Dad spent a lot of his time at home in the study, especially in the evenings. Whether he told me so explicitly or not, I came to understand that his habit of *knurring*, or reading at his desk, was at least in part a way to take his mind off thoughts of the past. The term *knurring* derives from a Yiddish word meaning to growl, snarl, or gnarl, but my father used it to imply, self-deprecatingly, a kind of overly intense occupation with study.[7] But his children were always welcome to interrupt him. That evening, when I came in to talk, I found Dad going through some papers that he had taken from the credenza. Among them was a document from his early days in the United States, and it listed him as a widower; it may have been his Certificate of Identity in Lieu of Passport, which allowed him to sail to the United States (figure 1). Now I see that the photograph affixed to the page shows the weariness in my father's face as he prepared to leave Europe. But at that time I barely noticed the photo as I took in the unexpected words. "You were married before," I said. He said, simply, "Yes." I saw his wife's maiden name: Serafima Meerowitz. I knew that Dad corresponded with a woman in Lithuania named Polya Meerovich. She always asked about me and sent me gifts, and I had thought of her for years as an old friend of my father's. I learned that night that she was my father's sister-in-law, the widow of his wife's brother, and later I learned the story of how they had caught the train to Moscow when my father and his family had not, a story, I would learn, that my father saw as the turning point of his life.

---

7. I mentioned this not long ago on the VICTORIA discussion list, when someone inquired as to early origins of the word *wimp*, and another asked whether *nerd* might derive from *knurd*, a term used by Violet Asquith in her diaries. There was certainly something nerdish about knurring. See post from Simon Poe in the VICTORIA archives, https://list.indiana.edu/sympa/arc/victoria/2013-11/msg00096.html.

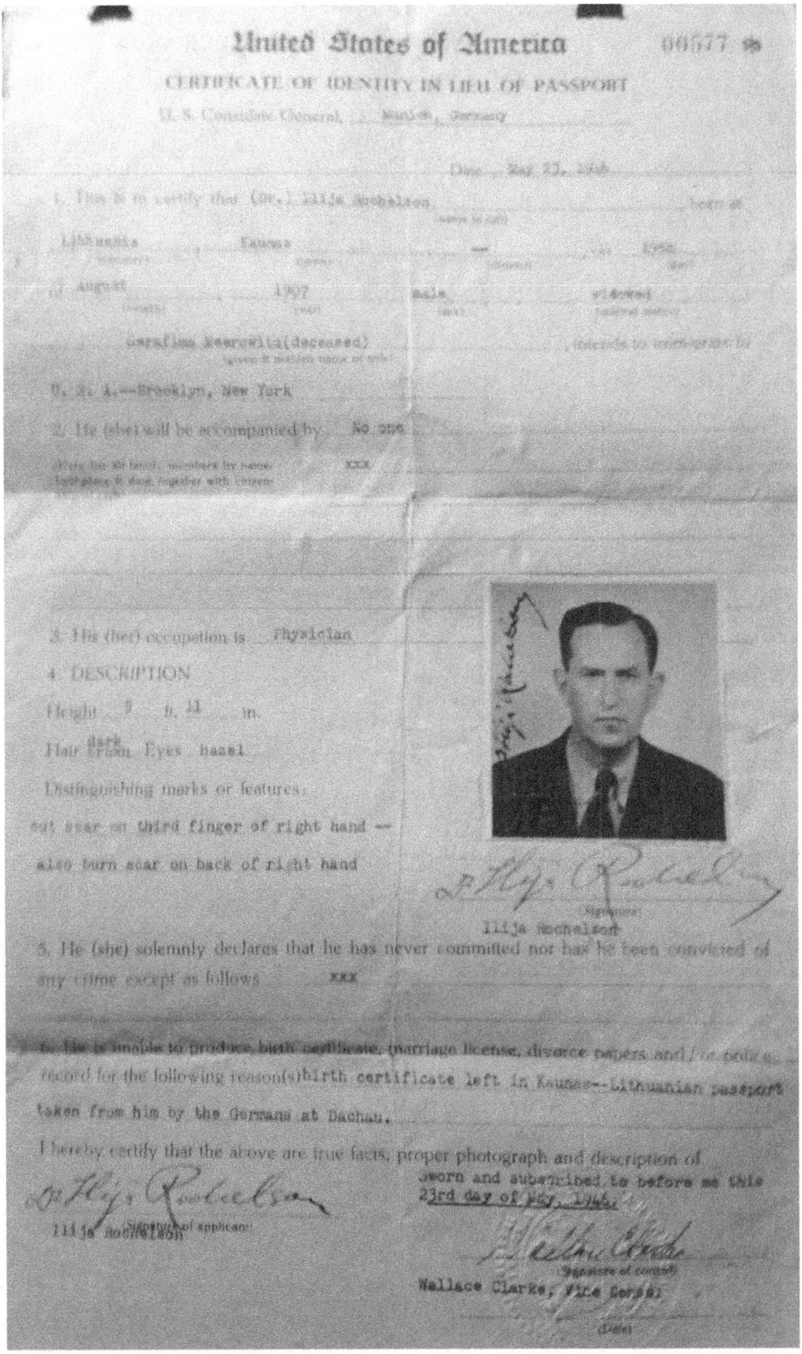
United States of America 06577

CERTIFICATE OF IDENTITY IN LIEU OF PASSPORT

U. S. Consulate General, Munich, Germany

Date May 23, 1946

1. This is to certify that (Dr.) Ilija Rochelson born at Lithuania, Kaunas, 1946, of August 1907, male, widowed, Serafima Kaurowitz (deceased), intends to immigrate to U. S. A.--Brooklyn, New York

2. He (she) will be accompanied by No one

xxx

3. His (her) occupation is Physician

4. DESCRIPTION

Height 5 ft. 11 in.

Hair dark brown Eyes hazel

Distinguishing marks or features:

cut scar on third finger of right hand -- also burn scar on back of right hand

Ilija Rochelson

5. He (she) solemnly declares that he has never committed nor has he been convicted of any crime except as follows xxx

6. He is unable to produce birth certificate, marriage license, divorce papers and/or police record for the following reason(s) birth certificate left in Kaunas--Lithuanian passport taken from him by the Germans at Dachau.

I hereby certify that the above are true facts, proper photograph and description of

(Signature of applicant)
Ilija Rochelson

Sworn and subscribed to before me this 23rd day of May, 1946.

(Signature of consul)
Wallace Clarke, Vice Consul

(Date)

Figure 1. Certificate of Identity in Lieu of Passport, May 23, 1946. Family collection.

We didn't talk much about Serafima that evening; in fact, we never talked of her much. But I did ask my father if he had had any children, and he said, "Yes, Boris." I don't know if it was then or later, but I can still hear him saying, "Boris, Boris," sadly, lovingly. It wasn't the name Boris that American children know from Rocky and Bullwinkle cartoons, but the true Russian name, pronounced with the accent on the second syllable and the *o* more like an *a*. Ba-*reese*. For a long time I tended to think of my father's first son as Boris, the name that my father had used. This was also how his name was transliterated in Yiddish on the birth record I received from the Lithuanian State Historical Archives. The Russian language and Russian culture were a bond between my father and me. From my childhood he told me stories from Russian literature, and in college I studied Russian for three and a half years, in the hope of becoming proficient in the language that my father so loved and that he spoke with his wife and child at home, before the war. I never gained the proficiency I sought, but my Russian was good enough that I was able to read short stories, plays, and novels in the original while taking intermediate-level courses, and, perhaps most importantly, to enjoy short conversations with my father in the language. Thus the name Boris, which seems odd and unfamiliar to most English speakers, has warm and endearing connotations to me.

My brother Burt, however, has a different knowledge of our brother. In his experience, our father called his first child only Bertchik, the diminutive of his Yiddish name, Ber, which is also Burt's Yiddish name. Josef Griliches, who knew our brother as a young child in Kovno and in the Kovno ghetto, has also referred to him as Bertchik in conversation with me. For Burt, this Yiddish name has warmer connotations than the Russian. In letters to our father after the war, Eli's surviving mother-in-law, Mariya Meerovich, referred to her grandson as Boretzken. Burt and I had many conversations on this subject, until the two of us reached a mutually satisfactory decision as to how I would refer to our brother in this book. When Eli sent photographs of his son to family in the United States, he wrote his name on the back as "Boria" or "Borya," the diminutive of Boris

in Russian. This was clearly a way in which Eli thought of him affectionately, and so Burt and I agreed that I would use this version of the name
most often in this book, the name that apparently was used often in the
family. It is striking that in the interviews my father does not call his son by
any of those names, or any name at all, although occasionally, as I describe,
he refers to him as Burt.

Eventually I saw photographs that my parents had kept hidden,
some in the plastic pockets of a family album behind other, more recent,
pictures: photos of Borya, alone and with his parents, and Borya with his
two *bubbies*, or grandmothers (figures 2, 3, and 4). We had those pictures,
as well as others that appear in this book, because they had been sent from
Kovno before the war to my Uncle Dave, my father's eldest brother, who
had come to the United States at the age of 17 in 1912. I'm sure he expected
the rest of the family to follow, and they probably intended to do so,
until time, life, and American immigration quotas got the better of them.
It was through finding those photographs that Burt first learned about
Borya's existence, and he was astounded that pictures of our father's first
child had been hidden in family albums. As an adult, he took the one of our
brother in the park and made 4x6 prints for the two of us and our mother,
and all of us found frames for them and put them on display. Our father
had died by this point, however. He never knew how much Borya would
become a part of Burt's and my lives, or how much we would think of him,
indeed, as our brother. When I was growing up, if I was nervous about
something, or afraid of what people might think of me in some situation,
my father would say, "Pinch your cheeks and make them rosy"; in other
words, put on your best face and don't let anyone know you're concerned.
I always found this heartening and helpful advice, since it implied that
whatever worried me could easily be overcome and, of course, the act can
become the reality. It was only in much later years that I learned that literally pinching one's cheeks to make them rosy was a way for Jews in the
Holocaust, facing selections, to try to appear healthy enough to work and
thus avoid extermination. Parents would also pinch their children's cheeks

Figure 2. Boris (Borya) Rochelson, age three, November 1937. Family collection. The site of this photograph is unidentified, although it seems to have been a popular place for photographs of children. The Ninth Fort Museum outside Kaunas displays a photograph of three girls in a place with virtually identical landscaping; only one of those girls survived the Holocaust.

Figure 3. Borya with his parents, Serafima and Eli, 1934–35. Family collection.

Figure 4. Borya with his *bubbies*, Henye Rochelson and Mariya Meerovich. Family collection.

for them, and no doubt my father had given his son the advice he would later give to me as I faced the ordinary stresses of youth.

It was in 1977, when I was a graduate student at the University of Chicago, that the idea of being a "child of a survivor" gained specific meaning for me. Since I was somewhat active in the university Hillel, I was asked to be the English department representative for the Jewish United Fund, phoning other graduate students in my program and asking them to donate. As I recall, nearly everyone pledged something. But one of my classmates had a question for me: he had read about a support group for children of Holocaust survivors in one of the Chicago suburbs, and did I know anything about it? I told him that I didn't, but if he found out anything would he share the information with me? We had been taking courses together for over a year and had enjoyed many friendly conversations, but this shared identity was news for both of us. We both soon joined the group at the Mayer Kaplan Jewish Community Center in Skokie, Illinois, and for the first time talked about commonalities and differences with others who shared our heritage. When Helen Epstein's *Children of the Holocaust* was published, her book tour brought her to our group, and a few of us—including me—participated with her in a WGN radio talk show. I remember sharing the kinds of details she discussed in her book, common to many survivors' children in their late twenties: feeling that our parents were overprotective, wanting to protect them and to make their lives perfect, wanting to achieve the best we could to help make up for all that they had lost, and wanting to keep the secrets they didn't want us to know. But I also spoke of admiration for my father, for the courage he expressed in starting again and in again bringing children into this world, and for giving us, his American children, a world that, though imperfect, was surrounded by his love.

I still feel that admiration, and for those same reasons. Yet as I have gone through life my "child of survivor" identity and my ability to empathize as an adult have brought me additional awareness. When I was a mother of infants, I remembered the stories of Nazis throwing babies against walls and terrified mothers stopping their children's breath so that people in hiding wouldn't be discovered. These were not specifically my father's stories, but I related them to myself. I thought of how fragile my children's lives were and how easily they could be lost. This was especially true with my firstborn; perhaps his successful development over more than four years gave me more confidence with the second. Then, as I delighted in my children's early years, I thought of how happy Borya's young parents must have been to watch him grow, how thrilled my father and his wife, Serafima, were to have this son. As each of my children lived beyond the age of ten, I breathed an inner sigh of relief. My first brother had been killed shortly before or after his tenth birthday. Having known my father as my loving parent, I could imagine the affection that he and his wife had lavished on Borya, and the dreams they held for his future. Since I experienced overprotective parents, I consciously allowed my children freedoms I never had. But also, knowing how easily hopes can be shattered, I tried to keep in check, as far as I could, my own dreams for my children's futures.

More recently, I experienced empathy of a different kind, less heartbreaking but in another way going to core issues of identity and loss. As I recount in the narrative, my father had a significant correspondence with the United Services for New Americans (USNA), an organization that paid for his dental work following immigration. The USNA report reflects my father's irritation at dentists who removed more teeth than he thought necessary, eight in all. From that time on, he wore dentures. When I read the report I felt angry that my father, an excellent doctor, had been subjected to what he saw as insensitive dental care, and I regretted that he had been put in a position to plead his case with a social service organization. Now, however, I understand even more about what that situation meant. Recently I lost four teeth in an accident; it was a minor event, and that was all I suffered. But two different sets of temporary space fillers proved to be extremely uncomfortable, and it was more than a year, in total, before my very expensive implant work was complete. In the meantime, I often thought to myself that this had irrevocably changed my life, and at times the phrase "ruined my life" melodramatically came to mind. I reflected that I used to have beautiful teeth that had never even needed braces. I found that often I couldn't eat properly, and that eating was just not that enjoyable anymore. And then I thought of my father. His life had been irrevocably changed and, yes, ruined, by something much more devastating than false teeth. He had lost wife, son, mother, brothers, cousins, friends, and everything that had made him what he was—a husband, father, son; a doctor; a happy man with good thoughts about his future. Then, although it may sound trivial, he had to wear dentures for the last thirty-six years of his life. I suppose he got used to it, but, at least at first, and maybe longer, he must have regretted the teeth he lost, the ability to eat all foods with ease and pleasure. If he was like me, it was another loss of who he had been, but for him it came on top of so many more terrible losses. I can understand, now more than ever, why he was so angry at those dentists.

I have often been asked what I think about the fact that, had my father's wife and son survived—or, had there never been a Holocaust—I might never have been born. The short answer is that I don't think about it very much now, although I thought about it a great deal when I was a child and teenager. Even before I knew of Serafima (also called Sima) and Borya, the thought that I might owe my life to the Holocaust was very difficult to accept. It was in the category of such thoughts as "What happens to us after we die?" about which I would reflect and lose sleep and cry quietly until I could no longer stay awake, and then in the morning the thought would be gone. As an adult I sometimes tried to think of it in a more serious way, so as to find some consoling explanation or meaning. I was not able to do so. The best I could do for a long time was rationalize to myself that if Dad and his family had managed to escape to the Russian Soviet Socialist Republic, as they had hoped to do,[8] Burt and I might have been born in Russia, but with half our DNA from Serafima, not Pearl, and with an older brother. Then again, our father, a Jewish doctor, might have been caught

---

8. See chapter 4.

up in the Stalinist "Doctors' Plot" of 1952–53, the culmination of years of antisemitic activity in the Soviet Union. Recent research has shown, however, that while many doctors were arrested, most of them were not Jewish, and although at least one Jewish doctor was murdered, very few actually lost their lives (Brent and Naumov 3–4). The fact is, my father's brother- and sister-in-law, Misha and Polya Meerovich, and his mother-in-law, Mariya Meerovich, with whom Eli, Serafima, and Boris Rochelson would have traveled, made it safely to parts of the Soviet Union never occupied by Hitler, and they returned to Vilnius after the war ended. Their lives contained hardship, but they were alive. At the end of the war, Sima and Borya were not.

I have found, however, that I can live with the complex and painful conditions of my origin, in large part due to what I know about the role of chance and uncertainty in my father's life. As he did, all of us make decisions based on the best information we have, as well as our personalities, our tolerance for risk, our attachments to family and friends, and our sense at any given time about what might be best for ourselves and others. Sometimes we make mistakes. Sometimes circumstances ruin our plans. The narrative that follows reveals many points at which things might easily have gone differently for my father and his loved ones, either for better or for worse. So it has been in my own life. For me, today, there is no point in existential "what-ifs." I know that no one has a "perfect life," not even those who seem to, although I also know I am probably more aware than others of how quickly everything can go bad. Maybe, in a way, that makes me more grateful (when I remember to be) for all that goes well, and for the fact that my father, having suffered and lost so much, decided to take a chance and give me the life I have.

∼

I have pondered why I waited so long, until my Uncle Dave, who had so many letters at one time, had died, and even my mother, who had surely talked with my father about his story, was gone. A major part of the answer is that I was afraid to open up old wounds and to create new wounds in my own heart. I wasn't ready to see tears, hear sighs of sadness or laments of unassuageable regret, or learn difficult truths, particularly if they revealed missed opportunities to save those who eventually were murdered. Even as an adult I found it hard to admit that, having had forbidden knowledge, I wanted to know more. I think there was another reason, as well, one that makes little sense rationally, but that makes complete sense to me emotionally. While my mother was alive, the past was alive, even my father's past. When my mother, at age ninety-four, prepared to move to Florida, I winnowed through her possessions and discarded items of hers that only two months later, after she died, I wished I had saved. The reality of inevitable absence did not sink in until absence was all I had.

And so I proceeded with this project as indeed I pursued my previous academic research, relying on interviews with others to flesh out the interviews of a subject unable to add anything more; combing through personal and published archives; and reading the works of historians and memoirists to gain context and perspective. At times my research became fascinating detective work, as when translated letters or unexpected documents revealed new connections between events, previously hidden relationships, and even an entire new branch of the family, or when my visit to Lithuania in 2003 gave concrete focus to events and places in my father's story. At times, as in investigating my first brother's fate, the search was all-absorbing although the results remained frustratingly beyond my reach. I have tried to convey something of the excitement of the search in each of these cases, but I did not want to make the book about my search, as Daniel Mendelsohn did brilliantly in *The Lost*. Mendelsohn and his brother Matt, who did the photography for that book, sought to bring to life the stories of relatives they had never known, victims of the Holocaust from the town of Bolechow, now known as Bolekhiv, Ukraine. Their travels and interviews in re-creating those stories become as compelling as the lives themselves in a powerfully written, detailed multiple narrative. In my case, however, as I wrote successive drafts of the passages that surround my father's words, I felt compelled to keep my stories of discovery in a place secondary to my father's story of remembrance. Unlike the victims whose experience Mendelsohn strives to re-create, my father survived the Holocaust, and the memories that he himself recorded about his life—before, during, and after the Shoah—would form the core of this biography. Engaged in a thorough work of reconstruction and re-creation, Mendelsohn still recognizes the limits of the belated approach: "I can look through the available sources and compare them, collate them, and from that arrive at a likely version of what probably happened . . . ; but of course I will never know" (226). That acknowledgment echoes my own, at many points and at this work's completion, and yet I still maintain hope of learning more—a feeling I suspect Mendelsohn and other chroniclers of Holocaust victim families share.

Thus my father's story adds to the growing collection of survivor memoirs and biographies, as it appears here both in first person and in context, and it contributes to understanding of the prewar and postwar lives of Jewish families and communities. Yet in examining the archival record and the published writings that I have used to fill gaps in my father's narrative, I recognize that both the effort of reconstructing events and the reality of accounts that confirm each other while differing in detail make the process of gap filling itself a kind of fiction, an attempt to shape the incompleteness that is inherent in the story. At the end of the book, in fact, I disrupt chronology with an epilogue that focuses on a problem I have not been able to solve, a story I have not been able to conclude: How, in fact, did my first brother—known variously as Boris, Borya, Borinka, or Boretzken and loved by devoted parents and grandparents—die? In that portion of the book, which recounts my various efforts at research, speculation, and frustration, I attempt to convey both my methods of re-creation and the limitations that necessarily accompany such attempts. I also reveal my own significant blind spots in growing up with my father's story, the way I could hear things but not take them in until considerably later in my life and work. The epilogue is a reminder that the stories of lives don't have clear chronologies. They go off in many directions, and in some ways they never end.

In the epilogue and, indeed, each time I insert an account of my research process or remark on my emotional response to an event, I hope that I am adding a significant perspective and not detracting from what is central. More directly, I hope that I am not deviating from my father's mandate to tell *his* story, although he is not here today to advise me as to how that story should be told. At all points, I try to take heart in James Young's assertion that what "received history" contributes is not displacement but addition, and I tell myself that if my father wanted me to tell his story, he also trusted me to tell it as I saw fit and with integrity. I hope that the two combine in what follows.

A Few Words about Transcription

The problems of memory in Holocaust narrative, as in all memoirs, have been amply studied by such scholars as Lawrence Langer and Alvin Rosenfeld. By the 1970s, too, my father had read and heard a great deal about the historical events he witnessed, and (as he himself at several points mentions) his narrative includes some information received at second hand. At least some of his memories combine with later understandings of events, and some have been weakened or altered by the passage of time. And yet, the more such narratives are published, the more information is available to complete the picture—or rather, many pictures—of Jewish life in Lithuania, Russia, the Holocaust, and the postwar world. New data may change or amend previous conceptions. Thus I have attempted to leave my father's words as he said them and to punctuate as closely as possible to what my hearing of the narrative suggests. This was not an easy decision, since my father was fluent in several languages—English, Yiddish, Russian, and German, and probably also Lithuanian—and it was important to him to speak and write accurately in each one. However, spoken language is never as polished as its written form, and the agitation of recounting painful events adds to disruptions in speech, repetition, and other verbal idiosyncrasies, not to mention inconsistencies and grammatical errors.

Thus, when I presented a portion of this transcript and commentary to colleagues in my department for their comments, I edited the transcript lightly. Yet many of those who read the excerpts and spoke or wrote to me about my project recommended that I not edit the transcript at all, that I leave my father's words intact to convey his voice as immediately and as transparently as possible. As a result, when I quote from my father's recordings in the narrative I transcribed, I leave the words and phrases as I heard them. I use punctuation to maintain, as accurately as possible, my father's pauses and emphases, as well as the clarity of his story. When there is a break in thought or an abrupt transition I have placed a dash after the broken-off phrase. Where a word or phrase is unintelligible, despite my best efforts, I indicate it as such in square brackets. I also use square brackets, sparingly, to add words that may be necessary for a sentence to make sense or to define words in languages other than English. Occasionally, when I am uncertain of a word or phrase, I indicate that uncertainty with square brackets and a question mark. However, when I omit any of my father's words I use ellipses without square brackets, to allow the narrative to flow more freely. I include the complete transcript as an appendix, for those who wish to read it in full. In the narrative, all quotations from my father are from this interview except where I indicate otherwise.

My procedure is slightly different when I quote from the NYPL interview transcript, which is, after all, a paginated, typewritten document. When quoting from that source, I use ellipsis to indicate a pause, as the typewritten transcript does. When I need to indicate an omission from that narrative (for reasons of either length or intelligibility), I signal that omission by ellipsis in square brackets [. . .]. Since my father himself edited the NYPL transcript in ink, I silently incorporate his revisions if they appear in passages I am quoting from that source, and silently also include corrections I made to the transcript while listening to the audio interview in full.

Many of the names and places mentioned in the audiotapes are in Yiddish, and I have transliterated them for ease of reading, generally using common English equivalents that are not necessarily the equivalents for scholarly use provided by the YIVO Institute for Jewish Research. Thus, Eli's sister is referred to as Chaye, not Khaye, and so on. Where I transliterate printed Yiddish, however (as in the documentation for a Yiddish newspaper article), I use the YIVO English equivalents for printed Yiddish letters.

The interview that I transcribed was recorded on four sides of ninety-minute audiotape cassettes. My son, Daniel Rochelson Mintz, transferred the tapes to digital audio files that I listened to multiple times as I transcribed their contents. An unanticipated pleasure of this project was listening to my father's voice as I transcribed his story. My father died in 1984; I worked on the transcription from 2011 to early 2014. I worried, before beginning the project, that listening to his voice might be too painful. In fact, although the content of what he said was often sad or even horrifying, it was not at all difficult to hear his voice again. I heard my father speak as if he were sitting next to me, exactly as I remember him. Indeed, when I was a child, my father often told me stories of the past, good stories from the times before the war. I wish I could reproduce for readers of this book that feeling I had, listening to the tapes. I wish I could re-create both the strength of my father's voice and the way it softens when he talks about the young son he lost. He refers to this son tenderly, and most often as "the child," as though to say his name out loud were to profane a sacred memory. I cannot help but mention that here.

1

Family, Youth, Education

EVEN THE BASICS are complicated. My father, originally named Ilija (Ilya) Gershon Rochelson, was born in Kaunas, Lithuania, on August 19, 1907. But Kaunas was known as Kovno (or Kovne) to the Jews for whom it was home, in some cases for centuries, and in 1907 it was not part of a country named Lithuania but rather a city in the Russian empire. The Jews who lived there, however, and in neighboring areas (many, like my mother's ancestors, in what is now Belarus) considered themselves to be Litvaks.[1] Moreover, August 19 was September 1 in much of the world, but my father's birth date was recorded under the Julian calendar, used in imperial Russia until the 1917 revolution. When in August Dad told us not to celebrate his birthday because he really was born on September 1, I never quite believed him, although perhaps I should have.[2] I thought it was just survivor guilt preventing him from fully enjoying the pleasures of his new life, the

---

1. Scholars of these turn-of-the-twentieth-century communities sometimes denote the geographic boundaries between Litvaks and Galitzianers (the other major Jewish cultural group in the region, largely in Poland) with a "gefilte fish line": east of it, Litvak Jews preferred their gefilte fish savory; west, the Galitzianers preferred it sweet (see Prichep).

2. Recently, doing research at the US Holocaust Memorial Museum, I discovered that my father's intake documentation from Dachau lists his date of birth as 1907.IX.1—September 1, 1907 (Dachau questionnaire of Ilija Rochelson, Individual Documents Dachau, 1.1.6.2/10266519_0_1/ITS Digital Archive. Accessed at the United States Holocaust Memorial Museum on January 23, 2017). It is repeated on some, but not all, of the cards in his International Tracing Service (ITS) file, perhaps because the relatives searching for him used his traditional birth date.

congratulations we all felt he deserved, even though I knew about the thirteen-day calendar difference. The August 19 date persisted in most of my father's official records, and it is the date that we, his American family, had carved on his gravestone after his death in 1984. Then, when I traveled to Lithuania in 2003 and obtained copies of vital records filed in the Jewish community archives, the Hebrew dates and an online Jewish/civil calendar[3] confirmed it: my father was born on the twenty-second of Elul, which coincided with September 1 that year. His *brit milah* (ritual circumcision) was performed exactly when it should have been, on the eighth day following his birth, the twenty-ninth of Elul.[4] I could only imagine the excitement in the house, and the nonstop preparations of his mother and other relatives as they prepared a family celebration for the day before Rosh Hashanah, the Jewish new year.

Jews are said to have lived in Lithuania since as early as the ninth or tenth century, CE, with extensive settlement beginning in the 1300s when King Gediminas invited foreigners to help build his empire (Greenbaum 1–5). Eli's family had been in Lithuania for generations. His grandparents, Eliyahu Gershon (for whom he was named) and Devorah (Dvera) (figure 5), were born between 1830 and 1833; his great-grandfather was named Moshe (Movsha on some records), and a number of records spell Movsha's son's name as Eliash.[5] During the childhood of my own

---

3. The perpetual Jewish Civil Calendar, http://wwwx.uwm.edu/cgi-bin/corre/calendar, is an extraordinary resource. There is now, of course, an iPhone app that also makes the conversion. I am grateful to Dr. Galina Baranova, now director of the Lithuanian State Archives, for providing me with copies of vital records documents, while I waited, on my last day in Vilnius.

4. This information is now in the Lithuania births database on JewishGen: LVIA/1226/1/2013.

5. I am deeply indebted to the genealogical work of Francis (Bob) Wilson, George Rockson, and Eric M. Bloch, whose combined efforts produced a detailed and comprehensive family tree on which I have relied while writing this book, and who compiled the extensive family history from which I have learned so much. I have also relied significantly on the All Lithuania Database of JewishGen.org, compiled through the efforts of LitvakSIG researchers who have translated and posted an

Figure 5. Formal portrait of Devorah (Dvera) and Eli'Gershon Rochelson, Eli G. Rochelson's paternal grandparents. Family collection.

grandfather—known in the family as Bere-Mikhel, but often Mikhel-Ber Rochelson in official records—the family lived in Veliuona (known by Jews as Velion), a town about midway between the two larger cities of Jurbar-kas (Jurborg) and Kaunas (Kovno). Eli'Gershon and Dvera's surname was Rochelson, but family genealogists have discovered that earlier generations used the name Michelson and, before that, Kielson. The standard expla-nation is that the name was changed when it seemed expedient to avoid compulsory service in the tsar's army, service that was particularly harsh for Jews.

At the time of Bere-Mikhel's birth, in 1864, his father was listed as owning a "drinking house" (LVIA728/1/873); indeed, being a tavern keeper was a frequent occupation for Lithuanian Jews, and Eli recalled his parents running a similar concern. A later record, of May 30, 1893, indicates that Eliash Gershon (Eli'Gershon) was a timber merchant who left Veliuona for Kaunas.[6] However, I became aware of his occupation decades before the internet made these records available, when an announcement of my marriage in the *New York Times* in August 1975 came to the attention of Manfred Rochelson, who lived in Queens, New York. He contacted my parents in Brooklyn, and they met for the first time. My mother told me that Manfred's resemblance to Eli was uncanny. He spoke of the German branch of the family, based in Berlin, and mentioned a family story that each Hanukkah they received a smoked goose from relatives in Lithuania. My father had no recollection of such gifts, but a phone call to cousins

---

extraordinary number and variety of records online. Spellings of names and specific dates can vary from item to item, as they still do in our supposedly more accurate age. I have tried, wherever possible, to indicate the sources of this information in the Kaunas Regional Archives (KRA) and the Lithuanian State Historical Archives (LVIA), as indicated in JewishGen and LitvakSIG documents.

6. JewishGen Tax and Voter Lists, KRA/I-222/1/2/134; see Bloch, "Rochelson Family History," endnote 16. Eric Bloch more recently brought to my attention, from the Kaunas Research Group databases, that Eliash Rokhelzon (another spelling of the name) had five hundred rubles in property in 1892, making him one of the wealth-ier Jewish property owners in Veliuona at the time (KAU-VEL-1892 Box Taxpayers List, Kaunas Research Group of LitvakSIG; e-mail to author, August 26, 2017).

in Tulsa (the descendants of Dina Sanditen, one of my grandfather Bere-Mikhel's seven sisters) confirmed that Lithuanian Rochelsons had sent a smoked goose, as described, every year. Manfred also confirmed that the German Rochelsons were in the lumber business, receiving timber from the rich forests of Lithuania via the Jurborg-Velion-Kovno branch of the family. Bere-Mikhel was born on July 17, 1864 (old style); internal passport data shows that his wife, my grandmother Henye Lubovsky Rochelson, was born in Naumiestis in 1869.[7] Naumiestis (New Town) was a place called Naishtot (Neustadt) by the Jews, and there were in fact several Lithuanian towns by that name. Henye's—Kudirkos-Naumiestis—was close to East Prussia, home of Königsberg, which became Kaliningrad in Soviet times and is now again an enclave of Russia.[8] Kudirkos-Naumiestis is in the district of Šakiai, where my grandmother was living at the time of the Nazi invasion, and where she died at the hands of Lithuanian partisans.

Bere-Mikhel was the only son among eight siblings who lived to adulthood, and he died prior to the Holocaust, in 1932. His sister Dina Glike,[9] emigrated to the United States and became the matriarch of the large Sanditen and Fenster family in Oklahoma; one of her descendants, named Deana after her, confirmed Manfred Rochelson's story of the Hanukkah goose. Dina's eldest daughter, Rivka (also spelled and pronounced Rivke or Rifke) lived for some time as a teenager with Bere-Mikhel and Henye's family, going to school in Kovno. There she became close to their daughter, Chaya (Chaye, later Anna). If Eli was alive at that time, he would have been a baby, but in the United States he had fond memories of his cousin Rifke, whom he certainly knew in later years; she, her husband, and her two eldest

---

7. Mihkel Ber's date of birth is in the All Lithuania Revision List Database, Part I, of JewishGen, Family List KRA/I-197/1/1. For Henye's most likely year of birth, see internal passport record KRA/66/1/738; dates in the JewishGen records differ.

8. See articles on "Shaki (Sakiai)" and "Naishtot (Kudirkos-Naumiestis)" by Joseph Rosin.

9. In Yiddish names such as this one, which end in an *e*, the final letter is pronounced as a separate sound, something like a short *i* in English. The sound is more obvious when the final *e* follows a *y*, as in Henye or Genye/Genya, which are variations of the same name.

Figure 6. Chaye with the Fenster family, shortly before their emigration to the United States. Chaye is dressed in white, on the left; Rivka (Rifke) is standing; her husband, Gershon Fenster, is reclining on the left, and the two very young children are their son, Louis, and daughter, Rosalee (later Minsky); their youngest child, Irving, was born in the United States. I cannot identify the other two people. The message on the back reads, "For my beloved and dearest ones, brother [David] and sister-in-law [Ida], from your sister, Chaye" (translation from Yiddish by Rivka Schiller). Family collection.

children left for Tulsa as late as 1922 (figure 6). All of us met Rifke in 1960, a year before her death, when we visited the Tulsa family for Thanksgiving. Greta Minsky, one of Rifke's granddaughters, suggests a reason for the bond between Eli and Rifke: "they both loved Chaye."[10]

Eli was also close to the children of his mother's brother Mordkhel (Mordechai), some of whom I came to know as well, since his daughters Genya and Riva survived the war in the South of France and later lived in Paris. Eli's maternal grandfather was David Lubovsky; I do not know his maternal grandmother's first name, although my father mentions her, too, affectionately, in his account. Only recently did I discover the existence

---

10. Greta Minsky, e-mail message to author, April 26, 2017.

of a sister of my grandmother, someone of whom I had never been aware although she immigrated to the United States in the late nineteenth century, losing her life in a Brooklyn trolley accident in 1909. I have met several of her descendants, and together we've confirmed the connection. That story comes later, as do the stories of other cousins.

When Eli was a child his family lived on Yatkever Gass, the Yiddish name for the "street of butchers," where many Jews lived in the Old Town (Senamiestis) of Kovno. It is now called M. Daukšos Street, and I easily walked the length of it when I visited the city, from its origin in a walkable branch of the major artery Jonavos Street to its termination at the Nemunas River, which Jews called the Niemen (see the map of Kovno and its environs in appendix A). I had no idea where on the street my grandparents' home had been, but I assumed I had walked past it. My uncle David Robinson, Dad's eldest brother, who was born in 1895 and lived in Miami Beach during the last years of his long life, told my son that one of his earliest memories was of seeing a circus parade with an elephant in the town square in Kovno, when he was a small child living in Yatkever Gass.[11] In the interview with his son Burt, Eli talked about his early life there, too, recounting memories of home and family (see figures 7 and 8):

I had one sister and five brothers. My sister's name was Chaye, and then the brothers were David (who changed his name for Robinson), then Maishe, Mottel, Avraham, and I.[12] Then I have another sister, she died of a childhood infectious disease; as far as I can remember, I was told that she had diphtheria. My [surviving] sister Chaye had scarlet fever, and she developed

11. My son, then in elementary school, had been assigned the task of interviewing an elderly relative. He chose Uncle Dave as the oldest person he knew, and I was amazed and delighted at this story from a past I had never imagined. Uncle Dave died on July 19, 1993.

12. The Yiddish names of the family are derived from Hebrew names. Chaye is a version of Chaya, meaning *life*, and can be translated to English as Eve, although my aunt's European name was Anna; Maishe (also Mishe or Misha) is Moshe, or Moses; and Mottel (also known as Motteh) is Yiddish for Mordechai. My father's name of Ilija is Eliyahu, or Elijah.

rheumatic fever with a severe rheumatic heart disease.[13] My father, at that time, when I was born, was working, at one time, in a brewery, by letting out the beer and counting, and by, when they came back from selling the beer, counting how many empty bottles they had, and how many they sold. After a while, he opened, we called it in Jewish an *akhsanye*.[14] This I don't remember, but I was told, it's like a little motel, a hotel; I would say I would call it a rooming house. Of course it didn't have the character, at that time, like it has here the motels. Now, then we moved, in a small street in Kovno called Yatkever Gass, where my parents opened a restaurant. I started to remember events, I think, when I was five years old. My brother David, at that time, it was in 1912, he was carrying me, I remember, on his shoulders, and going around all over, the rooms and in the streets. . . .

We had, as I said, opened a little restaurant, where we had different type of high-cholesterol food, but very tasty. Every breakfast we had, let's say, the fricassee from chicken, or from geese, boiled in soup with cereal, and then we had piroshkes made from dough with meat. That was our breakfast. There in this *birele*, or we call it restaurant, where we sold liquor, which we didn't have a license to sell, and David had to—the police were coming in often to check if alcohol is sold. And many times my brother when he saw the police he threw away the bottle . . . , and they couldn't do anything because they didn't catch him with alcohol. . . .

Among Eli's earliest memories were happy times with his extended family, especially his aunts and cousins:

We had there Tante Sarah with her children; her children were Feyge, Leiye, and Taibke.[15] And then Minne had children, it was Uri, Grunye, and Paike. There was another boy, Yankele, who died, who drowned while swimming

13. Chaye died from complications of this disease, as I will discuss in its place. According to a birth record in JewishGen (LVIA/1226/1/1993), the sister who died in early childhood was named Gitel.
14. This is the word for *hostel* in modern Hebrew.
15. Also spelled Feige or Faige, Leya or Leah, Taube, etc. Although spellings of names may be inconsistent in the narrative, I hope the reader will understand. All of these names were originally spelled in Yiddish, in Hebrew letters.

Figure 7. Formal portrait of the Rochelson family, ca. 1913. Left to right. Mottel, Ilija (Eli), Henye, Chaye (Anna), Bere-Mikhel, Maishe (Mishe), Avraham. The photograph on the table next to Chaye is of David, who was already in the United States. Family collection.

Figure 8. Formal portrait of (left to right) Avraham, Mottel, Maishe, Ilija (Eli). Family collection.

in the Niemen. Sarah is my father's sister, and Minne is my father's sister.[16] Almost every Saturday, holiday, either we visited them in their house or we were going out, on the Naburus[?], that means near the river, where we were running around, taking wildflowers, and having a good time, I would say. For some reason or another I remember the flowers which have a very round type of appearance, and when they blew, it flew away.... And after a couple of weeks there were a tiny button-like green fruit which was not edible. But we had a song, "run around the beigelach," we called [it]. Then also there were yellow flowers, and different wild flowers.

The park at the confluence of the rivers, close to Kaunas Castle, still hosts outings for city families on Saturday afternoons, and is called Santa-kos (Confluence) Park (figures 9a and 9b). It may also have been the place where Eli, his lifelong friend Joseph Kushner, and two other young men were photographed after a swim in the river in 1929 (figure 10). Lithuania is filled with natural beauty, and Eli's love for nature, the countryside, and even the ocean, which he called "the sea," began in that childhood life before the First World War.

Eli was just under seven years old when World War I began. As he described it, "In August 1914, we children were playing near the Niemen River, and we heard news that a war started." He spent his childhood in Kovno until he was nearly eight, when Russian authorities, fearing that Jews who lived near the German border might be a fifth column as the German army advanced, expelled Jews from Kovno and elsewhere in Lithuania in early May 1915.[17] Eli's maternal grandmother traveled with them from Kovno. He described her fondly as "very sweet," a woman who hid kopecks (pennies) and candies for the children to find, and to give to them as rewards. He remembered that during this time of travel or exiled

16. See the family diagram in appendix B. Uri Kanter made aliyah to Israel, probably in the 1930s, and his family survives there.
17. Dov Levin lists the dates of the expulsion from Kovno as May 2–5, 1915; if these dates are according to the Julian calendar, then the dates in the rest of Europe would have been May 15–18 (see Levin, *Litvaks* 107).

Figure 9a. Where the Neris and the Nemunas meet. Photograph by author on visit to Kaunas, 2003.

Figure 9b. Wildflowers in the park at the confluence of the rivers. Photograph by author on visit to Kaunas, 2003.

Figure 10. Friends at the river, 1929; Joseph Kushner is at right, Eli Rochelson is next to him; the other young men are unidentified. Gift of Joseph Kushner to the author.

settlement, "she got very sick, and she died from pneumonia, and this is very—This I remember clearly." The family resettled in Russia, staying in Rostov-na-Donu (Rostov-on-Don), a large and historic port city in southern Russia, until 1921. Eli's account describes the journey and his family life there and in other towns along the way:

> Within 24 hours we had to leave Kovno. . . . [W]e put everything together, our pillows, and blankets, and pots, whatever we could, we loaded on a horse and carriage, and we went to our relative. That is another sister of my father, Yente; there were two daughters she had. We went to [a place] called Žežmary.[18] I wouldn't know how many miles it was, but I do remember that the horse got stuck in the deep sand, like dunes, and it was unable to go. We pushed the carriage, we pushed the horse; finally we came there and we stayed there for a short time, and we returned back to our house, to our house in Kovno. But seems to be there was another order from the tsar[19] that

18. I am grateful to Josef Griliches for identifying this town east of Kovno, nearly halfway on the road to Vilna. Its Lithuanian name is Žiežmariai.

19. I have not found additional information to confirm two orders, but this was Eli's recollection.

not only from Kovno but [. . . Jews from many areas] have to leave Lithuania. Because they suspected that the Jewish people, by knowing Jewish language, which is similar, the derivate from German, may become spies for Germany.

Then we again went through the same ordeal. We went to, all the Jews went to the railroad station, we went to a train, and we were traveling a day or two. As a child, at that time I was six years old, I would say already seven. When we came, I remember vividly, when the train stopped, and they said, "You can go out now." It was a small town, and the light was visible, the light over the leaves of the trees, and to me it was a fascinating picture. At night, the electrical light and the trees. We slept overnight at the railroad station. And then, the next morning, the Jewish organizations which were there, in Khorol, a little town near Kharkov . . . ; they helped us out. We stayed for a while in Khorol but we didn't like it. And then we moved to another small town called Izyum. Izyum is a little provincial small town belonging to the county of Kharkov.[20] This town Izyum—the word "Izyum" means a raisin, but that was the name. Now in Khorol, also I remember, we rented a little apartment which was near a river. In the spring it was flooding, and we had to make, erect like little bridges with plain boards over wooden horses to walk out to the streets, because there was water, and in the house was water.

In Khorol and Izyum, where they stayed a bit longer, Eli continued the Jewish education he had begun in Kovno at age five or six, and enrolled in a tsarist Russian-language school. His sister Chaye, a young teenager when Eli was born, encouraged him to study Russian: "She was the one who guided us all through the years," he remembered, "and even taught me and my brothers Russian, how to write and how to read." Chaye continued to encourage Eli, nurturing his ambitions as he matured, and remaining an important influence in his life.

At school in Izyum, Eli experienced antisemitism for the first time. He recalled the school as having 90 to 95 percent non-Jewish students, who recognized the few Jews by their appearance:

---

20. This route would have taken the family southeast from Kovno, through what are now Belarus and Ukraine.

Of course we looked differently, maybe we didn't have a *payah* and yarmulke, but I wore tzitzis, and I was making *tefillin* every day and praying three times a day.[21] But when we came there, there was the icons on the walls, with a big cross, and a pope was coming, and they also had, so-called coaching into the Russian religious topics. And they had, let's say, with special writing in Russian Slavyonic [Slavonic] type of script.[22] I had to learn that, and when we tried to say we are Jewish, they said, "never mind, you have to stand up, you have to pray." The only thing, we didn't have to cross ourselves. That they didn't compel us. But what I remember, going home each time, I had to go different streets because we Jews—I personally remember on me they were throwing stones, attacking you, beating you up, . . . Usually we were attacked by kids the same age, maybe a little older, one or two years.

With help from local Jewish organizations as well as from vendors, Bere-Mikhel had opened a grocery store in Izyum. But the family didn't like the life there, and when they heard from friends in Rostov-on-Don, they decided to go, hoping the larger city would offer better economic and educational opportunities. Oleg Budnitskii reports that Jews made up 7.2 percent of the residents of Rostov-on-Don in 1914, a population that grew to 9 percent (or 18,000 out of 200,000) by 1918, playing "a significant role in the economy and public life of Rostov" (16). The family lived in a suburb called Nakhichevan, known for its sizable Armenian population. That the Nakhichevan Jewish community was considered integral to Rostov is evinced in the name of one of its mutual aid organizations, the Association of Jewish Refugees in the Cities of Rostov and Nakhichevan-on-Don

---

21. These are items and rituals associated today with Orthodox Jews. A *payah* (pl. *payot*, or *payis*) is the lock of hair that remains unshaven or uncut on the side of a man's or boy's head. Tzitzis (or tzitzit) is a word that means *fringes* and refers to the fringed garment worn by men under a shirt, generally with the fringes visible. *Tefillin* are known in English by the equally obscure word *phylacteries*. They are small leather boxes containing words of scripture that remind the wearer of the commandments. They are worn at weekday morning prayers, affixed to the head and arm by narrow leather straps.

22. Church Slavonic, the script of which differs from the more modern Cyrillic alphabet.

(Budnitskii 22). Eli recollected with pleasure how, in this town of southern Russia,

[w]e established in Nakhichevan a little . . . ice cream parlor, with a candy store and fruit. I remember we children, at night, we had our fruit, and watermelons, and grapes, and all type of tropical food, outside the store and inside, people were coming from all over the city because we did a very good job. We had different type of ice creams, and early in the morning we had by hand, we had to turn metal drums, with the sweet cream and sugar, vanilla or chocolate, and there we had also different kinds of pastries, and we made a very nice living. It wasn't near our apartment house, but it was, oh let's say, about, fifteen minutes or a half-hour walk to our house.[23]

The Russian school that Eli attended in Rostov was run by Iliya Shershevskii, a Jewish community leader who in 1918 helped found a Jewish Culture and Education Society. According to Budnitskii, the Shershevskovo Gymnasium[24] was one of his greatest achievements, "a mixed (boys' and girls') private Jewish gymnasium, the first of its kind in Rostov" (Budnitskii 22). Eli studied Hebrew there, as well as Russian. He also continued religious studies at the local synagogue, where he attended services every Sabbath and on the holidays and sang in the choir. Since he was there until 1921, he would have celebrated his bar mitzvah in that synagogue. I remember him telling me once that the reception consisted of women throwing raisins and candies at him from the balcony, where they sat. If I had the opportunity today I would ask him many more questions—about the bar mitzvah and so much else. In his interview Eli recalled that, as a newcomer, he was harassed by some of the other boys when they played in the shul (synagogue) backyard. Finally, when he had had enough of one

---

23. When my son was in high school, more than eighty years later, we hosted an exchange student from Azerbaijan. Alex mentioned to us that his family had lived for a while in Rostov-on-Don; what he remembered most about it were the ice cream shops.

24. The Russian gymnasium was a high school, but students started to attend earlier than in the United States.

particular boy, a redheaded, freckle-faced child who was older and stronger than he, young Eli said to the others, " 'Look, boys, I will show you that this guy will never go to me near.' And I gave him such a beating that since then I became one of the heroes and became friendly with this guy." Telling the story to Burt, years later, he concluded, "If a person goes too many times . . . , you finally react." He remembered a game called *yampolke*,[25] which they played in that backyard, which involved hitting a stick on the ground with a larger stick and then hitting it again when it was in the air. He recalled hanging onto the backs of trolleys when he didn't have money for the fare or when he was saving the money for a treat and thought he'd take a chance.

All was not to continue in this ordinary way, however. The Russian Revolution and its aftermath had a major impact on Eli and his family. Many Jews, inside Russia and elsewhere in the world, at first welcomed the revolution as an end to tsarist oppression. Eli remembered "excitement in the streets," parades, people carrying red flags, singing the "Internationale," calling out " 'Down with the capitalists, with the murderers, . . . with the tsar. [Long live] the proletariat, . . . Trotsky and Lenin. . . . We children were watching" as adults celebrated "the new regime of the proletariat [pronounced in the European way, with stress on the last syllable], and the eventual victory of the Communism." Right after the revolution, however, Rostov-on-Don became a major battleground in the Russian Civil War. As Eli described it,

> the tsarist army, or the White Guardians,[26] . . . occupied Rostov-na-Donu. There was fighting going on, you could see dead people on the streets, dead horses, horses who died and killed by compression the people who were riding, and it was terrible. Then, then again fighting in a couple of weeks; the Red Army took over, and then again it went to the White. Several times

---

25. The name of this game may be derived from the Russian word *yama*, which means *hole* or *pit*. In the interview Eli explains that the smaller stick was placed on the ground on top of a stone.

26. This group of anti-Communist forces is more commonly known in English as the White Guards.

the city changed the hands, till finally of course the Red Army was victorious, and they settled there.

At that time, Eli's brother Maishe (or Misha, as he was known in Russian) was mobilized and taken into the White Army. Eli recalled the day he came home:

> Early in the morning, we heard a bell, ringing. I came out first, and I saw there was an old-looking man with a beard and I didn't recognize him, till finally it hit me that it was my brother Maishe. Seems to be, he escaped from the White Guardians army, where he was doing the telephone lines, taking care of the telephone lines, and he escaped; he deserted the White Guardian army. . . . He came back to our house. He was with a beard, and completely unshaven, dirty, with plenty of lice. And my mother cried, everybody cried.
>
> And then there was the Red Army. Then again, attack, and this White Army started to attack Rostov-na-Donu. My brother decided, because he was a deserter, he was afraid they may catch him, and that would have been terrible, went to this, our ice cream parlor, . . . in the back room, . . . where he was hiding and covered himself with a lot of boxes and cans, they shouldn't find him. And imagine, at that time when the White Guardians came, they were in the backyard of the store, but they didn't open the [back room]. They were all looting. And what we did at that time, to make appear that it was looted already, we opened the front door, we took out and broke the windows. And he was hiding there, while the door was open, and therefore they didn't touch anything, and they didn't look in the back. Then finally the Red Army took over, and then he was able to go out of the hiding, and he became an ardent Communist. When we came back to Lithuania he didn't want to go back. He wanted to stay in Russia.

Eli's account of the preemptive "looting" of the house is reminiscent of similar actions taken by Jews, then and earlier, to avoid oncoming pogroms. Maishe (known as Misha thereafter, his Russian name) was at that time the oldest son at home with the family. They remained in touch with him at least until the start of World War II, and he remained an ardent Communist, at one point sending his brother Dave, in the United States, a

Figure 11. Maishe (Misha/Moshe) Rochelson and a young woman (his wife or future wife) in workers' clothing, reading *Pravda*. Family collection.

photograph in the style of socialist realism (figure 11).[27] The woman in the photo is unidentified, but she looks very much like Misha's wife in a later image (figure 12). As I will relate, my father disappointed Misha when he decided to go to the United States instead of the Soviet Union after the Holocaust, but Misha contacted him again many years later.

Despite early optimism among many, the Revolution did not bring with it the hoped-for better life. Times became harder for the family in Rostov, and they began to think about returning to Kovno. As Eli described it,

---

27. The photograph is signed by Misha on the back, and dated /3/VIII/25 (3 August 1925).

Figure 12. Maishe
(Misha/Moshe)
Rochelson and his
family, probably 1930s.
Family collection.

[i]t was difficult with getting food, it was . . . famine or starvation . . . all over
Russia and in Rostov-na-Donu also. . . . . We had to close our store there.
[W]e couldn't get supplies, . . . [and] the Russians were looking at any people
who are enterprising as remnants of capitalism or capitalistic enterprises,
and they just—we were afraid and we couldn't get even merchandise. The
only thing we could do, there was like a marketplace in Nakhichevan, and
we, buying bread, let's say, and selling bread, . . . we make profit to have
for us at least a few slices of bread profit—bread—no money, but bread.
Otherwise if you ate . . . [all] the bread we didn't have money to buy it the
next day. . . . [T]hen we also had thread, needles, little tiny things which we

could sell. . . . But the Russians made many times, we called *oblava* [a raid], it means . . . they surrounded [us] . . . from all streets, and were catching those who were selling. They didn't like even this, they didn't want any enterprise, this already is the beginning of the capitalism. And to make the story short, they [had] rations, we starved. One day they would have dried fish, salty, the other day they would have salt, the third day they will have sugar, or peas or pea soup. That was all we could have, and we really starved.

Although summers in Nakhichevan could be hot enough for ice cream, the winters were extremely cold:

> Now our house was heated with a stove, a coal-burning stove, and also wood-burning stove. Now we had to supply these. I and my brothers were going, and I had to carry, let's say, I remember, a whole sack, a canvas sack, with coal I was getting, and bringing home, going for miles bringing home to have some for the coal stove; also wood we were getting, to keep warm. . . . [W]e didn't have water [in the house]; in the winter, we had to go to a pump near the house . . . , and imagine there [it] is cold like in Alaska. . . . You go with a pail, and you go up and there is a hill of ice; you go up, you have your pail and you try to go down: Bingo! Everything spilled out and you go again and you bring it.

While in Nakhichevan, Eli caught the Spanish flu during the great epidemic of 1918–19 that killed between twenty and forty million people ("Influenza Pandemic of 1918"). The disease infected one-fifth of the world's population, and was most deadly among people aged twenty to forty. Eli would have been between eleven and twelve years old: "I got sick; while in gymnasium, I had chills. . . . When I came home I told my mother I am very, very sick. She put me to bed, and I became delirious. The only thing I remember is seeing rats going over the chest across my bed, and various types of wild pictures, imaginary of course." Some months later he became ill again, and an Armenian doctor treated him for *typhus recurrentes*, recurrent fever, and then for spirochete of Obermaier, a microbe causing "paroxysms of high fever that last five or six days" (Stevens 260). "[T]his Armenian doctor, really," Eli recalled, "saved my life." There was a cholera epidemic at this time, as well, and, as he recounted later, people were dying of cholera within twenty-four hours. But the government gave the family cholera immunizations, and they were spared: "I still remember the pain [of the vaccine]," he reported; "I had sharp pain with swelling of the arm, but this saved me against cholera." Eli remembered these events in the interview as an adult and a physician, and he took pride in sharing the details with his son, who was about to begin his own medical studies.

With conditions worsening in Nakhichevan and relatives in Kovno urging them to return, the family traveled back, via Rostov-on-Don and Moscow, in 1921. Even today, that rail journey would take between seventeen and twenty-eight hours. Apparently many families were making the trip then; Eli recalled that children left the train when it stopped, and some did not get back in time. When his family arrived in Kovno—"so starved and so hungry"—they were greeted at the train station by an older cousin, Dora Ozhinsky (a sister of Genya and Riva Lubovsky), who brought hot chocolate, bagels, candy, and other treats: "Imagine what it meant to us. I still remember the taste."[28]

At the time the family arrived home, Kaunas (Kovno) was the temporary capital of Lithuania, which had become independent from Russia in 1919. Vilnius (Vilna), the traditional capital, switched hands between Russia and

---

28. Dora Ozhinsky and her sisters were the children of Henye Rochelson's brother, Mordkhel Lubovsky. According to Riva's grandson Pierre Pizzochero, Dora, Genya, and Riva also had a sister Essia and a brother David. David was killed in the action against intellectuals in the early days of the Kovno ghetto, as I will discuss, and in an e-mail Pierre confirmed that Dora (and, most likely, her children) was also killed in the Holocaust. Essia, however, had married a Russian and survived the Holocaust in Russia. She had a son who became a scientist and a professor at Lomonosov Moscow State University. As I learned from Pierre in conversation, Essia visited Riva and Genya in Milan, where they lived sometime before their deaths, and the sisters enjoyed a few weeks' reunion. As I will discuss, while researching this book I came in contact with other Lubovsky cousins, the Esner family, American descendants of a sister of Mordkhel and Henye of whom neither Pierre nor I had previously been aware.

Poland in the interwar years and was restored as the capital of the Lithuanian Soviet Socialist Republic when the Soviets occupied Lithuania in 1940. It is the capital today, while Kaunas remains the second-largest city. At any event, Eli enrolled in the Russian gymnasium in Kovno, as he had in southern Russia. Most of the Jewish teenagers attended either the Hebrew or the Russian gymnasium, not the Lithuanian, in part because of the intense Lithuanian nationalism in those schools, which alienated Jews. Additionally, as Eli pointed out in the interview now in the Dorot Jewish Division of the New York Public Library, when Lithuania was part of the Russian empire, before the first world war, "[t]he Lithuanian language was strongly forbidden and you could be jailed for studying or teaching the Lithuanian language" (Rochelson, NYPL interview 4). Eli's sister, as he mentioned, encouraged him to study Russian, and he had already received a good start in Shershevskii's school. That he did not attend Hebrew gymnasium thus may or may not reflect on his family's practice of Judaism, but it does suggest a desire to be part of the larger world. As Eli's account makes clear, however, in the early years of the twentieth century he and his family were observant Jews, although not ultra-orthodox, and probably like most of their Jewish neighbors.

In the NYPL interview Eli elaborated on his own language use, and on general language preferences among Jews in Lithuania. In his childhood home they always spoke Yiddish, but when he was a young man and when he married, he and his Jewish peers conversed in Russian (4). Later in that interview he indicated that he also knew Lithuanian well (69). Thus there is a real parallel in language use as well as degree of acculturation between my father's generation of Jews (at least those in urban areas), whose parents remained in Lithuania, and those of the same generation (for example, my mother), whose parents emigrated to the United States and other Western nations. Yiddish was their first language, but they were also fluent in the languages of the nations in which they lived. Modernity touched all of them, its course interrupted in Europe by the Holocaust. Those who perished and those who survived were as much a part of twentieth-century culture as those who built Jewish lives in American cities after the 1880–1920 great wave of immigration (see figures 13, 14, 15a, 15b, and 15c).

א‏ראשװ‏א‏ל‏עצ‏ק‏ס‏א‏ר‏ד‏ס‏א‏ב‏ש‏‏ם‏ ה‏‏וה ‏אופ‏ו‏ר‏,,‏ה‏ ב כ ת'‏‏‏,ת‏ה‏ ‏אװ‏י‏ל‏ץ‏ ה‏ק‏פ‏ל‏א‏ 1928.‏רא‏י‏.

Figure 13. Avraham (Abraham) Rochelson (seated, left) and other members of the sport club "Ha-Koach" (Strength, Power) in a 1928 formal portrait. Family collection.

Figure 14. Chaye (Chaya/Anna) Rochelson Arendt and Albert Arendt visiting Montevideo, Uruguay, 1928. Albert had relatives in Uruguay. Family collection.

Figure 15a. Avraham Rochelson, formal portrait, July 29, 1928. Family collection.

Figure 15b. Mottel (Mordechai) Rochelson, formal portrait, no date. Family collection.

Figure 15c. Ilija (Eli) Rochelson, formal portrait, August 5, 1930. Inscription on the back reads, "From your youngest brother, Ilija, whom you used to carry on your shoulders" (translation by Rivka Schiller). Family collection.

When Eli and his family returned to Kovno, his studies in Rostov were accepted and he entered the third year of a gymnasium formed by "a cooperative of former Russian teachers . . . who were tsarist" and had fled the revolution.[29] He described the curriculum, in which he also studied Lithuanian language and history, as including mathematics, geography, astronomy, general history, and German. Exams after the first four years of study allowed a student to go on to the fifth through eighth years. Eli remembered the German courses especially well, because they led to a high degree of mastery: "We already had to write about Goethe and Schiller, and even had to memorize certain things from Goethe. Heinrich Heine wasn't allowed, but we were reading Heinrich Heine too."[30]

---

29. Josef Griliches identifies this school as the Russian gymnasium that was near a Russian Orthodox church, on Vytauto Prospect in the eastern part of Kaunas. There were also Polish and German gymnasia nearby (telephone interview, October 2012).

30. Heine, a German poet of Jewish birth who converted to Christianity, was well known for his lyric and his satiric poetry, as well as his sometimes radical political views. He

When the family first arrived in Kovno from Rostov, they lived a semirural life, keeping two cows, a goat, and chickens in their backyard. The animals shared a pasture with those from several other houses and, as Eli told the story, each cow knew where to come back to at night. Once when he became ill he was given goat's milk as a treatment—"[g]oat milk . . . and fresh air, and good food, and sweet cream, and cakes, all these carbohydrates. I think it was a good idea, too, after starvation." They had chicken, eggs, and milk from their livestock; they made sour cream and butter from the milk, as well as cheese, straining the milk through a towel. They sold some of the dairy foods they produced and thus were able to make a living and eat well themselves. Later they moved to Slobodke (also spelled Slobodka, or Vilijampolé in Lithuanian), a place renowned for its yeshivas, places of Jewish learning. It eventually became the site of the Kovno ghetto, after the Nazis occupied the city. When Eli's family lived there, he had to walk four or five miles, he estimated, across a bridge over the Neris River to the Russian gymnasium, summer and winter. He told this story in his interview with Burt, but he also told it to me often when I was a child. I was a bit surprised when I learned later that a parent's tale of walking to school over ice and snow was also part of American childhood lore, that children with American-born parents would later joke about hearing similar stories of hardships in the "olden days." In Eli's case, he had to pay a toll to cross the bridge, and once he and his brother Mottel got into a fight with the bridge tender when they didn't have the fee. In spring, when the ice melted, the bridge was washed away, and they would give someone a few kopecks to row them across, about ten people to a boat, each way. After Slobodka the family moved again, to the center of town, near a fish market, when Bere-Mikhel worked for the Wolf-Engelmann brewery.[31]

---

was a key poet studied by Jews at this time, as well as by others. His own relationship to Judaism was complicated, and that, too, was part of his identity for Jewish readers.

31. Volfas Engelman brewery, now largely owned by a Finnish company, was in the 1920s also called Wolf-Engelmann. At that time it was responsible for 40 percent of Lithuania's beer consumption ("Volfas Engelman"). A Volfas Engelman beer is

Eli completed gymnasium in 1927:

> [W]hile in gymnasium, in the same class there was Misha Meerovich and his
> sister, Serafima. I fell in love with her; I was invited many times to her house
> because Misha Meerovich was my friend. We were talking together. . . . He
> was a very bright young man, a capable man, he was—he never prepared his
> homework, he knew when he was present at school, he remembered, he mem-
> orized, and he was, in all type of science, or literature, philosophy, he was very
> adept, he finished with high marks. His sister was also in the same class; we
> had, at that time, a co-ed school. Now, many times we were walking together,
> he was talking about Schopenhauer, and Nietzsche, and other things, and I
> would say, partly my education was also through him, and his education, he
> got from his father who was a pharmacist, a very intelligent, cultur[ed] man.

Mikhail (Misha) Meerovich was born in March 1910, making him nearly
three years younger than Eli; Serafima was one year younger than her
future spouse.[32] That they were all in the same class attests to the high
intelligence that Eli took pains to record (see figure 16).

About 30 percent of the students at the school were Jewish, 70 percent
were non-Jewish, and Eli had many non-Jewish friends: "We were going
out together, meeting each other, and there [were] no signs of antisemitism,
or any hostility" at that time. Teachers, too, showed no hostility, and, as Eli
remembered, "it was a very neat, close group together, . . . the students and
the teachers." In order to receive a "certificate of ripeness," essential for applying to university, students had to pass difficult written and oral exams, at the
latter of which a representative from the state education department was
present. Nearly fifty years later, Eli recalled how his German teacher, named
Pinagel, was surprised that after his excellent performance in class his written

---

apparently still distributed by the Ragutis company based in Kaunas. The original
Wolf Engelman was a Jew, and in 1940 the brewery owned by that "Zionist leader"
was confiscated by the Soviets ("Soviet Seizes Jewish-owned Brewery").

32. Misha's birthdate is recorded in a Kaunas draftee list, KRA F 219/2 1043, made
available to subscribers to the Kaunas District Research Group of LitvakSIG; Sima's
year of birth appears in the internal passport database of LitvakSIG, Kaunas District Research Group and JewishGen, KRA/66/1/40515, passport number 68/2603.

Figure 16. Graduation photograph, 1927, Kovno Russian Gymnasium of the Teachers' Association. Eli Rochelson's picture is on the extreme right of the third row from the top; Serafima and Mikhail Meerovich are second and third from the left in that same row. Family collection.

exam was not satisfactory. She apparently then graded his test generously, so that he would gain the certificate, and then examined him orally again to make sure he knew the material. In the end, he graduated cum laude.

Antisemitism existed, however, in higher education. Eli applied to the veterinary faculty of the University of Vytautas the Great (also known as Vytautas Magnus University) in Kaunas, "because I knew they wouldn't accept a Jew in medicine." After a year, however, he applied to the medical faculty and was accepted. He had to earn a living, as well, and he worked as a bookkeeper while taking one course each year, presumably yearlong courses. There was no time limit, as long as he paid tuition. When he was drafted into the Lithuanian army in 1935, his wife took over the book-keeping job and he took six weeks off from his medical studies for basic training. Photographs show Eli in his army uniform and with his unit in the snow; he would explain that he was the one wearing a fur collar because they had to keep the doctor healthy (figures 17 and 18). Some of the young army doctors (jokingly?) practiced their trade for the camera indoors (figure 19). In his interview Eli praised an encouraging colonel, "the doctor in charge of the [military] hospital," who told him that, for the year and a half of service required after the first six weeks, he could work in the hospital in the morning and then "take off your uniform and go to medical school." Eli did that, and by 1939 he had finished his military service and earned his candidacy in medicine; in 1940 he received his medical degree.

As with the colonel, Eli took pains to acknowledge the non-Jewish teachers, professors, and even a dean who showed him friendship and support as he pursued his education. Similarly, he spoke of the friendships he had with non-Jewish peers, especially up until the early 1930s. He wanted to explain the complexities of life in Lithuania, as well as its pleasures. It

Figure 17. Eli in the uniform of the Lithuanian army, January 1937. Family collection.

was important to him, and valuable to his story as history. Seven decades after the Holocaust ended, it is too easy and at the same time inaccurate to see the situation of the Jews in their East European homelands as an unremitting struggle against antisemitism. Yet Eli also exposed the antisemitism that he and other Jewish medical students suspected and encountered:

Figure 18. Eli (front row, third from right) in his military unit, February 1937. On the back he has written in Yiddish, "Not far from the shooting field. People are warming themselves by the fire. I am standing in the fur" (translation by Rivka Schiller). Family collection.

Figure 19. Army doctors with their patients, February 1937; Eli is at far left. Family collection.

We had eighteen subjects, and each time you had to pass [an] oral examination, and face the professor. I had an argument with the dean of the medical college, he was the professor of physiology. Each time he failed me. I had to go two or three times; he said, come in a month, come in a month, and in a month. At one time—and the people, usually the students were waiting outside, and [there] were one or two—inside he questioned, and the other[s were] outside. One time he said, you come in a month; I got mad, and slammed the door, and then he said—they told me after, a girl, a medical student told me—"You know, he made a remark about you, he said you got mad, he almost broke the window, but I will never let him finish the medical school." Of course I got upset and so on, but finally I passed with him the physiology.

Anatomy was a different chapter. The first year of medical school we had one part of anatomy, and the second year we had the second part of anatomy. We had to do all colloquiums, about thirty-six colloquiums. . . . [T]his professor, his name was Yelinski, he was a known antisemite, and people were going, couldn't pass from first year, many times, and to the second year, or from second year to the third year, because he wouldn't pass [them in] the examinations. And the Jewish fellows sometimes go three or four years, studying only anatomy to pass. But he was such a cruel man, that after you answered all questions, he says—[he] gave another question. If you didn't know: come in six months, come in three months. Anyway, one young student, already three or four years, and he didn't pass, he told him to come in three months, he jumped at him with a knife, and he wanted to kill him. But then the assistant Kropotky came out. And I was then in the building there, nearby. He came out and he saved his life. But the man [the student] was committed to an insane asylum where he committed suicide. And that was only an illustration how hard it was in Lithuania, especially when you are a Jew. I think Lithuanians, the natives, didn't have too much problems; they have their notes in Lithuanian language, whatever they had, and they passed them immediately.[33] It only was trouble with the Jews. Anyway,

---

33. According to Paulina Rosenstein, whose mother graduated from the same medical school, the language of instruction and the textbooks were in German. (Personal conversation, January 24, 2015.)

I overcame— . . . This man who attacked the professor was not crazy, he was just mad and he couldn't suffer anymore. That was the story.

Natalia Aleksiun, in research on Jewish medical students in prewar Poland, has found similar antisemitism toward Jewish medical students there, and specifically among professors of anatomy (see Aleksiun, "Christian Corpses for Christians!" "Jewish Students and Christian Corpses"). Šarūnas Liekis reports that, on December 12, 1939 (just months after Eli received his candidacy for the degree), "[t]he [non-Jewish] students of the Kaunas University medical faculty started to protest and to demand to establish *numerus clausus* [numerical limitation, or a restrictive quota] for the Jewish students. The Lithuanian students filed a written complaint stating that the Jews were not loyal to Lithuania and claimed that Jewish students were distributing leftist literature" (254–55, italics in original). The University of Vytautas the Great medical school was later known as the Kaunas Institute of Medicine, or the medical faculty of Kaunas University (figure 20).

Figure 20. Entrance to Kaunas Institute of Medicine in 2003. Photograph by author on visit to Kaunas.

2

Kovno in the 1930s

ELI ROCHELSON AND Serafima Meerovich married on January 22, 1934. Their son, Boris (Borya), was born almost exactly nine months later, on October 19.[1] Serafima lived at 35 Laisvės Alėja at the time of the marriage, on what was then and is now the most prominent street in the Naumiestis (New Town) of central Kaunas. Today it is a beautiful pedestrian boulevard (figure 21). Very close by is the one remaining synagogue in Kaunas, the Choral Synagogue, where the marriage ceremony, officiated by Rabbi Gutman,[2] may have taken place (figure 22). My friends and I

---

1. The marriage record, which is now on JewishGen but of which I received a copy during my visit to Vilnius, is in the Lithuanian Historical Archives (LVIA 1817/1/101). It records Serafima's year of birth as 1908. Holocaust-era records, such as her intake interview document from Stutthof concentration camp (Stutthof Individual Records), indicate her date of birth was June 25, 1913, but, as with many adult Holocaust victims, she lied about her year of birth to make herself seem younger. When family members, such as my father, searched for her after the war, documents showed her date of birth as June 25, 1908. She was thus about a year younger than my father. Their son's birth record, which I also obtained on my visit, is LVIA 817/1/1934/100/154#459/Kaunas. However, I had known before then that his birthday was October 19, exactly one week after my own, although I don't remember how I knew. Since Borya was a child during the Holocaust, his recorded year of birth was earlier, and his camp records show a birthdate of October 9, 1930 (as, for example, Individual Documents Dachau, ITS 1.1.6.2/124 34026432-0_1). Why the day is also changed is a mystery, or perhaps just a recording error.

2. Ephraim Gutman of Kovno, in his 1946 interview with David Boder, tells a story of unexpected mercy when he and his family were allowed to pass unmolested by a

attended a Shabbat service there in 2003, and a concert the following day. In the 1930s, Laisvės Alėja was the home of numerous other Jews, including the teenagers Josef Griliches, for many years president of the New York-based organization Assistance to Lithuanian Jews, and Nissan Krakinowski, who settled in Brooklyn, both of whom knew Eli. Josef Griliches recalled later that the Lithuanian government, in the interwar years, would send people from house to house to collect money for armaments. In 1938, the Griliches family was visited by a public official, a deputy minister of finance or member of parliament, for that purpose. In 1939 they were visited for this purpose by Eli Rochelson, an ordinary neighbor, and the Griliches family joked to one another that they had apparently declined in status.[3] Borya's birth record indicates that after the couple married they lived at 18 Maironio Street, perpendicular to Laisvės Alėja and just a few blocks south, close to the university. Today that site is occupied by a rather nondescript, possibly Soviet-era building. By 1941, however, the family had moved to 36 Maironio,[4] and the current structure may well have been the one they lived in when the Nazis occupied the city (figure 23).

In an unexpected way, I obtained a glimpse into the life of my father's family just a few years before his marriage. After my mother died in February 2010, I discovered among her belongings a travel diary and photo album kept by my aunt Ida Robinson when she and her husband, Eli's brother Dave, visited the family in Kovno in the summer of 1931. Uncle Dave had changed his name from Rochelson to Robinson (and his given

fascist partisan in the early days of Nazi occupation. The Lithuanian partisan "felt embarrassed and requested his comrades they should let us go because this was the family of the Kovno rabbi" (4). Ephraim's father may have been the rabbi who had performed the marriage ceremony for Eli and Serafima and whose name is listed in their marriage record as G. Gutman.

3. Nissan Krakinowski, interview, June 2, 2011; Josef Griliches, telephone conversation with author, June 1, 2011.

4. KAU-KAU-Jan-12–1941-Voters list Books 1–24, 333–57; 60–67; lines A15268-A15271. This list, which indicates that Avraham and Rose (and of course their daughter, Sarah) lived at that address, as well, was made available through a project of the Kaunas District Research Group, LitvakSIG.

Figure 21. Laisves Aleja, 2003. Photograph by author. The building with the pagoda on the roof is the Metropolis Hotel.

Figure 22. Kaunas Choral Synagogue, 2003. Photograph by author.

Figure 23. Maironio gatve (Maironio Street), 36, Kaunas, where the Rochelson family lived in 1941. Photograph © 2017 Google, Image Date June 2012. A project by Nick Nicholaou using the Google Maps API. Accessed on Google Earth.

names from David Yonah to David John) soon after he arrived in America in 1912. Various versions of the story are that he was encouraged to take a name that would be easier to pronounce by Americans and that he had been invited to the United States by people named Robinson, so that taking their name would be appropriate and helpful. I have never found out who these Robinsons were, although they may have owned the hardware store in St. Stephen, South Carolina, where David worked when he first immigrated. When Eli arrived in New York, thinking he would take his brother's surname, Dave discouraged him, saying that Robinson never really felt like his own name, even thirty-three years later. Dave served in World War I, in Europe, as part of the United States Army, and told me in later years that he believed he had been denied military promotions and recognition because he was a Jew. Indeed, in 2015 two other veterans of the First World War, Jewish and African American, were posthumously awarded honors they had been denied due to prejudice. Dave eventually had a hardware business of his own, in Brooklyn, and ultimately retired from a position at the Brooklyn Navy Yard. His wife, Ida, was born in New York and was a Sanditen by birth, related to our Sanditen cousins in Tulsa (figure 24).

Figure 24. Ida and David Robinson, either shortly before or after their marriage in 1920. Family collection.

She taught music in New York City public schools, and by coincidence was my mother's eighth-grade music teacher. Less strangely, as my aunt, she became my own first piano teacher, and she provided me with some of my earliest and most cherished literary books.

Ida and Dave's 1931 trip to Kaunas also included Berlin, Munich, Lucerne, Interlaken, Frankfurt, and Paris. Both their itinerary and Ida's travel notes suggest that, at that time, neither in the United States nor in Europe was the family especially anxious about world events. Ida and Dave were excited about seeing the sights of Germany as well as reuniting with relatives, and the relatives were eager to show them Kovno and its surroundings. The first pages of Ida's small blue leather-bound travel diary (figure 25) mention "at least 35" people who saw them off, and the gifts that filled their stateroom. The transatlantic voyage on the North German Lloyd steamship *Dresden* included fine dining, dancing, band concerts, and cocktail parties. The ship sailed to Bremen via Cherbourg and Southampton. Eli's and Dave's cousin Genya Lubovsky visited Ida and Dave in Berlin;

Figure 25. Ida S. Robinson's travel diary, 1931. Family collection.

she was living there at the time, practicing dentistry.[5] In the diary's pages are handwritten lists of sights seen and paintings viewed, pasted tickets and travel brochures. There is even a pressed flower between pages recording sightseeing in Berlin and a Potsdam trip, during which Ida and Dave "met about 300 sailors & officers from the States." In Berlin, Ida notes, they bought a handbag and stockings for Genya, ties for "Dave's 3 brothers," and

5. Genya later moved to Paris, and then she and her sister Riva spent the war years in Grenoble and Juan les Pins, where they were safe from the Nazis. Riva's husband, Max Kané, had been deported, but he survived the camps and all of them returned to Paris after the war (e-mail to author from Pierre Pizzochero, July 30, 2012). I met Genya and Riva in Paris in the summer of 1971, and Max when I returned with my parents the following year and saw all three. In the summer of 2013, in Milan, I visited with Pierre, Genya's grand-nephew and Riva and Max's grandson, whom I had met in the United States when he was working on his PhD in astro-nuclear physics, and (for the first time) I met his mother, Jenny, an artist, Riva and Max's daughter and Genya's niece.

a cushion for Dave's father—my grandfather Bere-Mikhel, who would die the following year of pulmonary disease (figure 26). The three brothers were Mottel, Avraham, and Eli; Misha had long been living in the Soviet Union, while Lithuania in 1931 was independent. On July 1, gifts at hand, Ida and Dave boarded the train to Kovno.

On July 2, soon after they arrived, Ida expressed dissatisfaction with their room at the Metropole Hotel; they were given a better room the next day.[6] But in the same entry she also described the first day of their visit, her first impressions of the family (figure 27) and their home:

> [Dave's] father understands & hears everything but his speech is very weak. Anna [Chaye] is lovely. They are all very fine! You go through a door in a fence, then thru a back yard & up a flight of steps. Five lovely rooms & a toilet.
>
> The servant does all the heavy work.
>
> Mottle [Mottel] & Eli came in later. Eli looks like the Sanditen boys— [. . .] Speaks a little English. Very sensitive!

The family went sightseeing in Kovno, much as my friends and I did in 2003:

> We went walking and saw the Nemen [Nemunas River] and the Velya [old Slavic name for the Neris] and walked to the Junction [probably the park, described earlier, where the Nemunas and Neris Rivers meet]. Saw many churches & old buildings. Walked & walked thru all the quaint streets. At night Dave's Tante Sarah came & then Abraham & his wife [who had been married the year before]. He is between Eli & Mottle. She is all eyes. (Rose) Pretty soon she will be having a baby but at the present they both are working.
>
> They all walked us back to the hotel at 11:30.

Ida's diary records that she took a walk with Eli when Dave and Anna went to see the film *All Quiet on the Western Front*. In Kovno they also toured

---

6. The hotel still exists, as the Metropolis, in the center of Kaunas; see figure 20.

Figure 26. Bere-Mikhel Rochelson, 1931. Photograph in Ida and David Robinson's travel album. Family collection.

Figure 27. The Rochelson/Robinson family in Kovno, 1931; left to right, Avraham, Rose, Mottel, Henye, Eli, David, Chaye/Anna, Minne, and another relative. Photograph in Ida and David Robinson's travel album, probably taken by Ida. Family collection.

museums, including the War Museum, where Ida was most interested in American Red Cross posters. As a family they made excursions to Pane-mune, Aleksotas, and Kulautuva, a popular place for rural excursions by Kovno Jews, a wooded area along the north bank of the Nemunas River about 20.5 kilometers (just under 13 miles) from Kaunas. It was a place where Eli and his friends had enjoyed traveling as teenagers and young adults. When the family went there with Ida and Dave on July 7, 1931, a scheduling mishap caused a delay that gave them a brief northern summer idyll. As Ida wrote,

> [a]t 10 went back to the hut & prepared to wait out the night. We told sto-ries, sang, & walked to keep warm. All the constellations were very clear. Then towards 1 a.m. it began getting daylight. The moon & the sun were out together at 1:20 [. . .].

The peaceful scene is followed by Ida's picture of the *dampfer*, the boat that returned them to Kovno in a pungent three-hour upstream journey: "Chickens, ducks, sheep & calves were tied all over the place. The baa-ing, chicking etc. And I mustn't forget the smells from the 'w.c.'" But at the end of it all, Ida wrote, "if I weren't so tired I'd have enjoyed it" (figure 28).

The Kovno section of the travel diary depicts a warm and loving fam-ily delightedly hosting relatives they had not seen in years—Dave, not

Figure 28. Ida and Dave with Eli (left), possibly in Kulautuva, 1931. Photograph in Ida and David Robinson's travel album. Family collection.

since he left in 1912, and Ida, whom they had not met previously but who had been married to Dave since 1920, eleven years before this visit. Ida refers to Dave's family as "the folks," suggesting a kind of easy intimacy as well as a very American colloquial frame of reference. They met many of the relatives Eli mentioned when describing his childhood—Sarah and Minne and their families, the young Leiye and Feyge (Sarah's daughters, who would survive the Holocaust, presumably in the Russian part of the Soviet Union[7]), and "Dora Oshinsky" and her "adorable" children: "charming hostess, lovely home and family." This was the Dora who had brought hot chocolate, candies, and bagels to young Eli and his family when they returned to Kovno from Rostov-on-Don ten years earlier. On July 12, Ida's entry reflected the inadequacy of words to express the abundance of familial warmth: "Other cousins, cousins, cousins." She had named quite a few, but in the end there were just so many.

Eli brought Ida flowers twice, red and white roses the second time. Anna brought candy, and Ida wrote, "wish they wouldn't," fearing, it seems, that they were using funds they could be spending in more practical ways. On July 15, Ida's birthday as well as the day they left Kovno, the diary entry ends with a list:

Flowers from Rose
Candy—Anna, Tante Minnie, Leieh
Cake & jelly—mother (What will we do with it all.)

Ida's hesitations and minor laments are typical and conventional responses to familial generosity, perfectly appropriate to the normal times that those were. Several days earlier, Ida and Dave had had dinner at Rose and Avraham's home, where Rose proudly showed them her wedding gifts. Photographs in Ida and Dave's album show the family picnic, as well as Avraham

---

7. Sarah's daughter Taibe (Taibke/Taube) also survived, immigrating to Israel. The Bloch family tree shows her date of death as 1957; she had married and had a son, born in 1950.

and Rose leaning out of house windows with lace curtains (figures 29, 30). Flowering plants are in the window from which Avraham looks out. There is no sense at all (and why should there be?) that this was a world about to disappear. Yet the "War Museum" that Ida mentions is the same military museum, in the center of Kovno, where ten years later Eli would see the Lithuanian flag hoisted ominously as the Germans approached (figure 31), and Aleksotas, which affords beautiful panoramas of Kaunas (figure 32), was the site of a labor camp to which Eli, Serafima, and Borya were sent from the Kovno ghetto. In 1931, however, both were places of interest to show visiting relatives, who would share city pleasures as well as country retreats (see figures 33a and 33b).

Letters and photographs sent to Dave by the family continue to fill out the picture of their prewar lives. Indeed, many of the photos reprinted in this book come from Ida and Dave's collection. Anna, as Eli's sister Chaye was then known, was married to Albert Arendt, a non-Jewish German,

Figure 29. Avraham Rochelson, dated on reverse August 27, 1930. Photograph in Ida and David Robinson's travel album. Family collection.

Figure 30. Rose Kagan (or Kaganov) Rochelson, 1930 or 1931 (no date indicated). Photograph in Ida and David Robinson's travel album.

Figure 31. Vytautas the Great War Museum, central Kaunas, 2003. Photograph by author.

Figure 32. View of Old Town, Kaunas, 2003, from Aleksotas; New Town in the distance. Photograph by author.

Figure 33a. Street in Old Town, Kaunas, 1931; the name F. Steinas over a doorway suggests a Jewish-owned business. Photograph in Ida and David Robinson's travel album. Family collection.

Figure 33b. Intersection of Vilnaius and M. Daukšos Streets, Old Town, Kaunas, 2003. Photograph by author.

and they lived in Berlin. That she went back to Kovno for Ida and Dave's visit shows how close she felt to the family and what an important part of it she was, even after her marriage and relocation. This observantly Jewish yet modern and loving family did not reject their intermarried daughter. Photographs inscribed "Montevideo, 1928 and '29," sent to Dave and Ida, show Albert and Anna smiling on the beach and in the city (as in figure 14, above). Albert had relatives in Uruguay, whom he joined in the late 1930s, unable to get a visa for the United States and unwilling to remain in Nazi Germany. When I saw those photographs, late in my research, it occurred to me that Albert and Anna should have stayed in Uruguay, and brought the rest of the family after them. But life and history were more complicated than that, and no one had the benefit of hindsight.

On April 14, 1934, Anna wrote a long letter in Yiddish to her brother and sister-in-law in New York, expressing sorrow that she had worried them about her health and saying she was feeling much better. She reported in detail about her brother Mottel's medical studies, prolonged because he had interrupted them to serve in the military. He had finished his coursework, and the family hoped that soon he would be able "to practice in a hospital and pass 20 exams," all of which, their mother had written to her, "he can do [. . .] in one and a half years." At that point, wrote Anna (who signed her name *Chaye*), "He has hopes of passing the exams, getting his diploma, and that he may become a good doctor and have a lot of sick people [to treat], but only sick people whom he doesn't know. And I, too, would like to live to see him become a doctor already."[8]

Chaye's detailed description of Mottel's studies suggests an extended process and gives insight into the family's hopes and perhaps worries, as his mother, if not Mottel himself, shared the details of his courses and curriculum with his sister in Berlin. In an obviously later letter to her son David, dated only January 29, Henye writes that Mottel has "completed his internship" and should, in around two weeks, "get papers that will grant

8. Letter of April 14, 1934. Translation by Rivka Schiller.

him the right to practice." She adds, "He won't stay in Kovno, because it is difficult in Kovno. All the young doctors go to the provinces. He doesn't have a great desire [to go there], but we will see where it will be."[9] Whether it was especially difficult for young Jewish doctors, Henye Rochelson does not say. Natalia Aleksiun has pointed out that in Poland there was a discussion at this time about how to get more doctors, in general, to work in the provinces; she believes that new doctors throughout Eastern Europe may have been encouraged to work outside the already well-served cities, but that the pressure may have been even more intense for Jewish graduates.[10] In my grandmother's letter, the adjective "Jewish" may have been left as understood. As Dov Levin points out, in the interwar years, despite antisemitism, Jews studied medicine in large numbers, and, at Lithuanian universities in general, in percentages greater than in the population as a whole.[11]

Eli, who received his medical degree in 1940, stayed close to the big city, working as a medical intern at the university and in a *krankenkasse* (a health facility for government workers) in Šančiai, southeast of central Kaunas, from the time of his graduation until the day the Nazis invaded. But in a letter written as late as April 1941, his mother reported that he was "doing his internship. He has three more months. After that, we don't know what will be—whether he will get a job in Kovno—or whether he will then go to the provinces."[12] Her January letter about Mottel, however, illuminates something that for years had been a mystery to me. She and Mottel were living in Plokščiai (known as Ploksh or Plogsh in Yiddish) on

---

9. Letter of January 29 (no year). Translation by Rivka Schiller.

10. Personal conversation with author.

11. Levin, *Litvaks*, 150–51. Levin writes, "By 1933, of the 4,613 students enrolled at Kovno, 1,209 (26.2 percent) were Jewish" (150), while only just under 8 percent of the general population in 1923 were Jews. In the prewar years, Jews were 13.8 percent of the Lithuanian population (128). According to Mordechai Zalkin, in the late nineteenth century, "most local medical services [in Lithuania] were supplied by Jewish doctors" (146); hence Jews and medicine had a well-established connection and history.

12. Letter to Ida and David Robinson, April 14, 1941. Translated by Rivka Schiller.

June 22, 1941, and they were killed after the German invasion by Nazis or, more likely, Lithuanian collaborators. I could not understand why a young single man would want to live in the provinces with his mother. Her letter makes clear that the location was not his preference; she likely accompanied him to help keep house. This decision made for professional reasons led to their deaths soon after the start of the war.

Another vivid account in Chaye's 1934 letter fills in the details of an earlier letter from Henye to Dave, concerning the death of his father, Bere-Mikhel, on April 5, 1932. At that time, Henye wrote of her husband, "It is very sad. He became ill with an inflammation of the lungs—[he] lay one-and-a-half weeks, and then died." She warned Dave not to write to Chaye about this, because Chaye was ill, and she told him very clearly the Hebrew date of his father's death, 28 Adar Bet:

> I will ask you, my child, that if you can, you should [try to] squeeze in saying Kaddish. After a whole lifetime [next words unclear], be well—from me, your mother, Henye. The children send you regards. My child, record [mark] for yourself when your father died, so you will know when the *Yahrzeit* is.[13]

Saying the Kaddish prayer in memory of a parent during the first year of mourning, and then on each anniversary of the death, is a basic and widely observed Jewish tradition. It is a way of expressing respect for the parent and keeping his or her memory alive; among some Jews it is seen as a way to increase the merit of the deceased, thereby easing the transition to the world to come. I sensed in my grandmother's letter her concern that perhaps in America children were less conscientious about saying Kaddish. The April 1934 letter from Chaye reveals that, in addition, Henye was fulfilling her husband's urgent deathbed request. In that letter Chaye sent condolences to Ida, whose father had died in January.[14] Remembering her own

---

13. Letter dated April 6, Kovno. Translation by Rivka Schiller.
14. I confirmed the date of Max Sanditen's death on findagrave.com—not the most scholarly of websites, but helpful, since the details matched what I knew of the

father's death, she wrote that it was especially difficult for "us" (presumably herself and David) because they were not "with our father during the final days of his life." Yet she records their father's words, which she may have heard while visiting him earlier in his illness, or which he may have said at the end of the 1931 visit: "Our father felt that he saw you for the last time, and calmly parted from you with his sick tears. And since you were away from home, he said, 'I wanted to ask David that he say Kaddish for me'; and he wailed the entire day. Who knew that this would be the last time we'd see him; one cannot believe it."

The Yiddish handwriting in Chaye's letter is strong and clear; she was approximately forty years old,[15] and nothing suggests that she would die only a few days later. However, her reassuring words at the start of her letter may have been simply to allay her brother's fears. Anna died in Berlin of rheumatic heart disease, a complication of her childhood scarlet fever, on April 19, 1934. Her death was a great sadness to Eli, who went with their mother by train to Germany for her funeral on April 23. In a letter to Ida and Dave, Albert wrote that Jewish burial "was her last wish, and all the action pr[e]scribed by the Jewish Religion will be executed"[16]; thus Anna was buried at the Jewish Weissensee cemetery (figure 34). Albert also wrote, regarding the circumstances of her death, that after a sleepless and pain-filled night, "Anna got two injections made by her physician, she felt better, but her heart was too tired, to[o] weak."

I find myself suspicious of a German doctor treating a Jewish patient with painkillers in 1934, but I do not question Albert's loyalty.[17] He wanted to leave Germany after Anna died, and in February 1935 he corresponded

---

family. Since he died before the advent of Social Security, there is no Social Security Death Record.

15. An internal passport record lists Chaye's year of birth as 1894 (Lithuania Internal Passports Database, 1919–1940, internal passport issued 3 May 1922, KRA/66/1/35092, JewishGen.org).

16. Letter of April 21, 1934; written in English.

17. Ida expressed similar suspicions in at least one conversation I recall.

Figure 34. Anna (Chaye) Rochelson Arendt's gravestone, Weissensee Cemetery, Berlin; photograph sent by her widower, Albert Arendt. Family collection.

with Ida and Dave about steps he was taking to emigrate to the United States, a process that in the end did not succeed, leaving him eventually to join his brother in South America. In June 1935, however, while he was still residing in Berlin, Albert visited his late wife's family in Kovno. On the back of a picture postcard of the Garrison Church, a large late-nineteenth-century neo-Byzantine church that intersects Laisvės Alėja, Albert wrote a cheery message in English to Ida and Dave in Brooklyn, his words surrounded by short messages in Yiddish from various family members. "*A hertzlichen geruss fun Sima un Borinka*" ("Heartfelt regards from Sima and Borinka") sends the wishes of Eli's wife and eight-month-old child. Eli wrote (in Yiddish, as well), "Sincere regards from all of us, and from our little son, especially"[18] (figures 35a and 35b).

A great poignancy underlies these loving thoughts from proud parents, one of whom later became my father. I can picture the family gathered with Albert, perhaps after a day of sightseeing, sending their wishes to a son and brother in America. Serafima's short passage, although she used her Yiddish name, Sima, is written with the large and clear letters of someone unaccustomed to writing in Yiddish; her learner's penmanship makes her entry the easiest for me to read. Dave probably read Yiddish well; he would have learned the Hebrew letters as a child, and Yiddish was the language in which he communicated with his family in Europe. He might have had to read the words to Ida, who spoke some Yiddish but whom I remember as being generally more "American"—although many American Jews of her generation spoke Yiddish, too. The Kovno family, with its two young children, Borya and Sarah (the child with whom Rose was pregnant when Ida and Dave visited in 1931), presents an even livelier picture than the scene in Ida and Dave's apartment; the Brooklyn couple were childless. In 1935 Dave was likely still recovering from the failure of his hardware business a year earlier: "It is far worse that you worked so hard for 8 bitter years and your business has now gone under," Chaye had written in

---

18. Postcard, June 20, 1935. I was able to read Sima's Yiddish and thus to translate it on my own. The rest of the greetings were translated by Rivka Schiller.

Figure 35a. Postcard of the Garrison Church, sent by Albert Arendt to Ida and Dave Robinson in 1935. Family collection.

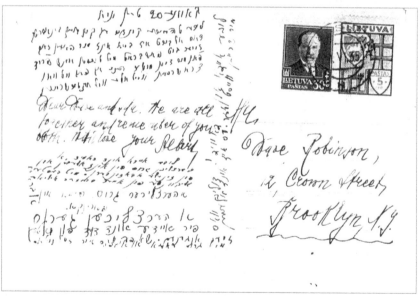

Figure 35b. Reverse of postcard, with family messages.

April 1934. By this time, of course, the family in Kovno knew that life was uncertain for them there; as Eli remembered, 1934 was the point at which antisemitism intensified. But at that moment, on that postcard, they were cheerfully sharing family happiness.

Historian Mordechai Zalkin confirms Eli's perception. Zalkin sees antisemitism in Lithuania as a phenomenon with a complicated history, moving from a "unique religious tolerance" in the late-fourteenth- and early-fifteenth-century reign of Grand Duke Vytautas (136) to patterns of antisemitic feeling that varied as economic needs and political regimes changed over the centuries and years. In the second half of the nineteenth century, Lithuanian nationalism combined with a sense that Jews were allied with Russians and Poles, who had been former rulers. Such feelings intensified anti-Jewish sentiments, violence against property, and other antisemitic acts. Yet, as Zalkin notes, the "classic pogroms" in other parts of Europe, characterized by the murder of Jews, were generally absent in late-nineteenth- and early-twentieth-century Lithuania (145). The era of independent Lithuania between 1920 and 1940 was characterized by ambivalence toward the Jewish population, in law as well as in common life, with antisemitism intensifying after the 1926 right-wing coup led by Antanas Smetona[19] and, again, increased antisemitic acts and attacks in the middle to late 1930s (148–50). Eli recalled that in the early years of independence there were even Jews elected to the *Seimas*, the Lithuanian parliament.

Eli discussed some of the ways antisemitism increased in Lithuania after Hitler was named chancellor of Germany in 1933 and "propagandists brainwashed the Lithuanians about the Jews, about the beauty of Hitler, victory in the future, and so on," but he said, too, that the antisemitism was "quiet." In the early 1930s, he recalled, "in my social life, we were going

---

19. Smetona was elected first president of Lithuania in 1919, but lost power the following year. He seized it again in the coup of 1926 and then fled the country after the Soviet occupation in 1940.

out many times, Sundays, or weekends, we were going to café, restaurants, drinking, dancing, having a good time." Then things changed:

[I]n 1937 and '38, it was dangerous to go on the street. . . . [W]e were attacked by the Lithuanians, the boys, and when we went to a cop, he says, "I don't see anybody." He turned his head, and they continued, and it was very dangerous to go out in the street. . . . Anyway, once we beat up a few. There was a Jewish man, a boxer, he beat up one Lithuanian and we went into the Monica restaurant, and then came out the whole group looking for us.[20] But because there were so many people, luckily, they couldn't see us. He came with other boys to beat up the fellow, the boxer.

---

20. The Monica was a popular restaurant among the Jews of Kovno. Josef Rosin writes, "In the winter of 1939, when Poland was divided between Germany and the Soviet Union, many refugees arrived in Kaunas. . . . Among the arriving people were authors and artists and they used to gather in the 'Monica' café" ("Kaunas [cont.]"; also confirmed in conversation with Josef Griliches).

3

War and Efforts to Escape

ELI RECEIVED HIS diploma as a doctor of medicine on June 15, 1940. On that same day, the Soviet Union invaded Lithuania, and by early August it had become a Soviet Socialist Republic, part of the USSR ("Annexation of the Baltic States"). Eli began working in the *krankenkasse* and held an internship at the university. As he recalled, "We didn't have any difficulty under Russian regime, because antisemitism was strictly forbidden, punishable by prison, and everybody was sweet and nice to us. But we knew that there is an underground favorable to Hitler. . . ."

In fact, from the late 1930s, the family had been trying to find ways to leave Europe, but the United States was largely unavailable as a refuge in the years leading up to the Holocaust. The Immigration Act of 1924, also known as the Johnson-Reed Act, passed at a time of intense nativism and xenophobia, reduced the total number of immigrants allowed to enter the country, and set quotas for each country of origin based on its representation in the United States in 1890. This severely limited further immigration from southern and eastern Europe, which had increased greatly in the years between 1900 and 1920. American secular ideology prevented designating Jews as a distinct population, but it was known that immigrants from certain countries after 1890 were predominantly Jewish. In 1924, the highest quotas were for Germany (51,227, which enabled Jewish German refugees to immigrate, at first), Great Britain and Northern Ireland (34,007), and the Irish Free State (28,567). All other quotas were in four figures or less ("Who Was Shut Out?").

The quota for immigrants from Russia was set at 2,248; for Lithuania it was 344. Whether or not the numbers were the same in the 1930s, this disparity between the two quotas was to have heartbreaking consequences for Eli, his wife, and their child. Serafima had been born in St. Petersburg in 1908 (Leningrad, by the 1930s), so she and Borya might have come to the United States in the Russian quota. As Eli described it in his interview, the US consulate "said she could go any time." Instead, however, the family decided to stay in Lithuania together. I don't when that was, or exactly how they envisioned the consequences of their decision. I don't know who persuaded whom, or if there was any persuasion involved. When my father mentioned this situation to me once, I was too afraid to ask him any questions; I suppose I thought probing might evoke unbearable pain. My brother, only about twenty years old when he interviewed our father, may have felt similarly. Thinking about it now, however, I realize I might have been more afraid for myself than for my father. Perhaps I was afraid to hear my father tell this story with its horrible ending. But he had already lived with the outcome of that decision for many years, and perhaps he would have been able to talk about it. He might have welcomed the chance.

We know, however, that as early as 1938 Eli's brother Avraham took steps to go to America. On January 2 of that year, he and Rose sent Dave and Ida an excited and optimistic letter:

> My Dear and Beloved Brother and Sister-in-law!
>
> I am glad that you are well and that you feel good and healthy.
>
> I thank you for your efforts, that you are concerned about us. I was at "HIAS,"[1] and they told me that it is easy to make up the papers if you have the means, or if we have friends with means. They say that they can make up the

---

1. The Hebrew Immigrant Aid Society, founded in 1881 to assist Jews from Europe to immigrate to the United States. It remained active throughout the twentieth century and, as HIAS, continues to aid refugees and support immigration reform ("HIAS").

papers in the course of four months' time, and they would be able to count us as part of the July quota for this year.

I want to ask you—if I am able to establish myself in America; according to my profession, I am a bookkeeper and a business manager. You will likely receive an inquiry from the New York "HIAS." The inquiry will be sent by the Kovno "HIAS" to the New York "HIAS," so that they may inquire of you about us.

Avraham encloses a letter from "Sorale" (little Sarah, around six years old; figure 36 depicts her at age nine), printed in Yiddish in neat schoolgirl handwriting. The note, in ink on graph-lined paper, begins, "Dear Uncle, I want

Figure 36. Sarah Rochelson, January 21, 1940. Family collection.

to see you," and then Sarah goes on to tell her uncle and her musical aunt that she does well in school and plays the *fidl mit klavier*, violin and piano. She carefully signs the letter "Sorale Rochelson." At the end of Avraham's letter, Rose adds a brief wish "that we may soon be able to speak with you in person," noting, "You would certainly like my Sorale. Bobe Henale [Grandma Henye, with a sweet diminutive ending] will already tell you that."[2]

It is hard to imagine how anyone could resist such an appeal, and maybe they did not. Ida and Dave had seen Avraham and Rose, then pregnant, less than seven years earlier. In 1938, did they feel they could not financially support their brother and his family? In fact, Dave's business had failed a few years earlier, and Ida earned a city teacher's salary. Did they think of contacting relatives in Oklahoma—cousins who generously assisted Eli after the war? Maybe they did, and those cousins, building a business, were unable to help, even if they tried. Among family genealogy files I have discovered a United States of America Affidavit of Support, filed with the Cunard White Star Line by David B. Pierce of Chicago, on behalf of ten members of the German branch of the Rochelsohn family in 1938, after Kristallnacht. Germans, as noted above, had the largest immigration quota under the 1924 law. However, out of the ten individuals promised sponsorship, only four were able to immigrate, two teenagers and their parents.[3] The rest were murdered in Terezin (Theresienstadt) and other concentration camps.

The family in Kovno did not stop trying. In a letter of April 1941, Henye Rochelson mentioned to Dave and Ida a branch of the family that lived in Brooklyn. She did not ask directly for their help, but about their health: "My child," she wrote, "I am suffering greatly on account of my

---

2. Letter of January 2, 1938. Translation of adult handwriting by Rivka Schiller; translation of Sorale's letter by author.

3. In later years, when we were all middle-aged, I came to know the teenagers, Hans Georg Israel and Inge Sarah, at that later time known as George Rockson and Ingrid Scheuer. George was instrumental, in fact, in connecting me with family genealogists, photographs, and information.

nephew—that he died. Indeed, he was still a young person. . . . He left behind a wife and children. In fact, he had a gold business [he dealt in gold], so he was wealthy. How is his brother, Moishe Esner, and how are his sisters—aren't they unmarried? Write me about them. If you see them some time [?] give them my regards."[4] At the bottom of the letter, in English and in Dave's handwriting, are the names and addresses of members of an Esner family, people I had not known of before seeing this letter recently. Following genealogical leads online, I found descendants of Moishe Esner, now new and dear cousins.[5] I asked Bill and Sandy Esner what they thought of this missed family connection, not only in 1941, but also over the many years Eli lived in the United States and, indeed, in the same city. Bill told me that if Dave had contacted the individuals whose names he had written down, they would not have had the means to rescue anyone in 1941. If that had been the case, we concurred, perhaps neither side felt they wanted to continue the connection. It is also possible that Dave, in the United States since 1912, had never contacted these relatives before, and then, years later, felt uncomfortable doing so when it was clear that he was asking for or even implying that they grant him an enormous favor. Perhaps Dave did everything he could have done when he received all these letters and possibly others. In the end, I just don't know.

Documentary evidence, however, supports what has become common knowledge: It was extremely difficult, if not impossible, for Jews to leave Lithuania in early 1938, and even more so after the war started, although

---

4. Translation by Rivka Schiller.

5. A query to the LitvakSIG listserv resulted in extensive, generous, and very helpful research by Bette Stoop Mas; a subsequent query to the Ellis Island database led me to the ship's manifest of a woman who had to have been my grandmother's sister, named Chaine (as the manifest has it) or, as in later documents, Sarah, a woman who came to the United States in 1897 and was killed in a trolley accident in Brooklyn in 1909. My grandmother's nephew "in the gold business" was Abraham Esner, a jeweler who died at age sixty in early 1941, and indeed the brother of Moishe. The relationships verified in conversation with Bill Esner were confirmed by death certificates that Ms. Stoop Mas helped me to obtain from the Family History Library in Salt Lake City.

Jewish organizations did what they could to repatriate Lithuanian Jews in the United States and elsewhere. The HIAS-HICEM archive at the YIVO Institute for Jewish Research offers a sense of both the strenuous efforts of HIAS officials to help Kovno Jews emigrate and the difficult bureaucratic situation they faced that was most likely unknown to refugees applying to leave.[6] Kovno had a population of between thirty-five thousand and forty thousand Jews in the years prior to the start of the war (USHMM, "Kovno"). A statistical document sent from the Kaunas office of HIAS-ICA to its Paris headquarters, the only such document I found covering a complete calendar year, illustrates how few of them were able to leave in 1939, the year after Avraham, Rose, and Sarah sought HIAS assistance. It was a year, too, in which Jewish refugees from throughout occupied Poland fled to Vilnius, once again part of Lithuania as of late September, and added to the workload of the Kaunas office, which served Riga and Vilnius as well.

In 1939, 5,119 would-be emigrants approached the office, of whom 3,475 men, women, and children officially registered; 1,554 of those intended to emigrate to the United States. Yet a final tabulation indicates that only 204 people, in all of 1939, went to the United States from the Kaunas office, with promised support. The total who arrived at all destinations (the second largest being Palestine, at 182) was 591. Thus only about 10 percent of those who approached the office at all, during a year when mobility might still have seemed possible, were able to leave their soon-to-be-occupied cities. When one realizes that support in the country of destination was only one step in a process that required obtaining a Lithuanian passport as well as a visa to the intended place of refuge, a ship's ticket that cost more than $300 per person, and transit visas—all of which, even today, involve expense and complicated application procedures—it

6. The HIAS-HICEM Archives, Series II France I, are in microfilm file MKM 16.7 RG 245.5 at the YIVO Institute for Jewish Research, Center for Jewish History, New York. HICEM was formed in 1927 by a merger of HIAS (the United States–based Hebrew Immigrant Aid Society), the ICA (Jewish Colonization Association, based in Paris and London), and Emigdirect (based in Berlin). The acronym combines parts of each organization's name; Emigdirect withdrew in 1934 ("HICEM").

is not surprising that many would-be refugees could not leave.[7] As Israel Bernstein recounted in his March 1940 report to HIAS and HICEM, "we must face reality as it is and confess that there are to-day no emigration possibilities even for a small portion of those interested. Since the catastrophe [of the Nazi invasion of Poland in the fall of 1939] there were at Lithuania issued visas: 91 for the United States, 205 for other countries, 250 for Palestine," smaller numbers, for the United States, than appear in HICEM's statistical tables, and of all those who were issued visas to anywhere, Bernstein indicates that only 258 had left at the time of his writing (page 4 of report).[8]

Bernstein also expresses, as diplomatically as possible, his frustration at the lack of awareness in America of the dire situation for Jews under both the Soviet and Nazi regimes: "Some time ago (and, perhaps, even now) a considerable faction of American Jewish opinion indulged in discussions as to which of both the captivities, the German and the Russian,

---

7. The statistics I cite are from YIVO file MKM 16.7, RG 245.5, folder 84, Kaunas HICEM statistics, 1939. I am indebted to Marsha Rozenblit, who helped me translate from the German, explained the relations of the various columns of figures to each other, and recounted to me the many steps an emigrant had to take from first approach to the committee to safe arrival in a land of refuge. The cost of a ship's ticket, $300 per person, is noted in the report by Israel Bernstein to the HIAS and HICEM offices in New York and Paris, March 22, 1940 (YIVO MKM 16.7, RG 245.5, folder 92).

8. Bernstein, on a fact-finding mission for HIAS-HICEM, recounted the sufferings of ten thousand Polish refugees newly arrived in Vilnius, most of them men uncertain of their future and afraid for wives and children they were forced to leave behind. Bernstein indicates that waits of five to seven years were anticipated for most visa applicants, and he is forthright about the horrific experiences of the refugees, whose stories "force the listener to cast down his eyes and remain silent. Painfully silent" (page 2 of report, YIVO MKM 16.7, RG 245.5, folder 92). While he is able to recount successes in providing temporary shelter, food, medical care, and clothing, he expresses frustration at not being able to answer the more pressing question of where the refugees and their families were to go. "It seems to me," he wrote, "that there is no other Jewish organization whose representative has, like the emigration worker, to face this problem in all its ramifications. For in prevalent conditions mere counsel and advice is less than not enough" (page 4). Later Bernstein coordinated HIAS-ICA activities in Vilnius, Kaunas, and Riga.

is the less cruel and more human. From my discussions with many prominent personalities [who had experienced one or both] . . . , I gathered the opinion that there can be no talk on where life is easier and better. [In] both it is 'worse'" (5). This was in 1940, after the Nazis had invaded Czechoslovakia and Poland. How much less could Americans in early 1938 have imagined the extermination to come? Moreover, the sums of money Avraham would have needed were probably beyond the reach of his American relatives. Even the wealthy Nathan Straus Jr. was unable to help his friend Otto Frank, Anne Frank's father, bring his family to the United States from Amsterdam (Rothstein C5). Without means or "friends with means," Avraham, Rose, and Sarah could not get on that ship in July. Many hopeful families like theirs found themselves without hope.

4

"Silk Stockings":
The Holocaust Reaches Kovno

THE NAZIS INVADED Lithuania on June 22, 1941, a date that Eli spoke of often. His experiences of that day and those following were memorable and harrowing:

> I was working in the hospital in 22nd of June, 1941, when we were awakened by explosions. When I got up, I was told that the Germans attacked Lithuania, and the airport is on fire, and there is a war. . . . I immediately left for home, and of course there was panic, and fear, and so on. As a matter of fact, the same day, the 22nd of June in the morning, about 12 o'clock, I would say, Lithuanians had already put their national flag (we lived near the military museum) with the Lithuanian anthem playing. Now, this was the most frightening picture, they removed the Russian flag. In other words, while the Germans were not there [yet], the Lithuanians already celebrate their independence, supposedly.[1]
>
> And when I came home at that time, everybody, the whole people, converged to our apartment, and we didn't know what to do. The whole streets were full with people, carriages, walking with bundles towards the Russians, towards east. And—But I for some reason didn't move, I was afraid to go with the crowd. And I stayed home, and that evening I got a call to come to the suburb of Kovno, Šančiai, to work in the *krankenkasse*, and I came

---

1. This was troubling because of the pro-German, antisemitic elements among Lithuanian nationalists.

there.[2] . . . [O]f course Red Cross didn't give me any cars, I had to walk some miles and miles. And there in middle of the night I called up the chief from the *krankenkasse*, and I asked him, how [is] the condition. He said the condition is bad, all Jewish doctors left and he would advise me to leave, too, because it will be problems. I said, "What can I do?" He says, "You have a car, at your disposal there, in the aid station; take somebody who gets injured and you go home." Luckily a woman was pregnant, and she and her husband came; I didn't have [the] right to do, but I told the chauffeur to go ahead. We took them to the center of Kovno, to the maternity clinic, a private doctor, and then I left and came home; that was already in the—late at night. We came home; of course the whole skies were, the skies were—It was late at night, there were explosions heard, and bright lights like lightning, from the German planes, illuminating, and looking for places to attack.

I came home, there were a lot of people in hysteria, wondering; I know, the day before a lot of people left towards Russia. Anyway. The next day, about 10 o'clock, we decided to go out and see what we can do, maybe we can go to the station.[3] And then, at that time, we were surrounded by Lithuanians. There were quite a few people with us in a group. And they [the Lithuanians] stopped us and they said, "It is enough to spill our blood on the holy land of Lithuania, and we'll take care of you." And they surrounded with guns, with rifles, but they started to search us. There was one man, Becker, an elderly Jew, and they found *tefillin* and a *tallis*. "Oh," they said, "he is not a Communist, let him go." And while they searched others we ran back, it was not far, not far from our house, and we went back in the house. The . . . same day, we tried to go to the [railroad station], my brother-in-law Misha, and his mother, and my wife and I— . . . We went to the house where her mother lived, and my wife remembered that she has no stockings, she forgot her silk stockings. I says,

2. See "Map of Kovno and Environs," appendix A, for the location of Šančiai and other places mentioned in this account. The Old Town of Kaunas, where Eli was born, may be recognized by its proximity to the confluence of the Neris and Nemunas (Niemen) rivers. His apartment in June 1941, at Maironio 36, is in the New Town, to the east, on a large north-south street in the central district of Kovno.

3. From Maironio to the central Kaunas train station would have been a distance of between three and four kilometers (approximately two miles), depending on the route taken.

"What's the importance, without stockings, in such a time?" "No, no, I cannot go." Then we came back, and an hour or two later we got a call from a man, who said that Mikhail Meerovich left a message that they left with the train that was the last train going to Russia.[4] And of course, everybody was crying and screaming, and we missed everything, and we didn't know what to do.

Eli often said that if he wrote a book about his life he would call it *Silk Stockings*:

> The whole life changed because of silk stockings. Because if my wife wouldn't have insisted about silk stockings I would have gone with my brother-in-law, mother-in-law, my wife to Russia, and the child, and of course the child would have been alive, and I would have been a doctor in Russia in the army like a lot of other people were;[5] that changed the life completely.

He was right, of course. This story on which the rest of the story pivots demonstrates the way small decisions can have profound consequences. Our father told this story to Burt and to me early in our lives, and this is the message we felt he wanted to convey. As we learned the larger message, the story's details, too, became ingrained in our experience. If I leave the house and realize I have forgotten something, I think twice before returning to pick it up. Burt and I both like to get to an airport an hour or more before departure time, and we don't mind waiting longer than that.

But, despite our father's statement of his intention, we debated whether *Silk Stockings* should be this book's title. Certainly, the event was

---

4. In the NYPL interview, Dad recalls the telephone number, 26–326. Although "all Jewish telephones were disconnected," his remained working (Rochelson, NYPL interview 46).

5. In fact, this was how Eli's friend Dr. Joseph Silber survived the war years. After finishing medical school, he was arrested by the Soviets for participating in a Zionist summer camp. The Soviet army needed doctors, so he was taken from prison and sent to the front, where he served as a surgeon; his family remaining in Lithuania were murdered. Stationed in Berlin after the war, Dr. Silber defected to the American Zone of Germany and eventually immigrated to the United States, where he reunited with friends from medical school, including Eli (Silber).

crucial to Eli's life, and the lesson it implies about life and chance are central to his story. However, we also understood that larger story's additional lessons: the importance of determination and what our father referred to as stubbornness; the need to hold fast to one's goals and not be discouraged by even the greatest tragedy; the imperative to value life over death and to move forward, despite a broken heart.

Thus, Eli's story may pivot on "silk stockings"—Sima's felt need to bring them to Moscow and Eli's ultimate assent to her request—but it is not the whole story. Just as there was no way for Eli and Serafima to know what was ahead when they decided to keep their family together, there was also no way to be certain that there would be no more trains to Russia. If they had even been able to cut through the chaos they likely found when they came back to Maironio Street, they might have grabbed the stockings and returned to the station. They did the best they could, without benefit of hindsight. I believe all the decisions that affected his family's fate haunted Eli throughout his life. He never discussed them fully with me or with Burt, not even in his interview. "Silk stockings" may symbolize them all.

～

On June 23, 1941, the family were back in their Kovno apartment, trying to decide what to do next:

> [I]t was terrible. In exhaustion, I went in the other room and I fell asleep, and then my cousin, Minne's daughter Paike, woke me up and she says, "Look! There is the Russians with the truck, they're going to Russia from the building." On the stairs on the fifth floor, there were living the Russian family, pilot family, and we went down to them to talk; they were taking the luggage. And he says, "No men, only women we'll take." And the women, when they left for the luggage, they said, "don't worry; you will go in the truck, and we will sit over you, they will not see you." That's the way it went, in the truck, there were soldiers with guns, and from both sides there were mounted Chinese soldiers with the guns ready, because the Lithuanians were ready to shoot any Russians. . . . [T]he Russian soldiers

were coming back from the front, exhausted, starved, and begging for water, and the Lithuanians wouldn't give it to them. And the Lithuanian partisan underground, when they were alone, not too many Russians, they were shooting them, just killing them, on the streets, wherever they saw them.

Eli, his family, and their neighbors knew that the situation in Kaunas was horrific. In Eli's words, "we already knew and felt, before we left with the truck, that the Lithuanians already started to surround the Jews wherever they could and kill them on the streets, in Slobodke and Kovno, and blood was flowing. Before the Germans came, they were just killing the Jews." Although Eli did not witness it firsthand, the next several days saw torture and massacres in Slobodka, the home of a famous yeshiva and one of the places where Eli's family had lived after returning from Russia in 1921. Samuel D. Kassow records that on one day, June 25, between eight hundred and one thousand Jews were murdered there (13). He also describes the brutality of the murders at the Lietukis Garage, in the center of town, where sixty-eight Jews were beaten to death with garage equipment or suffocated with high-pressure water hoses forced down their throats (13–14).[6] Nissan Krakinowski recalled witnessing some of this brutality as a child, when his father was taken from their home on Laisvės Alėja. Later Eli learned that the wife of the superintendent of their building had protected the Jews who remained at 36 Maironio by keeping them in her apartment; her husband was in Palanga, a seaside resort. Marauding Lithuanian partisans went from apartment to apartment, asking, where are all the Jews? She told them they had all left.[7]

---

6. A photograph of the Lietukis Garage massacre appears in *The Clandestine History of the Kovno Jewish Ghetto Police*, 152.

7. The assistance of the building superintendent was not an isolated case. As Sara Ginaite-Rubinson, a member of the Kovno Jewish resistance, writes, "Janitors played a surprisingly important role during those days and the janitor at Vytauto Prospect 28 was determined to protect the Jewish owners and their Jewish tenants" (17).

Meanwhile, Eli, Sima, and Borya had left with the Russians and witnessed chaos on the roads as the Nazi occupation took hold:

... Now we went with the truck ... with the highways towards Russian border, and the highways were full with people, trucks, tanks. The soldiers, the Russian soldiers were so exhausted and dirty, and from dust covered, you couldn't recognize their uniforms, or face, they were sleeping on the tanks, and everything was rolling back, many tanks were broken, many trucks were broken, and the German planes were firing from machine guns from the plane, and a lot of people were killed. Anyway, we intended to go to Ukmerge,[8] but we were told [it] is too late, because the German parachutists are there. Then in the middle of, while riding, the chauffeur and the Russian pilot from the truck came out, and they knew [we were there . . .], and they said, "out of here," and we begged them, we said, "look, what will you [do], leave us in the middle? What is the difference?" He said, "you better go out"; he put [out] the gun, he said, "we'll start shooting if you don't go, that's an order."

Anyway, we had to [leave the truck and] go with the other people walking, and we changed our direction. And wherever we go, there were the Lithuanian underground, where [they] cut off the road and they were surrounding the Jews. Then finally we turned over off the main road, and we saw a small farm, and we stayed there. There we stayed one night, and the man says, look, his son is a partisan, an underground, he will find you, will kill you. You better leave. . . . Then we went to another town, where we stayed overnight.

Now, there were a lot of Jewish refugees, and then a man came and asked who is a doctor, they need a doctor. They took me to the forest, a man took me with a gun—he had a gun, a rifle—he took me in a carriage and we went through the forest and we came to see his wife. And when I came to see his wife, she had meningitis. I told him she is very seriously ill, you cannot leave her here. She has meningitis. You have to take her to a hospital. [At this point the man apparently offered to drive Eli back, probably to where they

8. A city approximately forty-four miles northeast of Kaunas.

had met each other.] . . . In the farm, in the yard, there were a lot of young men with rifles, and they said to [the man who had made the offer], "What the heck you have to tell him? Let him go alone." He says, "No, I brought him, I will take him back." He gave me bread, eggs, and lard, or bacon, and we went back to the place; there I found out he was one of the chiefs of the underground in that section.[9] We slept overnight in a barn, and then early in the morning he woke up, the owner, he said, "Look, I cannot keep you. You have to go back. You have to go out, because there will be plenty of trouble. I am sorry. I know you are in bad shape, but you have to leave." And we started to go back to Kovno. It took us about two or three days to go back.

It may seem strange that they decided to go back to Kovno, when they knew how bad things were in the city. Eli's account reveals, first, his initiative and effort to try to find safety elsewhere, and then the helplessness and despair that led the group simply to return to the familiar:

I sent a little note to a doctor, Mishelski, who was not far from the farm, or the barn [where] we were, and asked him if we could go there to him.[10] The messenger brought an answer and he wrote, 'Please don't come back, because all Jews are killed, I am the only one alive, and I am not sure for my life.' . . . Now, where could we go? I was with my wife and child, and there also [were] other people . . . with their families; we couldn't go, no place. Because we were, from one side were the German parachutists, and from the other side, were the Lithuanian underground, the fascists, the Nazis who were looking for Jews and Russian soldiers, and we couldn't help it. We had to go back. . . .

Going back to Kovno, we saw a lot of tanks broken, dead Russian soldiers, dead civilian people, and the sight was horrible. Now coming near Kovno, some women, Lithuanian, stopped us and they asked where we are going. We tell them, "to Kovno." She looked at us, she cried, and she said,

---

9. As Eli tells this story in Tape 1, it is clear that this man was a leader of the right-wing partisans, who at other times might have been killing Jews.

10. Mishelski was the original name of William Mishell, author of *Kaddish for Kovno*, but I do not know if the two were related.

"Please don't go." Why? "It is bad, it is bad." But we had no choice, we had to come back because we were surrounded. We didn't have a place where to be. Nobody wanted to take us, and nobody cared and wanted to help us, because they were afraid of the Lithuanian partisans.

Eli described the "paradoxical situation" they faced when they returned, as the nationalist partisans had to decide whom they hated more, the Jews or the Soviets:

> . . . We saw that the Lithuanian partisans [were] very hostile to us, and while going there, going back, we were surrounded by Lithuanian partisans, in a little forest, and they told us they will come, more people, and take us away. And we knew that that's the end. In the meantime they saw two Russian soldiers on bicycles; as soon as one told the other, "Look, there is Russians," they said, "You stay here in the forest and don't move. We go after them." They went after the Russians, to catch them, and we went, [we] immediately ran away from the forest and were hiding, and we heard that they were looking for us, that time.

They also found themselves looking forward to the arrival of the Wehrmacht, the regular German army that would keep the Lithuanian partisans in line:

> The German soldiers were not involved in politics, they were not involved in killing Jews. They are looking for some Communists, they were fighting men and we were waiting with [or, for] them. And sure enough, as soon as we saw the German soldiers we had a feeling of relief. As a matter of fact, they gave candies to the children, they talked to us, and I asked him how to Kovno to go, and he said, "everything is free, the road, you can go, nothing to worry." And that time, they gave an order to Lithuanians, wherever they occupied, not to attack the Jews, and not to do their own justice, because they will do it; in other words, the SS will come later.
>
> Coming back, as I mentioned again, the Lithuanian women warned us what's ahead. There we stopped in a suburb of Kovno, quite a distance,[11]

11. Over two kilometers, about a mile and a quarter, southeast of central Kaunas.

called Karmelita, and there we came in; there was a lot of German soldiers
with trucks, and cars, and jeeps, and everything, and we asked one of these
men from the town, please let us stay overnight. He says, "You know, I
know your situation, but not now, while everything is full of Germans, still.
And you go ahead and hide somewhere around, and then come at night."
Sure enough, we came at night. He brought us food and he stayed with us.
And he says, "In the morning, before the sun comes up, start moving." And
we start moving, and we were going— . . . We were there, maybe ten people,
or twelve people. . . . We slept in a barn, with the Germans. The Germans
were in the same yard there, like in the lion's mouth. But we stayed there
overnight; he was very nice, this man—a Lithuanian man.[12] We were going
back, towards downhill, towards Kovno. . . . There some of the people said
they want to go through the bridge to Slobodke, and some said to go this
way [northwest of the city center]. I said, "Don't go to bridges. In case like
this, in a war, there are soldiers watching the bridges, and it's dangerous."
But they didn't listen. But we and some group went down, home. I, after,
heard that they had a very bad fate going to the bridge.

---

12. When Eli refers to "Lithuanians" he is talking about non-Jewish Lithuanians. He
takes pains, here as elsewhere, to acknowledge the kindness of people from whom
Jews might not have expected kindness.

5

Kovno Ghetto

When we came home, we found, of course, Germans were all over. My brother was with his wife there and we went to our apartment, and we stayed there. The killings from the Lithuanians stopped while the German army came. And then there was a notice to the people, to the Jewish people, in Kovno, that by August 15, we all have to leave our apartments, and go to the ghetto in Slobodke. And in August 15, by that time, around, we took whatever we could, our belongings, in a horse, carriage, and we went to Slobodke. In Slobodke we had a little tiny room, maybe twelve by ten, or even less, and the tiny hall in the front, and that was our quota.

JOSEF GRILICHES FOR some time lived in the same building with Eli in the Kovno ghetto. Josef was twenty or twenty-one years old in 1944, and he remembers that Eli was appointed to count the inhabitants of the building every evening and report the number to the authorities. It was a three- or four-story stone or brick building on Varniu Street, Block A, with no running water or toilets, only an outhouse and water brought in from a well. It had originally been built by the Soviets as low-income housing.[1] Their building was painted white; others were red. As Eli points out, one or two families lived to a room. Later, Eli's family lived in the one-room house he describes further on in the narrative, near the Catholic cemetery. Josef Griliches told me that this would have been made of wood (Interview, May 31, 2011).

---

1. See the map of the Kovno ghetto in appendix A.

The only family apart from his wife and child who were with Eli in the ghetto were Avraham, Rose, and Sarah, who lived in a different building. By that time, Eli and Avraham's father and sister had died, brother Dave was in America, and brother Misha was farther east in the Soviet Union. As for their mother and Mottel,

> when the war started, my brother Motteh was a doctor in a small town, and the mother was with him, and there was a man who told me after, in concentration camp, that he begged him to come back to Kovno. No, he said, he does't want to. It was near Shaktiel, near Shakiai, we call the town, a little town in Lithuania. And, I understand, they had the same fate like all other Jews in the small towns. There they were, they just came, and [they] were killed. . . . They were killed by the Lithuanian partisans.

In 1981, when I collected information on our family for pages of testimony to be sent to Yad Vashem, my father told me that his mother and brother Mottel were living in Plokščiai at the time of the Nazi invasion and were most likely murdered there. Plokščiai is in the Shakiai (Šakiai) district or county; the town of Šakiai is the county seat. I had long assumed that Mottel and my grandmother were killed almost immediately after the Nazi invasion. However, in 2011 Yad Vashem published testimonies from survivors of actions in rural Lithuania, collected soon after the war by Leyb Konuichovsky, himself a survivor. These testimonies suggest a different story. Einsatzgruppen[2] organized by the Nazis, but in fact often staffed by Lithuanian executioners, killed adult Jewish men in the weeks immediately after the invasion and later killed the women and children. In Kudirkos-Naumiestis, my grandmother's birthplace in Šakiai, and the closest town to

2. Literally, *mission groups*, the *Einsatzgruppen* were "mobile killing units . . . squads composed primarily of German SS and police personnel. Under the command of the German Security Police . . . and Security Service . . . officers, the Einsatzgruppen had among their tasks the murder of those perceived to be racial or political enemies found behind German combat lines in the occupied Soviet Union" (United States Holocaust Memorial Museum, "Einsatzgruppen," *Holocaust Encyclopedia*).

Plokščiai discussed in these reports, "On July 1, 1941, almost all the local Jewish men were shot in the cemetery. On September 16, the women and children were shot in a nearby forest" (Bankier 133–34). My grandmother and uncle may have been murdered on similarly separate dates; in between, on August 15, my father, his brother Avraham, and their immediate families entered the Kovno ghetto:

> The ghetto was of course already [set up; it] had barbed wire, there were soldiers around watching, we shouldn't go away. Then the Germans came, they had a speech, assuring us that nothing will happen to us, and that everything will be fine, and we shouldn't worry, the only thing, we should comply with their directives. We should work, and they will get a ration, and all sweet talk.
>
> They had a big speech about work, and about food, and about everything, but the first week they said they needed five hundred persons, intellectuals, to work in an archive to prepare the documents.[3]. . . They took, at that time they took five hundred men; among them was my brother [Avraham]. The police came to my house, and I wasn't there; and somehow happened, I was to Rosenthal, going as a—I knew them, somebody was sick, I went to their house. The Jewish police came and says, "We need your husband, to go to, to go to the archives." [My wife] says, "My husband is a doctor," she doesn't know [if] I will be able to come. He says, "He has to, but however, he is a doctor, forget about it. We will not touch him."[4] Among them was Avraham, he was working for the supply of food for this ghetto government.

Avraham's work as a bookkeeper qualified him as an intellectual for the selection; as Eli put it, "That was enough for that job [in the supposed archives]; he's not a laborer." In fact, Avraham had declined higher education to help further his brothers' ambitions: "He didn't want to go to any

---

3. The "Intellectuals Action," the first major selection in the Kovno ghetto, took place on August 18, 1941.

4. It was a recurring theme for Eli that being a doctor saved his life, both physically and emotionally.

school, he had a very nice, beautiful handwriting, he was intelligent, he finished five years gymnasium, and he says he wants to work and support the family, because I and Mottel were studying, and for the father is hard."

> . . . Now, Avraham was among them. . . . When they took all the men and they came there to a certain place and they counted, there were 502 persons instead of 500. The German punctuality: they said, "We don't need 502, we need 500." My brother and somebody else, [they] said, let them go back together. Among [those who did not return] was my cousin, David; he is Lubovsky, the brother of Genya and Rivochka Lubovsky. And the next day we found out they all were shot. That was the first action from the Germans, we all knew.

Some sources, including the US Holocaust Memorial Museum website, indicate that the number taken and killed was 534. A note to Avraham Tory's *Surviving the Holocaust: Kovno Ghetto Diary* points out that although the Germans asked for only 500, the work option sounded so good that more than the number needed volunteered, and all 534 were murdered (33, n.1). Ephraim Gutman, in his 1946 interview with David Boder, put the number requested as 530, but "they grabbed together . . . five hundred and thirty-four so that four went for good measure" (8). Eli's account, which differs from both of those, is his firsthand recollection, and thus should be part of the record.

When they first arrived in the ghetto, Eli worked as a doctor at the ghetto hospital.[5] However,

> . . . we didn't have any food and it was bad and I told the chief there, that I'd rather go to work [as a laborer at the airfield]. And he says, OK, if you want to go, go ahead. And I was going to work because there I could meet some Lithuanians and get some bread or exchange some belongings for bread, and bring home. (Rochelson, Tape 1)

---

5. Although he does not discuss this service in his long interviews, he mentions it at this point in Tape 1 and lists it in the file he put together to reestablish his credentials as a physician in the United States.

It was the largest labor force from the Kovno ghetto, working to rebuild and expand the airfield in Aleksotas. According to Samuel Kassow, "many Jews did all they could to avoid going there, and for good reason":

> . . . [W]orkers had to rise at four o'clock every morning to . . . make the three-mile trek to the worksite. The Germans did not provide suitable clothing or footwear, and . . . [m]ost of the work in the airfield was outdoors, and it took place in all sorts of weather. . . . Many workers suffered frostbite or heat exhaustion. While some of the German overseers were "decent," many of them were sadistic brutes who ceaselessly beat the Jewish workers. The work itself was exceptionally difficult. (29)

Eli recalled how he did "manual or physical labor, carrying cement back, mixing cement, and doing a lot of heavy work," but apparently the advantage of obtaining food through what was a dangerous illicit market made up for the hardships of the labor. As Kassow points out, eventually the Germans began day and night shifts at the airfield, and no shift could return to the ghetto until the next shift arrived, which meant that shifts could be much longer than anticipated (30). Still, Eli reported that Russian prisoners of war, while they lasted, had even worse conditions:

> [W]e could see in the morning that the Russian prisoners were brought, too, to work, and they were holding each other in a line going to work, and there were also horse carriages where the dead Russians were put there, to bury them. They starved terribly. They didn't give them any food, and youngsters, fifteen and sixteen years old, from the SS—I saw, like, a Russian fellow, soldier, went to—stole a cabbage head from a carriage, and he went to him, he took his [rifle] butt and killed this man, and they were killing for every little thing. They were going twelve hours, with almost no food. They were held in a certain barracks outside Kovno, and they usually went miles and miles by foot, and there, they lived there in very miserable conditions.[6]

---

6. William Mishell, in *Kaddish for Kovno*, similarly records the treatment the Nazis reserved for Russian prisoners of war. On the work details with inmates of the Kovno ghetto, he writes, "[t]hey were mistreated even worse than the Jews. Not

Eli remembered the official Russian reaction:

> I heard the speech while under German domination in ghetto, I heard the
> speech from Molotov,[7] who said to the Germans, "I know what's going on
> in the occupied lands, I know your attitude toward the Russian prisoners. It
> is against the Geneva Convention. But if you don't stop killing our prisoners,
> I promise you that no German soldier will be taken alive as a prisoner. You
> better stop." It seems to be that this helped. They killed, from one hundred
> thousand Russian prisoners, they say, about ten or five thousand were alive,
> the others were killed, or starved to death, or heavy work by the Germans.
> Then, as I said, I worked for a while as a laborer but, after, the ghetto got
> organized, and they appointed me and some other young doctors to work
> as a physician in the same place [the airfield], with the working crews in the
> airport building.

On October 4, 1941, the Nazis set fire to the ghetto hospital.[8] In Tape 1, Eli
explains how he saw it as he came home from the airfield:

> And once, coming from work, I could see that the hospital where I was
> working for a while was on fire. It seems to be that while all able-bodied peo-
> ple went to work, the Germans surrounded the hospital on the pretext that
> there was some contagious disease. They burned the whole personnel, the
> doctors, the nurses, and they surrounded with machine guns, that nobody

---

only did they work the same long hours we did, but in the evening they were
taken to their stockades, where they were kept under the open sky. Every day
when they returned from work, dozens of them . . . had to be supported on both
sides by somewhat stronger p.o.w.'s, since they were already too weak to walk.
The next morning they would be dead. . . . In a month or so, there were no more
Russians" (81).

7. V. M. Molotov was the Soviet diplomat who signed the Molotov-Ribbentrop non-
aggression pact with the Nazis in 1939. Eli and others would have heard the speech
via radio in the ghetto.

8. In his testimony, Ephraim Gutman gives the date of the fire as September 4, but Tory's
diary account on October 6 makes clear that it took place a month later. This probably inadvertent factual error is one of many reminders, throughout the accounts of
witnesses, that small details may differ while the larger story remains true.

can escape, and a lot of people were killed at that time. . . . I know my friends and some others were killed at that time, and even the patients.[9]

Soon after the war, in the typescript he prepared for his OSE testimony on medical atrocities, presented at the Nuremburg trials (appendix C), Eli wrote, "The Jewish hospital located in the section known as 'Klein Ghetto,' bearing the inscription 'Danger—Pest [*Seuche-Gefahr*: literally, *Epidemic/ Disease-Danger*]' was set on fire while the sick, the nurses and physicians were inside. In order to prevent any person to escape the blaze the hospital was surrounded by German soldiers, armed with machine guns. This act of arson was committed on orders of the Gestapo with the full knowledge and consent of the German medical authorities in Kaunas (Kovne)."[10]

There were more atrocities to come.

When we came the 27th of October, 1941, we found that the ghetto was in terrible turmoil, there were all over placards saying that all population, sick, old, and men, and women, and children, should converge in a certain place in ghetto for inspection or some other pretext, and anybody who is found in the house will be killed in his house. And if those who cannot, sick too much, they should take some carriage or carry him to the place. On the 28th— . . . We came there, 6 o'clock in the morning, it was a snowy, wintry day, cold, dark, of course we didn't have any lights, when we came to the

9. William Mishell describes a similar fortuitous survival by his brother-in-law, a doctor (85). For more detailed descriptions of the ghetto hospital fire, see Tory and *The Clandestine History of the Kovno Jewish Ghetto Police*.

10. The doctors' testimony was described at the time in an article in the New York German-Jewish newspaper *Aufbau/Reconstruction* (see Lubinski). The OSE was an "organization devoted to the promotion of health, hygiene, and childcare among Jews," founded in 1912 in Saint Petersburg, Russia (Beizer). Its original acronym, OZE, translates to English as the Society for the Protection of the Health of the Jewish Population. After the rise of the Soviet Union, the OZE became decentralized; a branch opened in 1921 in then-independent Lithuania. After 1933, the central office moved to Paris, where it remains and is known as OSE (Oeuvre de Secours aux Enfants [Children's Aid]) World Union. During the occupation of Paris and to the end of the war (1940–45) the headquarters temporarily moved to New York.

place, and we waited about 9 or 10 o'clock, till the Germans, SS, the Gestapo came, and they started to sort, one goes right, the other goes left. And at that time, my cousin, Shloimke, Minne's son—I forget to mention, she had a son Shloimke, and she has a son Eli, too; Eli left, [he] never came back, we didn't know, before the ghetto was established. But Shloimke became a Jewish policeman and he tried, wanted to make sure that they don't take us [to] the wrong place. We had a feeling, they took the old, and children, and sick people on one side, and the others, more or less healthy looking, they took [to the other]—

The event became known as the Great Action. Ten thousand of the twenty-seven thousand assembled in Demokratu Square were taken to the "small ghetto" and then killed, as Eli describes, at the Ninth Fort, the ninth of a ring of tsarist-era fortifications around the city of Kaunas. Those who survived the selection went to stand on one side of the square, and it was twelve hours before anyone returned home.

Eli wrote an article to commemorate the fifth anniversary of this action, and it was published in *Der Tog* [*The Day*], an American Yiddish newspaper, on October 28, 1946 (see appendix D for an image of the article as published). As he explained to Marsha Rozenblit, "I had an urge to put in the paper for the Jewish leaders what had happened on the 28th of October in '41. [...] I called them up . . . I said—I feel that five years of such a date shouldn't be left unnoticed and shouldn't be left without putting to the readers, American readers who were not in Europe, who are still talking Jewish—[an event they] should know about" (Rochelson, NYPL interview 72). The article had my father's byline (Dr. E. Rochelson, in Yiddish letters) and contained the following description:

All the 30,000 Jews had to be out very early in the morning, 6:00 in the morning, to make a census. Nobody will go to work. Nobody could stay in the house. Sick, old, and children—all must be at the assembly point. If somebody would stay in the house they would be shot. This is the way it sounded, the order from the Gestapo. We understood what this "registration" meant.

The 28th of October, 6:00 in the morning. It was a sleepless night. People were running [streaming] to the assembly point in the ghetto. It was dark, cold, and tragic (mournful). Small children in carriages, and carried by the parents, sick ones and old ones, all went to the place. We understood that this is the tragic moment which will decide the fate. People were screaming, crying, confused, and lost. We saw that people were so confused and so afraid, because they didn't know what would happen.

In a very organized moment the German police came. The Lithuanian bandits and the Gestapo worked as a team. Part of the soldiers went to the houses to see what was doing in the houses. We heard very well on the place, there was shooting, because they heard someone . . . The rest of the soldiers were standing and waiting for orders what to do. The ghetto was surrounded by extra people who came to look to make sure that everything should go the way they want. Behind the ghetto were standing a lot of non-Jews [Christians], and they were waiting, to look at the tragic game that was happening here. They were standing still, the 30,000, they were waiting. We were very afraid, like an electric shock. The Gestapo came and they started to sort, with cold, murderous faces. Sometimes they made a façade, they had a smile on their faces, when they were sending people to die. Right, left, right, left. We heard the orders from the Gestapo. Whole families were sent to the bad side. Like hungry wolves they were tearing the children from their parents. They divided sister and brother, old and young, sick and healthy. All were sent to death. All day the gestapo and the Lithuanian forest bandits were out of control. All day we heard the screams from the beaten, the cries of woe from the children, the parents and the children. Till the evening, 11,000 people were taken out, a third of the people. The next day in the morning we found out that all of the 11,000 people got killed with machine guns.[11]

In his interview, Eli described that aftermath:

... [W]hen we came back everybody was crying, and was a panic, and they found out from the Lithuanians over the barbed wires, or differently, [that]

---

11. Translated from the Yiddish by Nissan Krakinowski, 2 June 2011. Personal typescript.

they shot them; they put them on the mass graves which the prisoners had to dig themselves, and they were shooting machine guns, and those who was still alive they shoot again even in the grave, and that was the first action. Not only in Lithuania but it was in Latvia, Estonia, and other places of German domination. It was an order from Hitler, and it was the first thing.[12]

Eli continued to discuss life and death in the ghetto, including efforts he made to protect his child:

Then the ghetto was more or less quiet for a while. Of course before each Jewish holiday they always find a pretext to hang somebody, to kill somebody or some other atrocious act there performed. Every day we went out from ghetto, but we had to have some food. The ration what they gave was very meager; and as a matter of fact, after a time they even stopped giving that also. What we were doing, we were taking some belongings, shirts, ties, or socks, whatever we had, and if we didn't have our own we took from other inhabitants of the ghetto, for commission. . . . [S]ome people had a lot of good stuff, I would say, and for a certain commission you took it out and went, and we were trading with the gentiles, with the Lithuanians, and getting some food for that, and I had to return whatever we agreed to give to [in?] food. Sometimes there were searches at the gates from the German, even the Jewish police, and they took away whatever we had, [what] we brought to the ghetto. The conditions were terrible. We starved, we didn't have any food, and always in danger to our life.

I tried, some of my friends, Lithuanian friends, doctors, to meet, and I went out despite the fact there was an order if you go out with a Jewish star alone and they catch, the Gestapo, they will shoot you. But I had to go out. I went to Dr. Mayofski who was near the airport. I talked to him, he says he will do something to hide the child, and after a while he said no he cannot; if it would be a girl he would have done, but it's a boy he cannot

12. For additional firsthand descriptions of the Great Action, see Tory 43–60, Eilati, *Crossing the River*, 39–48, and *The Clandestine History of the Kovno Jewish Ghetto Police* 23–26, 132–46.

[because of circumcision]. . . . He cannot do that, and he doesn't want. In the beginning he was coming to the ghetto trying to help the people, his friends, with food, till the Germans told him if he comes again he will be arrested. [He was] a gentile. Mayofski. I went with the star to see him. And he went to help to the gates of the ghetto to see some friends and give them food and the guards told him if he comes again he will be delivered to the Gestapo, stop to come; and he stopped coming. I also risked once and went to Dr. Wishnievsky who was in the center of the city, but this time I took off my Star of David because in the city, a lot of Gestapo men, they will see a Jew with a star they will definitely catch him. I took it off but I took a risk and went to him and asked him what he can do for me. He said no, he cannot do anything, he cannot help me; he was afraid himself, he was a Russian, you know.[13] And that's that.

Then I was assigned to work for a short while in university, the same university where I was an intern. And there in this—while I was working outside I knew the ways in the underground corridors and the connections. I went through and some of these nurses saw me and recognized; they looked at me with such a pity but they didn't say a thing. I went to the pathologist—assistant pathologist—to his place, because Dr. Zacharin, a surgeon in ghetto, wanted to get something, and he was making packages for him, but this Zacharin never gave me a piece, what I risked with my life to go and bring him.[14] And I brought him several times, packages; after [that is, later], I stopped. He also gave me certain things to give it to him to sell, and get product[s from?] the gentile pathologist to sell [in the ghetto]. And that was one part of this way we had to make a living.

As Eli made clear, the Jewish police, as well as the Germans, would confiscate items that ghetto inmates had obtained at great risk. In the 1970s, as later, their role vis à vis the Jewish population was questioned and criticized; the 2014 *Clandestine History of the Kovno Jewish Ghetto Police*,

---

13. As discussed, Russians, too, were at risk from both Lithuanian partisans and Nazis.
14. Dr. Benjamin Zacharin was head of the health department in the Kovno ghetto.

written by members of the Jewish police force, reveals a complex and more favorable picture than had often been assumed. When Burt asked about the Jewish police, Eli's evaluation was mixed:

> Now, the Jewish police want to save their skin; the Jewish police had good food, and drinking, and cigarettes, and alcohol, and women, whatever they needed, because when they needed there are thousands of people coming from work; they just either told the Germans to search or they searched themself and took it away for themself, and they used the food, and food was a very important commodity, and for the food they could get anything, anything they wanted for food—liquor, cigarettes, even money. And the Jewish police, some were on the level and some were rotten.
>
> My attitude was indifference. I don't know. I was in a state of shock and fog and I couldn't analyze and think about them because—Of course when they took away from me the food I was enraged, but you couldn't open your mouth. Anyway, you couldn't go again and protest. Because they were the ones who were selecting people going to Estonia and Latvia, to concentration camp, and other places. . . . I knew a few of them. Berman, he was a classmate from the gymnasium, this is the man who recommended me a job in 1927. He was Alonka Berman, very nice fellow, he was on the level. . . . I would say they were not brutal. They supposedly, with the Jewish *Ältestenrat* and the police, they supposedly were working with the Germans for the benefit of the people. [The police and the *Ältestenrat* in Kovno were not ostracized by the community.] . . . Dr. Elkes, he's a good medical man, was also assigned in *Ältestenrat* and he did a lot of things for the Jews.[15]

15. The *Ältestenrat* was the Jewish Council of Elders, set up in each ghetto by the Nazis. Their behavior and attitude varied from place to place, but Dr. Elchanan Elkes, head of the *Ältestenrat* in the Kovno ghetto, was admired for his active devotion to his people. See Tory's account of his role in saving Jews in the October 28 selection and at other times, as well as his letter or "last testament" to his children, rpt. in Tory 503–7. Similarly, the *Clandestine History of the Kovno Jewish Ghetto Police* presents the actions of the police in a more positive light, as it takes into account the frequently impossible choices with which they were faced.

Eli's descriptions of feeling—at various times or all at once—indifferent, shocked, in a fog, and helplessly enraged say much about the personal impact of ghettoization. That a ghetto inmate could work in a university hospital, even for a short time, and yet no one there could rescue him or his family is something about which I have no comment. It just bears repeating.

Eli went on:

> [T]his continued more or less with certain atrocities until 1943 when an order came out that they need certain Jewish people to go to a concentration camp in a north suburb of Kovno, Panemune. . . . And it was a concentration camp, a *lager*, with a lot of barracks, but the way we heard they said there is good food, and they have to work, but it's not too bad.

They left in late November 1943, the moment of their departure preserved in a photograph taken by Zvi Kadushin, now well known as George Kadish, who recorded life in the Kovno ghetto with a camera hidden behind a buttonhole (figure 37a). Eli obtained this photograph directly from him; as he told Burt, "This man, he risked his life." Indeed, he risked his life repeatedly. Kadish's photographs form a large collection in the digital archives of the US Holocaust Memorial Museum and are central to its *Hidden History of the Kovno Ghetto* (55).

Another image recording this event, in a photograph taken from a slightly different angle, is reprinted in Tory, *Surviving the Holocaust*, with the caption "Jews being forcibly evicted from the Kovno Ghetto in 1942" (Tory, page 12 of the illustrations section). The date is a year earlier than when Eli and his family left for the labor camp. That same photograph appears in the public online photo archives of the United States Holocaust Memorial Museum, which indicates that it depicts Jews being deported "either to a work camp near Kovno" or Estonia (USHMM Photo Archives #81079). The phrase about the work camp was inserted when I wrote to the USHMM identifying Eli and his family on the transport and explaining where he had said they were going. Their names appear in the online caption, but the longer description is of the Estonia action only, which for most of those deportees was fatal.[16]

The work camp was at Aleksotas, which is near Panemune, and it was opened in late November 1943 (*Germany: A Memorial*); the airfield at which Eli and thousands of others from the Kovno ghetto worked was also at Aleksotas (see map in appendix A). Eli described the place, saying, "[w]hen we came there in the concentration camp in Panemune, the women, the husbands and wife and children could be in one place. There was a big room with bunks, and then my wife and child were together. And they had bunks." In the NYPL interview, as well, he mentions these bunk beds in the brick former barracks, but in both accounts he also reports that the family was able to live together. The barracks would most likely have been communal rather than individual living spaces, with the women and children in one barracks area and the men in another. They may have been "together" in that the airfield workers were not as far away from their families during the day as they had been in the ghetto itself. Eli emphasized in both accounts, however, that he and his family had gone to the camp voluntarily, hoping for better conditions. The inscription on the back of the photo, however (figure 37b), contradicts that significant point:

> The barracks of a part/section of the ghetto in the prisoners' camp, concentration camp beyond Kovne (Aleksat), on the 30th of November, 1943. We appear very bad off because prior to this, they terrorized the ghetto; [we had] not slept, not eaten, [and were] in terror, because we did not know where they were taking us, and the official statement/declaration we did not believe.[17]

---

16. A photograph identical to mine is in the onsite-only collections of the USHMM (Photo Archives #81079A). As of this writing, it contains only the information about the Estonia transport. Eli's inscription on the back of the photograph, however, along with the testimony of his interviews, confirms that this group had gone to a work camp not far from the Kovno ghetto. I have given a copy of my photo and the inscription to the photo archives department, and I hope they will make the change soon, if they have not done so already.

17. The inscription is in Yiddish, and in Eli's handwriting. Translation by Rivka Schiller. Square brackets indicate her insertions, with the one exception noted in the

Figure 37a. Eli, Serafima, Boris Rochelson, and others on a cart going from the Kovno ghetto to a work camp in Aleksotas, November 30, 1943. Photograph by George Kadish. This print, with annotations by Eli Rochelson, is part of the family collection. An identical photograph, without annotations, is in the United States Holocaust Memorial Museum Photo Archives, #81097A.

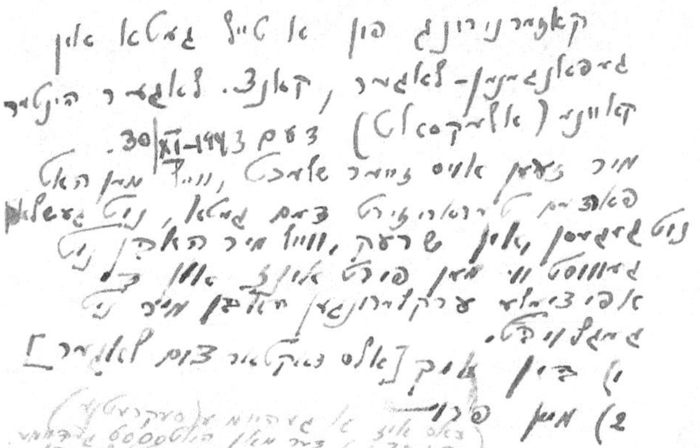

Figure 37b. Verso of Figure 37a. Most of the inscription, by Eli G. Rochelson, appears in the narrative. However, it also includes identifications paired with numbers written on the photograph and a brief mention of George Kadish, although not by name:

    1) Is me [as the doctor of the camp] *(brackets in original)*
    2) My wife
(This is a (secret) picture.) The man had 6,000 secret pictures of ghetto life.
[Translation by Rivka Schiller.]

It is not clear when Eli wrote these words, but since the photograph was given to him by Kadish it must have been after the war, although relatively soon after.[18] Much later, he would likely have written in English. The gap in time may explain why Eli describes the people on the cart as having just arrived at the work camp. If George Kadish took the picture, he would have taken it in the ghetto, before they left. Eli's remembrance, after the fact, may focus on the prisoners' depressed state at arrival, or it may reflect his own depressed state of mind after the war, as he remembers the people on the cart who had by that point perished.

As he describes in the long family interview with Burt, Eli, Sima, and Borya were in this work camp for approximately three months:

> Every morning we had to run to work with speed, and a German was stand-ing at the door and he said, *Los, los!*; make fast, fast. And those who didn't move got hit over the head. And as soon as the bell rang to get up they gave us five or ten minutes to have coffee and we had to run out to work. . . . No, the child did not work. He was staying in the camp. There were other children. Nothing. They didn't touch the children, at that time. But I can tell you when going to work many times in ghetto I took the child with me, because there were rumors that when we are at work they will surround all kids and take them away, or old men; then many times they went to meet you, they said you cannot take the child there.
>
> But there in Panemune concentration camp from 1943, December, till about the beginning of March—then my wife got sick and she developed diphtheria and again they gave permit to go to the Jewish ghetto, to the

---

caption to figure 37b. An earlier partial translation, done by Pearl Tucker, trans-lates *we appear very bad off* as the more colloquial *we look very bad*.

18. Kadish secretly developed his photographs at a German military hospital where he performed slave labor in the X-ray department. A high-ranking Jewish police offi-cer in the ghetto kept them safe for him, and did not disclose their hiding place even when tortured, ultimately to death. Kadish escaped from the ghetto and retrieved the hidden photographic evidence after the ghetto was destroyed in 1944. He later displayed his work in displaced persons camps, which may have been where Eli and other former ghetto inmates obtained their prints (USHMM, *Hidden History* 55).

ghetto in Kovno, and to admit her to the hospital because she had diphtheria. And we came back by horse and carriage and I didn't have shoes—I
had shoes with holes. And while, it took about three or four hours with
the horse and carriage to come, it was cold in the winter, and when I came
the same night I developed chills, fever, terrific pain, in the left side, and
I developed pneumonia, and Dr. Berman, at that time (figure 38), was a
physician in the ghetto and I was critical, I lost my consciousness, and they
gave me some sulfa, I could [take it], when I was awake. And they assigned
a nurse to my bed; I was two or three days unconscious, till I woke up and
the nurse screamed that I went out of my coma, and the relatives asked
Berman what will be. He says God can help him, he is very critically ill.[19]

Anyway, my wife had diphtheria and there was a doctor, a distant relative of my wife's, seems to be, Grinberg,[20] and he was the guy who was going
between the ghetto and Kovno city and meeting a lot of people, and he had
the diphtheria serum and I asked him to bring me some serum to inject for

19. Dr. Zelman Berman (as I knew his name), nineteen years older than Eli, forms an
important part of this narrative because he was an important figure in Eli's life.
Putting together information I have obtained from Josef Griliches and through
documents accessed via ancestry.com, I can confirm that Zelman-Moisse Berman (as he is listed on his American Joint Distribution Committee emigration
card) is the Dr. Moshe Berman who "headed the hospital . . . in the Ghetto at the
end of 1941, after the Germans burned down the contagious diseases hospital.
He was also an active member of the Council's health department. Before the war
he had been head of the Lithuanian military hospital and personal physician to
the Lithuanian chief of staff, General Zukauskas" (Tory 229, n. 1; Josef Griliches
mentioned that Gen. Zukauskas had also been a patient of his own father, Samuel
Griliches, a dentist.). When I was a child, our family often visited Dr. Berman and
his wife, Stefa, at their home, which was also his office, on the Upper West Side of
Manhattan. Dr. Berman was quite elderly and he suffered, I recall, from Parkin-
son's disease. He and Stefa were kind to us children, but I never fully understood
his relationship to my father, or his heroism, until I listened to this interview.

20. Eli pronounces the name Greenberg in the interview tape at this point, but he is
most likely the same Dr. Grinberg who at one time, like Dr. Zacharin, was head of
the health department in the ghetto. Dr. Zalman Grinberg's work in setting up the
St. Ottilien hospital for displaced persons after the war is documented in Hilliard
and elsewhere. He also served as chair of the Central Committee for Liberated
Jews in the American Zone of Germany.

Figure 38. "Kovno, Dr. Elhanan Elkes [left] and Dr. Moshe Berman." Courtesy Yad Vashem Photo Archive, Jerusalem. 4613/93.

the wife and he says they have to pay me, and I didn't have [anything] to pay, cigarettes or money, or something; I didn't have any valuables, I was a poor church rat. Anyway, somehow he did get it to me, somehow I gave him something, and he gave it to my wife. Then we found out that my son got sick, and they brought him to the ghetto [hospital].[21] Meningitis. The same story, meningitis antiserum, I think we got some anyway.

Then came the twenty-sixth of March, 1944. There was the famous and infamous children's selections [known as the *Kinder* Action (children's action, in German)], in all Baltic states, and all children have to be delivered to the Germans.[22] Imagine what it [was]. My son was sick, still, he was sick for a week already. And I tell to the doctor, Zacharin, look, bring the child here [to my hospital bed], he says I cannot. Anyway, I got the child without his

---

21. It is unclear from this account whether Borya traveled back to the ghetto with his parents or had remained at the labor camp.
22. The correct dates of this action were March 27–28.

permission. They were the Germans like wild dogs running all over the ghetto, looking for the children, going in the house. Women were fighting for the children, immediately shut the windows; they were fighting, surrounding the children, took them away, to Auschwitz, or somewhere, I don't know. Anyway, my wife recuperated, my son was feeling better, and . . . I took the liberty to take him in my room.

And I had him under my blanket, with my legs up, and he was laying there. He knew the danger already, it was in '44, he was ten years old, yes, ten years old.[23] I know they were coming, they came to the hospital, they looked in refrigerator, they looked in the basement, they looked in all rooms. Then they went—There was set partitions from cubicles for the patients. I was a patient after, recuperating after pneumonia. Then there was a doctor sick on the other side, an elderly doctor, Orbach, and his wife was around, and when they came they took him, and they took him away. And they were taking the children from wherever they could. And it was terrible, terrible tragedy. They took a lot of children, some were able to save. Now, they took this old Dr. Orbach, and they took him away from the bed, and we knew what it is, and his wife knew, too. She asked them, what are you doing? Why are you taking my husband? He is nothing wrong with him. No, we'll take him. No, she says, you cannot take him; he is healthy, and he is a doctor. She says, never mind, and she was fighting. So he says, OK, come with us. We'll give you a good place. And they took her away with the doctor.

Now they were going on inspection, and here is what [is] always in my mind, and I think about. They were going from cubicle to cubicle; in some places they found children, some guys, and they took it away. Now, I was laying there and, supposedly sick, and Dr. Zacharin, the chief of the hospital, introduced me to the Gestapo man. He says, this is a doctor, but he is a young man, he has a little cold, he will recuperate, he will be able to work. He was very nice to me, you know. I was probably white like this sheet of paper. You know, the Gestapo man gave a look under the bed, he didn't pick up the blanket, and he went out and said loudly, no, this room is OK,

23. In fact, he was about nine and a half years old. If he was murdered at the time most people have assumed (as I discuss later), he was murdered just a few weeks before his tenth birthday.

everything is OK. The other guys would hear, they shouldn't, you know—I have a feeling and suspicion that he intentionally didn't pick up the blanket, and he suspected that somebody is there but he let [it] go, I would think. I mean, it was one of those rare Germans who had some conscience and couldn't see that, but they had to comply with the law and the instructions from Hitler. And that was, I was able to save the child.

William Mishell reports that "Later in the evening," after he had hidden his own children at his place of work, he learned that the ghetto hospital was "surrounded and all the patients forced into the trucks and hauled away" (209). Eli's narrative makes clear that there were at least a few exceptions, and that he and his son were both fortunate and brave.

On March 26, 1944, the Jewish police were summoned for an inspection, and on March 27—the same day as the murderous action against children and the elderly—the Germans in control of the Kovno ghetto shot and killed 33 officers, including the entire police leadership (Kassow 2). Kassow explains that all 140 police officers had been summoned and questioned, since certain members of the force had been involved in resistance activities; those not murdered were permitted to return. Eli's friend Alonka Berman was among the murdered; his cousin Shloimke Kanter survived the police selection. However, as Samuel Kassow points out, "The murder of the police leadership meant the end of the Kovno ghetto police as it had been. To be sure, the occupation authorities set up a new force, but it was led by characters whom the Jews in the ghetto despised" (3). According to ghetto survivor Ephraim Gutman, they were hated because, at the time of the *Kinder* Action, a number of them saved their own lives by leading Nazis to the hiding places of children in many ghetto houses, but I have not found confirmation of this elsewhere.

A few months later, the Kovno ghetto was liquidated. Not long before that, the Nazis used Russian deserters to raid houses in the ghetto, and Eli recalled how he used the techniques his parents had used in southern Russia during the civil war to try to protect his own family from looting:

> We were in ghetto till about, I would say till the end of June, and beginning of July.[24] . . . We went from the hospital but we returned to our previous apartment we had. . . .
>
> [In the past, the tsarist armies sent] . . . out supposedly for searches the White Guard, and [now the Nazis sent] the prisoners, with lots of soldiers, the Russians who deserted to the German side. And here we had the same trick. We had cut a hole in the ceiling and camouflaged with the papers there; the whole ceiling was with paper.[25] We had a lot of, we put it inside and when they passed by we had the doors open like I did in Rostov-na-Donu; the doors were open, everything was empty, disarray, and when they came in, the Russians, the soldiers, they said—Oh, they cursed, nobody's there. . . . And then we are hiding upstairs and we heard them; [they] came there, "nobody is there." And another time when it was we were hiding beneath the table, they couldn't see us, they came in, they opened and they left. Then they broke the door from a little closet outside, a little place where you keep a lot of supplies, a pantry, they broke this, looked there for the people. . . . And we were in this apartment, and staying there in hiding, . . . but we were able [to survive].
>
> In the beginning of July we heard rumors that the Russians in 1944 [were] doing very well, and they were chasing the Germans all over, going to the Baltic States. The Germans felt it was getting bad and they wanted to have the Jews from the ghettos from the Baltic States deported farther into Germany. And then they decided the time is ripe to liquidate

---

24. The Kovno ghetto, by this point KL (Concentration Camp) Kauen, was liquidated by the Nazis in a six-day period beginning July 8, 1945 (United States Holocaust Memorial Museum, *Hidden History of the Kovno Ghetto* 248).

25. Although he describes this place in the interview as a "one-room apartment," the way they hide in the attic suggests it may have been the wooden house near the Catholic cemetery. It is unclear exactly when Eli's family moved there from the apartment block on Varniu Street.

the ghetto. As a matter of fact before that they took from little towns where they still have a few Jews working for the Germans, they brought them all in the ghetto. . . . Most of them, 90 percent, were killed, the Jews in the towns. But this working force, they took people from [that] . . . working force, they brought them to the ghetto. We knew that something is cooking very bad.

At this point, hearing about how the situation worsened, Burt asked Eli about resistance: whether he knew of any attempts in the ghetto to resist the Nazis, and whether he had ever been approached to join a resistance effort. Eli told him about Chaim Yellin, the leader of the Jewish resistance in Kovno, who was captured in April 1944 and killed by the Nazis in May 1944. A textual note by Dina Porat in *Surviving the Holocaust* suggests that Yellin may have committed suicide after his capture (Tory 500), something that Eli mentioned, as well. Chaim's brother, Meir Yellin, survived the Holocaust and died in Israel in January 2000; he coauthored *Partisans of the Kovno Ghetto*.[26] Eli knew both brothers, and mentioned that their father had been the director of a Kovno library before the war.

However, Eli was never approached to join the resistance. He recalled that they mostly enlisted young unmarried men and women whom Chaim Yellin had specifically invited. But he also said that he and his friends had not been interested in joining, in any case, although they admired what the resistance had tried to do:

People were afraid to talk, and they didn't talk, and they were not in the mood to talk. They were depressed, starved, and in fear. In ghetto was only passive resistance and organizing these people who would go fight against Germany in the woods. And about the resistance in the woods and

---

26. Eli owned the original Yiddish publication of this book, and referred to it in his interview. Its title (transliterated) is *Partizaner fun Kaunaser geto* and WorldCat shows its authors as Meir Yelin and D. Gelpernas (or D. Ghelpern). The only copy of the English translation is held at the United States Holocaust Memorial Museum library; the translator is Robin O'Neil.

the trouble the partisans, the anti-Nazi partisans, did to the Germans was known. They derailed trains, there was shooting. They [the Germans] were sending out the native Lithuanians to fight with them in the woods because the Germans were afraid, themsel[ves].

Eli also told Burt about the famous revolt at the Ninth Fort at Christmas 1943, when a group of sixty-four *sonderkommandos*, four of whom were not Jewish, got the German and Lithuanian guards drunk and escaped. The *sonderkommandos*, prisoners in forced labor, had the task of burning bodies as the Nazis began to hide the evidence of their acts. The revolt was something Eli had not witnessed firsthand, but it belongs in any account of resistance in Kovno. Eli believed that all the escapees had survived, but, in fact, only a small number managed to return to the ghetto and join the partisans. As Martin Gilbert points out, however, the survival of these few "provided witnesses of the fate of tens of thousands of Jews" (646; see also "Messages scrawled . . ."). Eleven of them produced a document now available online through the Shoah Resource Center of Yad Vashem, testifying to the opening of mass graves and the burning of over twelve thousand bodies, seven thousand of those estimated to be from the Kovno ghetto ("Evidence of Jewish Escapees . . ."). In all, "[a]n estimated 40,000 [people], were shot to death in Fort IX between the fall of 1941 and the spring of 1944" ("Messages scrawled . . ."). It had become the major killing center for the Jews of the Kovno ghetto, as well as for others transferred to it from many parts of Europe.[27]

In September 1943, at around the same time the burning of the bodies began, the Kovno ghetto came under the direct control of the SS, who began the process of turning it officially into KL Kauen, a concentration camp.[28] At the beginning of July 1944, as the inmates suspected, the Nazis

---

27. Today the Ninth Fort is open to visitors as a major site of Holocaust history and commemoration. See the map of "Kaunas (Kovno) and its Environs," in appendix A, for its location outside the city and the ghetto.

28. The abbreviations KL and KZ are used interchangeably, depending on the document, to indicate *concentration camp*. According to the chronology in *Hidden*

began to prepare for its liquidation and the transfer of the Jews to other camps:

> In the beginning of July there was an order that the Jews will be deported, but we should go voluntarily. And they gave a certain date. At that time people started to dig underground, and tried to save themselves. My [aunt] Minne and her children and Shloimke . . . there was an apartment house in the middle of the ghetto and they dug under the basement. And they told me to come to give a look, maybe I can [join them] with my wife and child. I went there, there were thirty [or] forty people in a small dungeon under, and there was no air, and there was no heat, and no water, and I thought we will die from starvation. I wouldn't do it. And I said, I will not do it. We knew that the Russians are coming, anyway. Then we saw that people were voluntarily going, the Germans surrounded, took them to the train. . . . As I told you, we had an opening in the ceiling. And we decided instead to get killed there from suffocation we will go upstairs and hope for the best. The same stair. My brother, and his wife [and child], and I and my wife and child went up. . . . We went upstairs and took the ladder and covered up, and there, you see, this was a one-room house, the whole house was in one room, and there through the opening of the boards I could see what's going on, and observe; and we were observing. We were there about two or three days. [We had no food], nothing. Whatever we had we tried to keep it going on. Maybe we had water. We had a well in our backyard; maybe we ran out at night to get water at the well. Then in a few days we saw the ghetto, explosions and fires. We lived near the Catholic cemetery, nearby. . . . One part of the ghetto nearer to us, [were] more fires, and then loudspeakers went that all those hiding should go out, because we soon will put dynamite, will explode, and put on fire. And I said no, let's wait, maybe they will not. As a matter of fact, we tried to run through the fence on the Catholic [cemetery] side, which was not too bad, but there were Lithuanian soldiers who said, what do you have? You give me, I'll let you go through. They took away whatever they had, valuables, and they reported [those who tried to escape] to the Germans.

History of the Kovno Ghetto, the SS took over on September 15 and it was officially declared a concentration camp on November 1 (USHMM 247).

And we found out that was no sense to go because they [the soldier guards] are traitors. They wouldn't let you go through. They took away everything and that's all, and that's the reason we were staying, and couldn't escape.

When they came, the loudspeakers, the next day, near us, we decided to go out.[29] And as soon as we go out we were surrounded by German soldiers. They didn't beat us up, nothing, we go to this point I think near the Jewish hospital, and there they took us when a lot of people were collected, they took us to the train, and in the train we were like cattle, in cattle wagons with no water, with no food, and they locked up the gates and it took us a week till we came. . . . We thought we are going to be shot. To kill us. That was our feeling.

They were on their way to the concentration camps of Stutthof and Dachau, the destinations of all those from the Kovno ghetto who left in that transport. What happened then formed a new epoch in Eli's and his family's experience, and will form the next chapter of this narrative. But in telling the story to Burt, Eli paused near this point to relate the fates of those who had attempted to hide beneath the ghetto buildings:

[T]he Russians came about five or six days later [to liberate the ghetto]. . . . Now I would say that a lot of people were digging underground holes to hide themselves, and among [those] killed were also Minne and her children, were killed there, in the bunker, because they exploded the apartment house. . . . [T]here was . . . one [other] group who dug enough a passage underground [far enough] in[to] the middle of the yard, where they survived. But the trouble is they didn't have—couldn't go out, because the apartment house was demolished; there [was] no way [to] escape till one person knew—a Jewish man, I don't know how—he told the Russians, look, there are people hiding in the middle [of the yard], dig 'em out, and they dug them out, and they took them out alive. They were [there] for five or six days. . . .

29. In handwritten notes on the transcript of the NYPL interview, Eli wrote, "With loudspeakers on trucks the Germans warned that if we don't come out they will explode the buildings. We had no choice [but] to leave the hiding place and surrender" (Rochelson, NYPL interview opposite page 17).

Winick and others,[30] a few people. . . . After the liberation we heard the story. [But Minne and her children] all died, because of the explosion and fire . . . ; the Germans were going, and ripping up all, house by house.

As Kassow writes, "Two thousand Jews ignored the deportation order and tried to survive in hideouts specially constructed beneath the houses of the ghetto. The Germans systematically set fire to almost every building in the ghetto, and all but ninety of the Jews who had hoped to survive to see the liberation perished just a couple of days before the arrival of the Red Army" (52) (figure 39).

Figure 39. "Ruins of the Kovno ghetto." United States Holocaust Memorial Museum Photo Archives #81133. Courtesy United States Holocaust Memorial Museum.

---

30. I have been unable to identify Winick and others who are mentioned by name in the interview. I leave the names in, however, in the hope that surviving family members might discover them.

6

Dachau, Stutthof, Auschwitz

ELI'S STORY CONTINUES:

We went for about five, six days, in the train, they said all women should go out. And we had our child with us, he was ten years old, and I said to my wife, what should we do, should he go with you or with me? She said, let him go with you, better. She gave me what she has, rings, earrings, other valuables, keep it with you; take it. And I took him with me. She was left in Stutthof, near Danzig; I'll tell you about that, too.[1] And we went from there. When we came to the concentration camp Dachau, it was a big field, the Germans met us, and they put immediately to work on barracks. There were barracks already erected but they made more barracks. After a while, a couple of weeks, they started to have bunks for us. . . .

We came by train to Dachau, we came there, there was a big speech from the *lagerführer*, it means this man in charge of the concentration camp. And he said, you fellas should remember, you came here to work, and if you don't work we know what to do with you. And if we Germans lose the war, don't be so happy about, because you will lose, too. That was the greeting speech.

---

1. From "And we had our child with us" through "I'll tell you about that, too," our father spoke in an especially soft and tender voice, in a way noteworthy enough for me to mention it here. The moment he records here is the last time he saw his wife.

Eli and Borya arrived at Dachau on July 15, 1944 (Dachau Concentration Camp Records, JewishGen[2]). In the NYPL narrative, Eli elaborates on conditions in the camp following the *lagerführer's* speech:

> Again, [there was] an order to give away your jewelry and whatever valuables you have. And they had—succeeded—they shoot some people to show they mean business. One of them, Dr. Berman—they took him and go to the latrine, you know, and at that time it wasn't like here, but plain holes and the whole fecal material was there, with the worms. They had to go nude there and clean it out . . . Because the people were throwing the jewelry and gold there instead to give it to the Germans, they were throwing it down there and they had to fish it out and clean it out. Then they beat them up there and killed a few [unintelligible] and hanged and did everything to create terror. (Rochelson, NYPL interview 20)

Dr. Zelman Berman, whom the Nazis so brutally humiliated, was the kind and dignified man who became Eli's lifelong friend. Dr. Lazar Goldstein, a Kovno medical school friend of Eli's, described the confiscation of valuables in his own memoir:

> After the first relatively peaceful night of sleeping on the bare floors of the tents, groups of us were searched by a[n] S.S.-man. On a large table that stood near a barrack, each one of us had to place all his belonging—money, watches, papers, photographs, everything. It was all taken away by the S.S.-man, who placed the money and the more valuable items in special boxes. Anyone who dared to ask permission to keep a document or a photograph was beaten by the S.S.-man with his truncheon. (Goldstein-Golden 75)

---

2. Although I initially accessed these records through JewishGen.org, scans of the relevant documents are also available in the digital collections of the International Tracing Service, accessible at the United States Holocaust Memorial Museum. The names of Ilija (appearing as Hija) and Boris Rochelson are on "Zugang am 15.7.44 von KL. Kauen [Arrival on 15 July 44 from Kaunas Concentration Camp]", 1.1.6.1, folder 43, List Material Dachau/Document #9898796_0/ITS Digital Archive. Accessed for me at the USHMM on September 6, 2010, by Sara-joelle Clark.

Indeed, among the papers Eli compiled to reinstate his medical credentials is a cover letter in which he writes, "While in the concentration camp at Dachau (Germany) . . . all original documents including the diploma of Doctor of Medicine were taken away by the Germans and destroyed" (appendix E). That Jews were able to keep such items, as well as jewelry, with them in the Kovno ghetto, hidden or not, underscores the trauma of the change when they were confiscated at Dachau.

For a long time I thought that Eli and Sima had made an individual decision to let their son, nearly ten years old at the time, go with his father. But eventually I learned (first, from Shalom Eilati, in an e-mail correspondence, and then from oral history testimonies of children who survived) that a large number of families, when the train arrived at Stutthof, made the same decision. They felt that boys who looked old enough to work would stand a better chance of survival with their fathers than with their mothers. Arnold Clevs (originally Abraham Klavarsky) reported that when the trains were loaded in Kovno, men, women, and children were together. In cattle cars, eighty to ninety sat with no food or water, and when they arrived at Stutthof the men and women were separated. A train with the men and boys took them to Landsberg, a nearby subcamp of Dachau, but the boys were separated from their fathers and taken to a different hut. Leo Zisman reported that the boys went to Lager 1 in Landsberg and the adults went elsewhere. However, the ITS (International Tracing Service) arrival records indicate that the men and boys arrived together, before they were separated; Borya and Eli were assigned prisoner numbers 81992 and 81993, respectively.

Eli's interview indicates that the fathers and sons could see and communicate with each other, until their final separation on July 26:

> [T]he Germans said that all children should be in the morning in a certain place, and they will take them to a child camp where they will have all good conditions and be fine. And there was Dr. Kaufman, had a child, and I, and a lot of people had children, and the next morning they put all people in

the—for counting, the people, and the children, too. While we were waiting for the count or *appel*, I ran out; he was in another column. I said, Burt, go ahead and take the sweater.[3] And stupidly enough I didn't tell him to stay there. Because they were all going outside [to the supposed "child camp"], the Germans will come and kill them out. And he went for the sweater; I asked, after [later], this man there, who was the supervisor of the bunk, he says, My son? Yes. Did he take a sweater? Yes. I says, you are lying, he probably wasn't here, he took the sweater for himself. He says, Yes, he came and he took, and he went.

The children, all boys, came to be known as the 131 Boys of Kovno. The camp they were taken to was Auschwitz. Arnold Clevs, Moshe Kravetz, and others have reported that two of the boys jumped off the train from Dachau; one got away, but the other was shot, and this discouraged similar attempts. They arrived at Auschwitz on August 1, and were sent to barracks in Birkenau. They were there until at least mid-September, when 90 of them were murdered in selections; those who survived were later sent to other camps (Waltzer). Of course, when the children were taken away, their fathers did not know where they were going. The name of Eliezer Kaufman, possibly Dr. Kaufman's son, is listed among the murdered and memorialized in Eilat Gordon Levitan's "131 Boys from Kovno."[4]

The men who as boys survived the fall selections pondered why they were spared the gas chambers on arrival and instead kept in Birkenau in a quarantine camp for about six weeks, counted and fed meager rations but not working, until the selections took place (Lewin). Arnold Clevs

---

3. Here and later Eli seems to have meant his first son, but he uses his living son's name, which is similar, in telling the story. Art Spiegelman records a similarly jarring yet poignant confusion on the part of his father at the end of the second volume of *Maus*, when Vladek calls Art by the name of his lost brother.

4. Eli and Dr. Kaufman both survived and remained in touch in the United States. According to Joseph Griliches (interview May 31, 2011), Dr. Kaufman, like my father, later did physical exams of survivors for the German consulate, to be used in calculating restitution payments. The consulate had found that survivors did not want to be examined by German non-Jewish physicians.

attributed their reprieve to their disciplined demeanor, "like little soldiers," as they marched off the train, led by one of their group who gave commands (Greene and Kumar 124, and testimony). Jacob Lewin attributed it to overcrowding, saying three thousand Jews had arrived the night before, and one thousand had been gassed and cremated earlier on August 1. Sol Lurie remembered that they had been given soap and towels and were told they would be going to the showers, but were soon given back their clothes and sent to a barrack at Birkenau because of a pending equipment deal that led camp officials to hold off on executions for a while.[5] Moshe Kravetz told me he had no idea why the boys were spared at that time; he suspected the Nazis just didn't know what to do with them. According to Ralph Codikow, they were the first transport of children who had been led into Birkenau alive, and they were thus an object of much curiosity and attention by the older prisoners.

At Stutthof, Serafima was given prisoner number 44346; her sister-in-law and thirteen-year-old niece, Rose and Sarah, received the numbers 41314 and 41313. I was unable to locate Rose's prisoner intake card, but Serafima's and Sarah's are in the digital archives of the United States Holocaust Memorial Museum[6]; Serafima gave her age as five years younger than she actually was, and listed her occupation as bookkeeper. Sarah's year of birth made her one year older than her actual age; such subterfuges were common, as both children and adults sought to ensure survival by appearing robust and the perfect age for work. Borya's papers made him four years older than his actual age, and listed him as a plumber's apprentice. Young Sarah's card at Stutthof identified her as a seamstress. Eli related that all

---

5. According to Jacob Lewin, when they came out of the showers they were given other people's clothes. Again, these disparities in detail tend to confirm the larger picture. The many interviews I have been able to listen to are but a tiny fraction of the many that are available.

6. Individual Documents Stutthof, Prisoner Questionnaires O-Schk, I 185 6, OCC 25/9 ID/1, AII 55, items #4612923_0_1/ (Rochelson, Serafina [sic]) and #4612920_0_1/ (Rochelsohn, Sara). ITS Digital Archive. Accessed at the United States Holocaust Memorial Museum on January 23, 2017.

three women died close to the end of the war, but he knew little about their experience in the camp. Women who survived, however, left testimonies that offer some clues.

Nesse Godin, who was from Shavli (Šiauliai), Lithuania, reported that she entered Stutthof alone at age sixteen, and after being sent to a shower was subjected to an invasive medical exam and strip search. It was the spring (cold in northern Europe), and the women stood outside naked for hours. The women were given prison clothing (some pants, some a dress, according to Rachel Gordon, from Kovno) and slept on bunks in barracks. After a while they went to a work camp, where they stayed and performed hard labor, digging trenches. Rachel Wise reported that it was very cold and they slept on straw, which was never changed. They had no shower after the first, and she washed her hair in the coffee they were given. These women's testimonies often emphasized social connections. Godin related that, in the midst of her traumatic arrival, nice Jewish ladies[7] held her hand and gave her hope. Rose and Sarah Rochelson were together until their deaths.

Soon after arriving at Dachau, Eli received his work assignment. In a bizarre paradox that carries a certain poetic justice, a major work site at the camp was an underground airport that the Nazis were constructing:

> After that they started to have groups, finding out what profession, what type of things they can do. At that time you should remember there were already not very old people, because the old all were killed. And they were sending to work. I was assigned in the beginning to Moll construction company, about six or seven miles from the concentration camp, where I was doing as a laborer work; as a matter of fact they assigned me once on the scaffolding for underground airport, to work with cement and picking up these pails with cement and letting down by rope, but I couldn't work because I couldn't stand any height, and I told the Jewish supervisor that I can't go. He said,

---

7. I would like to be able to put this phrase in quotation marks, but since they are not in my notes I treat it as a paraphrase.

never mind, you'll come the next day. But next day I joined another group, I didn't have to work this way.[8]

. . . Dr. Berman after the war made a remark; he says to me, Look, I have everything in America, he says, food galore, anything I want, and life is good, he says, but you remember when we got the watery soup in concentration camp, and we found a little potato, don't you think that was the best treasure you ever had? And that was the most fascinating remark, and truthful, because there were [it was only] water! In the morning you got a slice of bread with black coffee, and in five minutes you had to run out to go to line in the columns and they counted you ten times, for hours sometimes, because each time they count was a different count, to make sure nobody escaped. Who could escape, the stupid Germans? . . . In ghetto, maybe, not in Germany. Anyway, then you got, you went to work. You came back 5:00, you didn't have anything to eat; maybe, I don't remember, in the lunchtime maybe they gave you a piece of bread; then you were, your supper, and they gave you the piece of soup, and that's all.

And several times I want to be smart—and the Jewish concentration camp inmates worked in the kitchen, I had one like aluminum military can and the other is a plate. What I did, the plate I was hiding under my shirt, and the aluminum can I took it out first to get soup. I got the soup, I put it in my belt like this, with a hook, across my prisoner uniform, it was blue and white, the prisoner jacket, and then I went with the plate. And one of these *chikhak* [?] says, look, I notice you do it every day, several times; I will fix you up, I will report you. This bastard. After, he was sick, and I took care of him. After liberation, he broke an ankle, and before liberation in the concentration camp I give him a medication, Kuprex called, like now you use Kwell, for delousing—you were full of lice, after liberation—but he didn't allow me. . . . But he knows, he was avoiding me. But these guys, you see what [was] happening: they were taking the food from the prisoners, whatever there, they had all day, trading for other goodies, and taking away

8. For as long as I knew him, my father had a fear of heights. Estimates of mileage, numbers of inmates, and so on are from Eli's memory. The most accurate statistics will be found in published sources such as those listed in the Bibliography.

from the concentration camp people, and he's telling me, You're taking too much, there will not be left for the others. . . .

By December 1944 Eli was working as a physician in a camp hospital, assigned to a quarantine of people who had typhus. Dr. Zacharin, the same doctor who had been in the Kovno ghetto, secretly gave him and Dr. Berman immunizations against typhus, which kept them from contracting the disease then or later. But it was because the conditions of labor had made Eli so sick, in the first place, that Dr. Berman helped him get reassigned to the hospital in the camp:

I was going every day to the Moll, back and forth, and I'm getting weaker and sicker, going out from the concentration camp going to work; there was a little hill, and I couldn't make it. And once Dr. Berman saw me and he says, Look, you look sick; . . . [I say], Look, Dr. Berman, I am sick. I am starved, the legs are swollen, the scrotum is swollen, the belly is swollen, I cannot last anymore. And I knew that a lot of people, when they came to this stage, they developed a diarrhea, colitis, [unintelligible], and that was the end. I told Dr. Berman, I will not be able to continue it; I am very bad. He said I will try to make an opening for you in the *krankenreview* [a small hospital within the concentration camp] and sure enough I was there relieved from the duties going to the construction company, and I ate better, and after a while there, in December, [when prisoners] developed the typhus, they assigned me to this place in a separate quarantine within the concentration camp. And as I said before, I was immunized.

There was another doctor, Greenberg, I can tell this, who was having a very good job outside the concentration camp, and having food and having everything.[9] He was one of these guys who were able to accommodate to each condition and not to suffer. Anyway, after the quarantine ended, in January or February, he wanted to stay in the hospital, but the Germans had a certain quota, how many doctors. And Dr. Berman told me, you know what, I cannot help it, he gave cigarettes to Dr. Zacharin, you didn't have it, I will put him on

---

9. This was probably, again, Dr. Zalman Grinberg, who was able to get the anti-diphtheria serum to the Kovno ghetto and later ran the DP hospital at St. Ottilien.

the place of you but you can still be in the hospital and when the Germans come for an inspection you will hide in some of the barracks.

Eventually, Eli was assigned to a first-aid station for the Moll construction company, in the woods, "where I had wood for the wood stove to burn in the winter, but I didn't have any food; I really was starving." His hunger led to one of the few incidents of abuse he recounted in his interview:

[A]t one time there were three shifts, there were working about five or six thousand people from different concentration camps, you know. One of—a Jewish supervisor came and he tells me that, hey, he will give me some food. What does he send in? He sent me the peel of the potatoes. He has the food plenty, but he gave me the peels of the potatoes. I had a stove, I boiled it, I ate like a horse, and then I got very, very sick. I remember I had palpitations, I got weak, I couldn't move, and then Dr. Goldstein (he doesn't remember that), Dr. Goldstein came and he says, look, they all come, to—already ready to go, they're missing the doctor.[10] They cannot know, what happened to you? I said, I got sick. [He said,] You better go, you'll be in serious trouble. We were without guards, you see. Then I went out and came there; everybody was waiting for me. And one of the guards went and gave me *whoosh!* and I fell down, but I stood up because otherwise they would kill. And then the other German guard told him that he was wrong, I am a doctor, he shouldn't have hit me, and that's all.

Every day going to work, going back, we were singing Russian songs—Russian—and the Germans loved it. They asked us to sing the Russian songs, one of those peculiar things—Because it's a good melody, and hundreds and hundreds of people singing, you know, it fetched them up. And that was the ghetto for a while—the concentration camp. . . .[11]

---

10. This is the same Dr. Goldstein whose memoir, published after his death by his widow, Esther, describes the confiscation of valuables at Dachau.

11. Here, as later, Eli uses the word *ghetto* when he means *camp*. Eli also described another time he was given twenty lashes, when he asked to be moved with some other prisoners. The sequence of events is not clear, but beatings were far from limited to one or two episodes.

Avraham continued with Eli to Dachau after his wife and daughter, Rose and Sarah, had been left at Stutthof. Eli was in lager 1 and his brother in lager 2, but, Eli recounted,

> I was able to communicate with him, with my brother, and sometimes send him bread. He was very honest. He wouldn't take a thing more than his ration, but he was assigned to give the bread to the prisoners. And once in a while he gave it to me a piece of bread.

At one point, when they were in lagers (subcamps) far apart, Eli learned that his brother was trying to send him bread through an agent, but the agent never gave it to him. Through an intermediary, Eli asked his brother to stop.

> . . . And then I told him that maybe he should come to lager 1 . . . [T]he liquidation of [Avraham's] lager started, then they liquidate there, and there he could have a choice; he could come to lager 1, or lager 4. Lager 4 was infamous, we call it an elimination camp, where they killed the people by starvation, not by shooting. And to come here—but anyway, I found out, after, that they assigned [him] to go to Czechoslovakia.

Avraham entered the Flossenbürg camp on January 7, 1945. Flossenbürg was somewhat to the west of the Joachimstahl region, in western Czechoslovakia, known for its mines, and while Flossenbürg employed slave labor in granite quarries, it also had subcamps in Czechoslovakia. Eli learned only after the war of Avraham's fate, from a friend, Marc Rubin,[12] who had been in lager 2 with Avraham. Eli attributed his brother's death to harsh conditions that aggravated existing ailments: "He had a lot of varicosities, and he had a little infection in the concentration camp. And he went to the mine, Joachimstahl mines, famous with uranium and other things, and

---

12. Marc Rubin and his wife, Dorothy, were close friends of Eli and Pearl after the war. They lived in the New York area and Marc ran a lab that my father used in his medical practice.

there he got an infection, and he died from starvation, exhaustion, and later—not fit to be a miner."[13]

At one point, Eli was selected to go to lager 4, but because he was a doctor those in charge told him to stay in lager 1. At another time he was recommended to work as a doctor in a Belgian camp. Dr. Berman discouraged him, saying he was better off staying with his own people:

> However, I had an appointment there, and, imagine, I went with the guard outside the concentration camp to the so-called, this *militaristube*, the house where they had the guards. And I went there and I waited for appointment. Then a German doctor, a big shot, came in and he says, who is the doctor, he has an appointment? They says yes, then another went to him, one of these low-echelon military men, and says, you know, he is a Jew, you know that. Oh, he says, if he is a Jew, then forget about. And that was fortunate enough, and lucky. . . . Because if I had gone there in Belgium, and they found out, after, I am a Jew, they would say you hided your identity, and I would be exposed to mistreatment and a lot of trouble.

13. The evidence of Avraham's transfer date is in the JewishGen Holocaust Database, as well as documents in the USHMM digital archives, including "Lists of Lithuanian and Latvian Jews who were Transferred from Dachau to Other Camps," List Material Dachau, 1.1.6.1., folder 0157/Document #9921059_1/ITS Digital Archive. Accessed for me at the USHMM on September 6, 2010 by Sara-joelle Clark. Archival materials differ on his date of death. Two documents in the digital archives, copied from original files, indicate that Abram Rochelson, Dachau prisoner #85000, died at Leitmeritz (Litomerice), a Czechoslovakian subcamp of Flossenbürg, one on February 19, 1945, the other on March 28, 1945 (Central Names Index Card, Flossenbürg, item #34026444_0_1 and Death Certificate issued by Special Registry Office in Bad Arolsen, CNI section 0.1, item #34026440_0_1/ITS Digital Archive. Accessed at the United States Holocaust Memorial Museum on January 23, 2017). The Third US Army record of his death lists the place as Flossenbürg, but agrees with the date as March 28, and includes Avraham's Flossenbürg prisoner number—as in the earlier document with that date—43019. (Individual Documents Flossenbürg, CNI card #34026437_0_1/ITS Digital Archive. Accessed at the United States Holocaust Memorial Museum on January 23, 2017). Disparities are understandable when crimes of such magnitude are being documented. Whichever date is correct, however, it is clear that Avraham died close to the end of the war, and after the liberation of Auschwitz at the end of January, now a significant commemoration date.

Considering both episodes, Eli concluded, "You know, you never know. But to go into unknown places in a camp is dangerous."

As spring came on, unusual events occurred in Dachau:

> About end of March or beginning of April 1945—A German soldier was coming and talking to me, bringing me one day potato, the other day bread, and trying to be friendly. I was frightened with this goodness, here there's something suspicious, probably from Gestapo an agent. He wanted to find out, he asked me questions: What do you think, the Germans will lose, or no? I said, I don't know, I am here a prisoner, I don't know what is. [He said,] Look, I am telling you, we are losing. And I didn't make any reply. Then he opened [his coat]; he says, Do you think I am SS man? I have SS man's uniform; here, look, I am Wehrmacht; I am soldier, military. . . .

The NYPL interview transcript records more clearly that "beneath [the SS uniform] he has the Wehrmacht uniform. . . . He was already ready to change his uniform beneath his coat . . . after defeat he shouldn't be killed. And he wanted to have somebody, a good word, in case . . ." (Rochelson, NYPL interview 26). The NYPL interview also records Eli's reaction to the Allied bombings that were taking place around that time: "In spite of the tiredness and starvation and the misery, at night we heard flashes of light and the sounds of explosions, and I and others were happy[14] . . . And we got up—and there was an order at night, we could never go out to go to the latrine or wherever we had to . . . We couldn't. [W]e had to stay in the camp. We looked through the windows and enjoyed—the Americans are bombing . . . and flashes. This was the best music. We, I enjoyed so much, you have no idea . . . The Americans are bombing . . ." (Rochelson, NYPL interview 25–26).

---

14. Eli edited this part of the typescript in ink in a way that is worth mention. The typescript of the audio reads, "we heard flashes of light and the sounds of explosions, and I was happy" (26). Rereading the text, he added words to make clear that he was not alone in this feeling, but his original "I was happy" remains powerful.

About the twentieth of April the guards didn't pick us up to take to the concentration camp [from the work site]. We were waiting, and waiting, and they didn't come. We know that something is cooking. And, sure enough, after about five, six hours they came to pick us up and we came to the ghetto, there was the *lagerführer*, the chief of the concentration camp, [who] says, Voluntarily, whoever wants, we will transfer him to another place. And there were a lot of volunteers who agreed to go. I . . . agreed, too, and Zacharin says, You go as a doctor with them. I had already everything ready. And I will never forget, a guy from Kovno comes to me and he says, You are so stupid, Why the heck you have to go? Isn't this better to die in ghetto or going there to the Alps and be shot in the Alps? At least you have two or three days life here in ghetto—in the concentration camp, I mean. You are better off. Don't go. And I listened and I listened, and I think, He is right. Why should I? OK, then, I took off my rucksack and didn't go. Berman [more likely Zacharin] found out, he was mad like a dog; I said Look, I don't go, and forget about: I will not go.

. . . Two days before, I exchanged my ration of bread with a Russian prisoner. The Russian prisoners were also [there], too, but they have a separate part, and theirs a little better. I gave him bread and he gave me potatoes. The potatoes were rotten, but he gave me a whole bag of potatoes and I kept it and then I took from the hospital pharmacy a lot of tablets, Decalcit, called, it is a Swiss vitamin D and calcium tablet, which has a lot of sugar. I took about five hundred pills. Then came the last call and the *lagerführer* says, Look, only the sick and unable people will stay there. The others should leave the concentration camp. There was no choice. If you are the old and left, you will be shot. Then we went. . . .

7

Liberation and Landsberg

ELI TOLD THE next story often, from the time Burt and I were quite young, and in my mind I titled it "Escape from the Train":

I saw there is no choice, I had to go and we went by train, some type, we didn't know which direction. And there, the next morning, the train was attacked by English planes, or American planes. And they killed the engineer of the locomotive and each time there was an attack the Germans told us to go out, and when the attack subsided they told us to go back. A lot of people were killed at that time and one of these running away for shelter. I and another guy, Baikovich,[1] I saw him, I says, look, there is no sense, let us go back, and the Germans said to [us, go] back. We couldn't go to the left because the railroad station was burning; other places, I heard, with those people who went there, the native Germans shot at them, probably they shot at them, they were afraid, and there was shooting and fire—I suspected, [but] I didn't know the war was over.

But then we went under [the] train elevation, through a, like a sewer pipe, ... we went on the other side of the elevation, and there we felt entirely different atmosphere. It was quiet, and peaceful, and we start to walk through the forest—then we went with another few other refugees, I know Dr. Lichtenstein, he lives in the Bronx, and some other people—and we all went together and we slept overnight in the woods. Baikovich was very hungry and he says, I want to go to a German house and get some food. I says, You are crazy, you will be killed and reported; don't do that. And I remember when we are

---

1. This may be the same Mr. Baikovich I met once at our home, when I was a child or teenager.

going already to this place we heard a truck coming. And we went down the elevation into a ravine, with boxes, cans, and something to hide, and we saw that there are German soldiers and higher, there were [unintelligible] driving. I get out at night and then we were hiding somewhere and there are two houses, and we saw a German soldier came and his wife came out and she was crying, and crying, and she says don't go, he says, I have to go, and he left and then we saw it is dangerous. So what we did, we went . . .—That was the first day, I think. It started to get a little light, and we went, we saw a chapel, we saw a chapel in the road, and we tried to hide in the chapel.

And, sure enough, we came up and there was, you know, there, religious artifacts, and pictures and everything, a little tiny room for prayer, what they have it all over Europe. And I went up on the shoulders of another and tried to open the boards to go up and hide. We couldn't, we couldn't open the boards. Then we left to the woods, and the forest, and we slept all night and the rain was raining. We heard shooting all over, from all places, and we knew that the Russians already or Americans are near, and we were sleeping there. Then, middle of the night I saw—. . . . I heard voices, and I give a look, and then I see, the sun didn't come up yet, the two shadows coming out covered with protecting colors [camouflage], canvas, what they have. Usually the military, the German pilots had it, airplanes. And sure enough we heard them talking in a foreign language.

And we got up—We were frightened, and, after, we saw the insignia[?]. And one guy took out cigarettes, the other took out bread, and he said, Here you have it. It was the biggest feast we had for a long time. Then as the day came on more people came in, more refugees came in, and then on the third day, I think, like, twenty-ninth of April, a guy, a Polish guy . . . came out and said, the Americans are down the field, in the forest. I said, you are a dirty liar. And he said, you, doctor, are stupid. I am telling you that these are the Americans. And then he says, I will prove it to you. And he comes an hour later with a lot of food. And I said to the other guys, you know, this fellow there, he didn't get it [from the Americans?]. He says, You know what? You want to stay there, stay.

To make sure enough, another guy went and we found out the Americans are [there], and he saw the American soldiers, motorcycles—and American motorcycles, and soldiers, we kissed them, and so on. And he went into a German place, and he says, Give us place for these people. And the German, you know, he still didn't want. He put us [in] the attic. And then [in] the attic this doctor—Mr. Koton, came, and he started to choke me. He was a Lithuanian [Jew], I knew him—his father, his son—he got crazy, you know. And I took and I was fighting, till others separated us, and then we went down and they gave us food. He got out of his mind, just like that. Suddenly he's free, and you know he didn't know what to do. Loss of senses, I don't know. After, he was embarrassed. They separated [us]—He just choked me. Then we went down and they had us meat and pea soup and eggs, of course, and other people got sick, got diarrhea, but I was able.

In Tape 1, Eli elaborated a bit: "We went to the attic . . . there were quite a number of prisoners, about ten people. We went to the attic and the hay; it was good. At least we had a place to warm up. . . . I ate like a horse and I couldn't finish, one plate after another."

Although Eli told us little about Dachau or the Kovno ghetto when we were growing up, Burt and I knew well the story of the escape. It was happy and heroic, so we thought of our father as someone who had gone through horrible things but who was not essentially a victim. It was difficult learning more, hearing of lashings and humiliations, hard-earned supplies of food obtained at great risk, then taken away at the ghetto gate—stories that I remember as unbearable when I heard my father tell them, the frustration returning in his voice, but which appear in the recordings in a matter-of-fact way. The escape from the train, however, was a story of heroism and personal victory over the Nazis. Eli wrote it up for the *Landsberger Lager-Cajtung*, the newspaper of the Landsberg displaced persons camp, in a "humoristic" way, as he described in the NYPL interview (Rochelson 73).[2] He was wise to make that the first detailed story of the Holocaust that he shared with his children.

Eli and many others who were liberated at Dachau and in the surrounding forests ended up in the Landsberg-am-Lech displaced persons camp in the American Zone, the part of Germany controlled by the US

---

2. This article was published in the *Landsberger Lager-Cajtung* (later titled the *Landsberger Jidisze Cajtung*), the newspaper of the Jews in the Landsberg DP camp. Eli saved a large collection of these papers, which now crumble at the touch. I have so far had no success in finding the article, which he mentioned often, either in his collection, online, or in microfilms at the YIVO library.

Army after the war. Landsberg had been the site of a subcamp of Dachau, and in the town was the prison where Hitler, in the 1920s, had written *Mein Kampf*. After the war, Eli recalled, the *lagerführer* of Dachau 1, who had given the prisoners the big speech upon arrival, was hanged at Landsberg after his trial. The camp was the second largest DP camp in the American Zone, and, after October 1945, it housed only Jews.

In the DP camp Eli worked as a doctor, setting up the outpatient clinic. He worked closely with Dr. Solomon (Shlomo) Nabriski, also a Holocaust survivor from Kovno, who established and directed the Landsberg hospital, and with Dr. Jacob Oleiski, an agronomist from Kovno who had served as director of ORT in Lithuania from 1927 until the Nazi invasion (see "History of ORT"). Dr. Oleiski survived Dachau and became a leader in establishing ORT schools in the displaced persons camps, and he had a sig-nificant role in Landsberg as chief of the Culture Section. Both Dr. Nabriski

Figure 40. Doctors, nurses, and others on the staff of the hospital at the Landsberg-am-Lech displaced persons camp. In the center row, seated from left to right, are Drs. Rochelson, Orlinskaya, Goldstein, Berman, Nabriski, Oleiski, and Poretsky (later Perry). The photograph is from the family collection, but it also appears in the *Landsberger Lager-Cajtung*, December 31, 1945, which pro-vides the identifications. See "Fun Unzer Bilder-Galerje."

and Dr. Oleiski appear with Eli in a photograph of the Landsberg hospital staff, as well as Dr. Berman and others mentioned in this narrative; Eli also saved less formal photos (figures 40, 41a, 41b, and 41c).[3]

Figures 41a and b. Less formal photographs of Eli at the Landsberg hospital. Family collection.

Figure 41c. Eli at Landsberg or in New York soon after arrival. This photo was taken at the same time and place as another photo in which he is with Jacob Oleiski, and thus it might have been taken in either place, since Dr. Oleiski spent time in New York. Family collection.

---

3. Dr. Nabriski and Eli were close personal friends as well as colleagues. Both Dr. Nabriski and Dr. Oleiski emigrated to Israel, where they continued their distinguished professional careers, Dr. Oleiski with ORT and Dr. Nabriski as head of gynecology at a hospital in Kfar Saba (Tory 386).

How do people set up a hospital in a former concentration camp right after they, themselves, have just been liberated? As Eli explained, they took beds, medications, and equipment from the Germans, who at that point could deny them nothing: "we went to the Germans . . . we took it. We didn't ask any questions. . . . They had to give us" (Rochelson, NYPL interview 31). He went on to explain that "over 25,000 people went through our dispensary [the outpatient department] in about 9 months" (31), a number that would have included repeat visits, since the population of the camp was around five thousand. Many of the patients had lice, typhus, and typhoid fever, as well as dysentery and diarrhea. Many of them died, but many were brought back to life.

Many years later, Burt and I got to know one of our father's Landsberg patients. In late October 2010 I went to the annual meeting of Assistance to Lithuanian Jews, in New York, at which my mother's recent passing was commemorated. Josef Griliches leads this organization, the annual meetings of which are held on the weekend closest to the anniversary of the Kovno Great Action; that catastrophic event is remembered along with members of the organization who have died since the last meeting. At the door I saw and greeted Thelma Silber, widow of my father's friend from medical school, Dr. Joseph Silber. Thelma didn't recognize me at first, so I told her who I was. Just then an elderly gentleman entered. We had never met before, but when he heard my name he came up to me and greeted me with both enthusiasm and disbelief. "You are Rochelson?" he exclaimed. "Your father saved my life." Nissan Krakinowski had been seventeen years old and liberated from a subcamp of Dachau, when he became sick from overeating. Then he developed pleurisy. Both his parents had been murdered, his father at the very start of the German occupation of Kaunas. He went to the infirmary at Landsberg extremely frightened. Sixty-five years later he remembered my father's kindness and reassuring words, which helped him as much as his medical care. He told me that after talking with my father, those many years ago, he knew that he would be all right. When Nissan and I spoke in 2017, after I had listened to the audio of his Shoah

Foundation interview, he confirmed what he had mentioned then, that he had been in the DP camp hospital for a year and a half. He also confirmed what he had told me before, that my father had saved his life both physically and emotionally.

Eli's account of his time at Landsberg gains in detail both from files that he compiled and saved after the war and from archival and published sources. The documents that Eli used to reestablish his medical credentials contain a typewritten page, in English, documenting how he was invited by Dr. Nabriski to "assist in the establishment and operation of a hospital in the DP camp," and that the hospital, when established in May 1945, included an outpatient department, which Eli led, two hundred beds for inpatient care, and a dental clinic.[4] As the many printed hospital forms in YIVO Institute files make clear, DP Hospital 2014 was a highly professional institution from the outset, carefully tracking admissions and immunizations and issuing health certificates for patients examined.[5] On February 9–11, 1946, Eli participated in a conference "of the delivered Jewish Doctors of the American Zone," held at Landsberg.

A sense of the daily life at Landsberg can be found in the published letters of Major Irving Heymont, the Jewish American soldier who, assigned to run the camp for the US Army, became its chronicler. Heymont, in Landsberg from September to December 1945, published his detailed letters to his wife in *Among the Survivors of the Holocaust* nearly forty years later. He explains how he came to realize how much the effects of concentration camp experience influenced the lives and decisions of displaced persons, even making them reluctant to be transferred from the barracks of Landsberg to more amiable housing at Föhrenwald, another camp nearby: "To most of the people of the camp, the very mention of a 'transport' or move brings back bitter memories of when a transport or

---

4. This and subsequent information appears in a typewritten page among his papers, a summary of information he provided to a medical certifying group.

5. YIVO file R294.2 MK.483.62 (hard copy and microform numbers) contains numerous examples of blank forms.

move to another camp meant that many were to die. . . . Now, they want to be secure in one place unless they know the move is a definite step along the path leading out of Europe" (75).[6] Early on, by October 1945, Heymont succeeded in getting non-Jewish refugees moved to other camps. The goal of non-Jews was to be repatriated near their former homes, whereas for the Jews at Landsberg the goal was to leave Europe as soon as possible, and there had been friction between the two groups (17). Heymont was less draconian than other officials regarding black market activity in the camp, viewing arrests of small traders as unnecessary harassment when "all Germany is one black market" (60; see also 97). He recognized the paradox of trying to establish reasonable living conditions in a place that was, ideally, a very short-term way station, and yet intensive efforts were necessary.[7] Although most displaced persons had emigrated by late 1949, the Landsberg camp did not close fully until October 1950 (108). Eli was there until late March 1946.

The camp was run jointly by the US Army and the United Nations Relief and Rehabilitation Administration (UNRRA). Several observers castigated the military and UNRRA governors for inadequate food, clothing, cleaning equipment, and sanitary supplies. Dr. Lee Srole, a sociologist on leave from Hobart College who served as chief welfare officer at the camp, sent a letter of resignation in protest against conditions that he saw as resulting from official negligence. In the midst of an itemized list of concerns, Srole protested against both a weakened UNRRA and a US military government,

---

6. Ruth Gay, in *Safe Among the Germans*, includes a photograph of Föhrenwald, which eventually became the third largest DP camp in the American Zone (71–72). Landsberg was the second largest, after Feldafing.

7. Keith Lowe's *Savage Continent* provides a context for less than perfect conditions, black market activities, and even attacks on former *kapos* in the DP camps. The horrifying conditions of concentration camps, discovered by the Allies at the time of liberation, could not be transcended overnight (78–93); however, what American and UN inspectors saw as anarchy and filth was mild and orderly in relation to much of what Lowe documents throughout postwar Europe, where refugees of many nationalities found themselves adrift.

which, "contrary to the letter and spirit of General Eisenhower's Directives, on the one hand tends to protect and often coddle the Germans, and on the other callously neglects elementary human needs of those who were the first declared enemies of Nazism" (page 2 of report).[8] Similarly, three months later, Judge Simon Rifkind prepared a report to the chief of staff in which he urged the American military to insist that Germany do its part: the Jewish displaced persons "object to American food given to them as an act of grace. They prefer German food delivered to them as of right" (Rifkind 6).

For all their sympathy for the concentration camp survivors, Major Heymont and others were appalled at sanitary conditions in the camp, in particular at the filthy conditions that persisted in camp kitchens as well as latrines (Heymont, 10–11 and frequently throughout; see also Smith).[9] Apart from being disgusted aesthetically by overflowing toilets and excrement in corridors, observers feared the spread of disease and epidemics. In his account of the Landsberg DP camp, Major Heymont praised the hospital as one of "two bright spots" in terms of sanitation; the camp schools, including the ORT schools run by Oleiski, were the other (11).

Regarding sanitation specifically, Eli's typewritten summary of his contributions confirms the hospital's "strict enforcement" of policies

---

8. Heymont disputed Srole's allegations, saying they were either exaggerated or "founded on misinformation" (104). He conceded, however, that Srole wrote in good faith, and that his charges served their purpose of calling attention to disturbing conditions—adding that he hoped Srole would withdraw his resignation (107). I have found no evidence that Srole did so. Heymont refers to Srole as Leo, but the name on Srole's typescript in the UNRRA archive is Lee.

9. Heymont often expressed frustration at the difficulties in obtaining such basics as brooms and toilet paper (27, 58, 71, and elsewhere). To this day, commentators criticize the US Army for the treatment of displaced persons in the camps; in 2015 Eric Lichtblau in the *New York Times* described displaced persons as "jailed by America." Yet Atina Grossmann's account reinforces the comment of one of Lichtblau's interviewees that "[c]ompared with the Nazi camps, 'it was heaven'" (Lichtblau; Grossman 181–82). Eli's experience, too, suggests this more complex picture.

promoting sanitation. No one was admitted without being first "deloused and bathed," and after three violations of sanitary rules, "the violator might be evicted from the camp." In March 1946, UNRRA staff conducted a "Sanitary Month,"[10] at the end of which the Sanitation and Health Office held a "festive closing" at which both Dr. Nabriski and Dr. Rochelson presented lectures. A 4″ by 6″ card in Eli's personal archive contains the program for this event; it is written in Yiddish but, like the newspaper and innumerable posters and flyers, printed in Latin type (figure 42).[11] Dr. Nabriski spoke on "Abortion as a Social Problem" and Eli gave a lecture on "Sexual Diseases, Their Rise and Prevention."[12] Awards were given to contest winners in art and writing, presumably on subjects concerning sanitation, as well as for the cleanest rooms and corridors. The event was designed to appeal to all ages, and the program suggests a lighthearted and celebratory tone, even given the serious lecture topics.

The last item on the Landsberg hospital's sanitary colloquium program is a performance by the orchestra of St. Ottilien, a musical group made up of survivors in the DP camp and hospital at a former monastery of that name. The orchestra is best known for having played at the Liberation Concert of

---

10. UNRRA file S-0436-42-6.

11. Heymont, writing about the first issue of the *Landsberger Lager-Cajtung*, notes, "We did not succeed in finding Yiddish type even though we scoured the whole American occupation zone" (42). Ruth Gay points out that in this case necessity may have been a virtue, since many of the young people in the DP camp spoke Yiddish but could not read it in Hebrew letters (72). The transliterations of Yiddish in these documents were made according to the Polish alphabet, not the German, as if the German language itself had become anathema. Eventually, but late in the camp's existence, Yiddish type was found and used at Landsberg.

12. Atina Grossmann writes about the continuing need for abortions among survivor women even at a time when the birthrate among Jewish DPs was exceptionally high. The abortion rate was low, however, and Grossmann reports that "Jewish medical and religious authorities condemned abortion and encouraged births as part of the surviving remnant's collective responsibility" (192). The doctors were also perhaps responding to the many abortions they had had to perform on Jewish women during the Holocaust, when pregnancy was punishable by death.

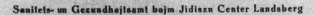

Sanitets- un Gezundhajtsamt bajm Jidiszn Center Landsberg

Ajnladung

Der Sanitets- un Gezundhajtsamt hot dem kowed Ajch ajnculadn cu der fojerlecher szlisung fun dem propogande-monat far zojberkajt un hygiene welche kumt for milwoch, dem 27. III. d. j. in kino-zal, punkt 19 azejger in ownt lojt folgnder program:

1. Referat fun dr. Nabriski ojf der teme: »Abort als gezelszaftlecher problem«
2. Referat fun dr. Rochelson ojf der teme: »Di geszlechtskrankhajtn, zejer antsztejung un farhitung« (mit lichtbilder)
3. Partejlung fun premies far di gewiner fun di konkursn far dem bestn bild un far di beste szularbetn.
4. Partejlung fun premies far di zojberste cimern un koridorn.
5. Szluswort.
6. Orkester fun St. Ottilien un zejer repertuar.

SANITETS- UN GEZUNDHAJTSAMT

Figure 42. Program of closing events for a public conference at Landsberg, underlining presumably by Eli Rochelson. Family collection. The translation (of the transliterated Yiddish) by Rivka Schiller reads as follows:

Sanitation and Health Office at the Jewish Center Landsberg

Invitation

The Sanitation and Health Office has the honor of inviting you to the festive closing of the propaganda month for the cleanliness and hygiene that will take place Wednesday, March the 27th of this year, in the theater hall, at promptly 7:00 o'clock in the evening, according to the following program:

Lecture from Dr. Nabriski on the subject "Abortion as a Social Problem."

Lecture from Dr. Rochelson on the subject "Sexual Diseases, Their Rise and Prevention" (with photographic slides).

Distribution of awards for the winner of the contests for the best picture and for the best schoolwork [i.e., essays].

Distribution of awards for the cleanliest rooms and corridors.

Closing word.

Orchestra from St. Ottilien and their repertoire.

Sanitation and Health Office

May 27, 1945, an event held at St. Ottilien and led by Dr. Zalman Grinberg.[13] It was considered to be the first formal gathering of Holocaust survivors (Hilliard chapter 1). Documents in the YIVO Institute files attest to a wide variety of organizations at the Landsberg camp, including *landsmanshaftn*

---

13. A film has been made about this orchestra, *Creating Harmony: The Displaced Persons Orchestra at St. Ottilien* (2007).

(organizations of survivors from towns in Eastern Europe, which frequently held memorial meetings), sports clubs, and chess clubs. A historical commission undertook a folklore survey of camp inhabitants, and parties were held on Hanukkah and other occasions.[14] I have no idea which, if any, of these events and activities Eli might have participated in. In later years, although he joined various organizations, he was not an especially active member. He had little interest in team sports, and only discovered the Sports section in the *New York Times* during the 1972 Bobby Fischer/Boris Spassky world championship chess competition. Had he still been at the camp, he might have enjoyed the "First Jewish Chess Olympiad," a competition among representatives of sixteen DP camps in the American Zone, held in September 1946, but that was three months after he left for the United States.[15] (The opening ceremonies for this event, too, featured a concert by the St. Ottilien orchestra.) Eli did not live in camp housing but rather in a private boarding house. However, if there is no evidence that he participated in group activities other than medical, the letters he saved from his time at Landsberg and after attest to close relationships with colleagues and others.

In Landsberg Eli had what he always described as a platonic relationship with a teenaged girl, Masha, but it was clear that the friendship was tinged with romance. He was very open about this friendship, and our family albums included photos of Masha as a lovely young woman, one of which is inscribed on the back in Yiddish, "As a sign of good friendship I give you my picture. For you, Ilija. Your handed-over [*ibergegebeneh*] Masha." The inscription is dated Landsberg, 26-VII [July]-46, more than seven weeks after Eli left for America, and it seems to have been written with humor and affection (figure 43).[16] However, a letter dated June 6, from Regina Keller, who rented rooms to both Eli and Dr. Nabriski, suggests a

14. YIVO file R294.2 MK.483.62/861/507 contains an example of a memorial meeting announcement File R294.2 and microfilm rolls MK 483.61 and 62 include samples of posters and flyers advertising a variety of meetings, clubs, parties, and appeals.
15. See YIVO files R294.2 MK.483.61/834/239–42, 252.
16. Inscription translated by author, with help from Marsha Rozenblit.

Figure 43. Masha Zulzberg, July 26, 1946, Landsberg-am-Lech. Family collection.

difficult parting when my father left Landsberg. Regina writes of Masha, "I'm sure she will answer your three letters and two telegrams which I brought to her," and adds that, as Eli had asked her to do, she gave Masha "a beautiful bouquet of roses and carnations together with your business card. Her happiness was really huge."[17]

When our family traveled to Israel in 1968, we visited Masha, her husband, and her children. I still remember the extraordinary cakes she baked for us, and Eli's and Masha's delight at seeing one another again. Recently, as I began working on this book and Burt and I combed through our father's papers that were among our recently deceased mother's belongings, we decided to try to find Masha again. We located her via the internet, and visited, separately, with her and her family in the winter and summer of 2013. Masha told Burt of how our father had taken her to a movie theater outside the camp to see Robert Young and Dorothy McGuire in *The Enchanted*

---

17. Translation from German by Roland Pabst.

Cottage—dubbed in German and titled *Mit den Aügen der Liebe* (*With the Eyes of Love*)—a romantic film about two damaged people transformed by their love for each other. When I spoke with her, Masha reminisced about how the DP camp, to its younger inhabitants, was a remarkable liberation after wartime life, and how they laughed at but enjoyed the mismatched shoes and oddly sized clothing (so criticized by camp inspectors) that came to their barracks.[18]

Dad never mentioned another woman from Landsberg, whom Burt discovered when he asked a German-speaking friend, Roland Pabst, to translate some letters and a small hardbound notebook containing a handwritten diary. We have been able to reconstruct that she was a German woman who worked as a nurse at Landsberg and lived at the monastery of St. Ottilien, which, as noted, had also been converted to a hospital for Jewish displaced persons. She wrote to Eli at breaks in her workday and while on the night shift, and it is clear that their relationship was sexual. Atina Grossmann has written that "relations between Jewish men and German women remained a troubling and contentious issue for survivors" (228). Yet while such relationships were often resented by Jewish women and used by young men as a way to gain sexual experience, there were cases, as Grossmann reports from a male survivor, "of 'deep reciprocal feelings' in which 'the answer would simply have to be that a man and woman met and fell in love" (230). From the evidence we have (and it is all from the woman's perspective), this was the case with Eli and the nurse. As he prepared to leave for the United States, his lover acknowledged the temporary yet instrumental quality of their relationship. In a letter dated April 15, 1946, she wrote,

> The bridge which I built you is done. You're standing at the big change in your life, you have to build bridges again and you have to walk over those bridges

---

18. Interview with Burt Rochelson, January 2013; conversation with author, June 2013.

and it will take years like this year. You have to go through your life, believe
in it, trust in it and from time to time, just a little bit, think about me.[19]

She asked Eli to write to her from time to time; whether he did or not is
unknown.

Of course, after the liberation Eli joined all the survivors in looking for
their relatives, and this, too, was part of life in the DP camp. He placed ads
in camp and survivor newspapers and wrote to the International Red Cross
and American Jewish relief organizations. In an ad placed in a column of
the first number of the *Landsberger Cajtung* titled *Mir Zuchn Krojwim!* (*We
Seek Relatives!*) Eli mentioned that two weeks before the liberation his wife
Sima had been seen in "lager Praust," one of the work subcamps of Stutthof.
In 1947 he contacted the World Jewish Congress about Borya, and Ruth
Saffron, of their Child Care Division, wrote to the Central Committee of
Liberated Jews in Europe, noting that, while most of the 130 children in
his transport had perished, some survived; "Perhaps this unfortunate child
is among those who are alive."[20] The Central Committee returned disap-
pointing news. Even as late as 1950—when his second wife, my mother,
was pregnant with me—Eli wrote letters inquiring about his first wife and
son. I suspect that, in some sense, he never stopped believing he might
find them again.[21] Others were searching, as well. The digitized files of the
International Tracing Service, accessible at the US Holocaust Memorial

---

19. Translation by Roland Pabst.
20. Letter from Ruth Saffron and reply, Individual Documents Boris Rochelson, ITS
    Digital Archive items #84458147_0_1 and 84458149_0_1. Accessed at the United
    States Holocaust Memorial Museum on January 23 and March 24, 2017.
21. The cover of Boris Rochelson's ITS Correspondence file is item #91706475_0_1/
    ITS Digital Archive, Accessed at the United States Holocaust Memorial Museum
    on January 23, 2017. While cards on file show inquiries beginning at the end of the
    war, this cover sheet logs in all requests beginning in 1951. These extend through
    1989 and 1990, when I contacted the International Tracing Service at Bad Arolsen,
    as news spread that more records were becoming available. But inquiries were
    logged in, before that, as late as 1961. A copy of the letter from June 10, 1950, is in
    the family's personal collection.

Museum, show multiple requests by Eli's cousin Genya Lubovsky, and by Erich Arendt of Goettingen, Germany, searching for every family member by name. Albert Arendt, Chaye Rochelson's husband, would have been in Uruguay by that time. I suspect he asked a brother or other relative, living closer to the tracing bureaus, to look for all the members of his late wife's family, and Erich seems, from the existing record, to have searched devotedly. A document from the British Red Cross, dated June 11, 1947, indicated that they were not able to find any of the people he was searching for, including "Elias."[22] Whether Erich ever located Eli, I do not know.

Eli's own searches would continue for years, but, in fact, he received information early on about his wife's and son's fates:

> About my wife, people were coming to Landsberg-am-Lech from all places, and there, women told me that she—my brother's wife and child, Sarah, [were] in different places [in Stutthof]. My wife got dysentery. My wife was free—no, she wasn't free. They had a march.[23] The Germans took them to another place, and while this she got dysentery, and weak, and she died from exhaustion, starvation, and disease. My brother's wife had the same fate from Stutthof, in a different section, where they told me that she also got dysentery. And she was on a march with the Germans; she died from starvation, disease, and exhaustion. And when she died, and a witness told me, that her daughter Sarah—she was then thirteen or fourteen years old—so she saw her mother died, she just lost her consciousness and she died at the same time.

---

22. ITS Correspondence item #86498950_0_1/ITS Digital Archive, Accessed at the United States Holocaust Memorial Museum on January 23, 2017. English translation, item # 86498950_0_2.

23. When Eli told this story in the NYPL interview, he said that his wife died after the liberation: "Later on I heard that she died from starvation and colitis . . . after the liberation . . . she was liberated . . . she couldn't take, it was the same way [with] my sister-in-law and her daughter" (Rochelson, NYPL interview 32; ellipsis as in transcription). That he corrects himself about this in the interview with Burt suggests that he may have heard two different accounts but believed that she died on the forced march.

There were, in fact, numerous forced marches out of Stutthof, beginning in January 1945 and going through April. In some of them, prisoners were forced into the sea and shot or allowed to drown (USHMM, "Stutthof"). Since Eli heard that Serafima had been seen two weeks prior to liberation, he must have assumed that she died late in the war. In his inquiries to the ITS he indicated her date of death as March 28, 1945.[24]

When Eli was in Dachau, he received what he believed to be reliable news about his son from prisoners who had been transferred from Auschwitz before its liberation:

> I was very happy when in November the Hungarians came from Auschwitz, and they looked for me, and I said, how do you know to look for me? They said your son sent regards and he asked us to look for you. That he is fine. . . . I got a *geruss* [regards] . . . that he is OK, and everything is fine, . . . he's playing chess with the other boys, and nothing wrong. . . .

But he received very different information after the war. In the NYPL interview Eli explains that "After the liberation I met people who were in Auschwitz and I confronted them . . . young boys, fifteen, sixteen, and I asked them what happened to my boy. Many didn't know. One knew and he says, look . . . I tell you the truth . . . I cannot . . . it's hard to tell me . . . but he's gone" (Rochelson, NYPL interview 32), and this survivor told Eli that his son was murdered after contracting measles. In the interview with Burt, Eli describes that moment:

> I couldn't believe it. I was hysterical, I was crying. I said, it doesn't matter, give it up. Then I talked to others, they were concerned. I had to face reality; that's that. I said, they told me in November he is alive. He says, look—As a matter of fact he had a brick with him to stand up to look taller. He knew what it is to be a little shorter. He was a tall fellow, anyway, and he was able

---

24. Not knowing the exact date, he may have chosen the date of his brother Avraham's death, which had been documented.

to escape the fate until he got the measles. Came the measles, came into the doctor, the doctor needs to give an order. That was the terrible tragedy.

The transfers of prisoners to Dachau in November were a prelude to the liberation of Auschwitz on January 27, 1945. The Hungarians may have been trying to spare Eli's feelings, or keep his spirits up—or, in fact, his son may have survived the selections at Auschwitz and had measles sometime later, as Eli seems to have assumed. I discuss these possibilities in the epilogue to this book, "Searching for Borya." I never stopped searching for him, either.

8

Leaving Europe, Arriving in America, Restoring Identity

IN MARCH 1946, Eli registered with the Joint Distribution Committee to go to America.[1] He explained that it was not a simple decision:

> [B]efore that I didn't know where to go, go to Israel or to Russia.[2] I decided to go to Russia, still look for my relatives, because I wasn't sure about the fate of them—my wife, my child. I didn't know yet, till after a while [it was] confirmed. But I registered with the Russian major there, and [he] put me on a list to go back to Russia. And trucks with flowers and orchestra, and music, went towards Berlin, to Russia. And then, I knew [my brother] Dave's address, 12 Crown Street, and I saw a man, Poretsky, this is Dr. Perry's brother, a soldier, American soldier.[3] And I gave him—he says he went to the States—I said, give a letter to my brother. To Israel I didn't want to go, and I will be frank 100 percent. I had enough in ghetto and I had enough in concentration camp; there was a lot [of] injustices from the Jews against

1. A file card for Ilia Rochelson (with correct birthdate, location, etc.) from the American Joint Distribution Committee indicates that Eli registered with them on March 27, 1946. Accessed on ancestry.com, "Munich, Vienna and Barcelona Jewish Displaced Persons and Refugee Cards, 1943–1959 (JDC)."
2. That is, the Soviet Union, of which the Lithuanian SSR was at that time a part.
3. Dr. Alex Perry was another doctor from the Kovno medical school with whom, and with whose wife, Lily, and family my parents and our family remained close in the United States. Others were the families of Dr. Simon and Ruth Brandwein, Dr. Joseph and Thelma Silber, Dr. Leonard and Janina Pace, and Dr. Lazar and Esther Goldstein. Lazar Goldstein and Thelma and Joseph Silber are mentioned earlier in this narrative. Joel Poretsky was the full name of Dr. Perry's brother.

their own Jews and I didn't feel like going there.[4] I had enough suffering and
I decided either I go to America or to Russia. But as the time passed, a couple
of weeks, there were coming people, who were ardent Communists, crying
and begging, not to go to Russia because as they came to there to the points
of destination the Russians searched them, questioned them, treat[ed] them
as criminals, and said if you are alive that means you were collaborating with
Hitler; and the younger men they sent either to the army or to Siberia, took
away all their belongings, whatever they had, little, and they said not to go.
Of course, then I changed my mind. And I got a letter from Dave, I should
come to America, he would give me money for a plane, and so on, but of
course no private people could go by planes, and to make a story short I went
to München, to Munich, in March 1946 and there I waited for the calling to
the American consulate.

Eli then expressed anger and disgust at the American authorities who
delayed his departure from Europe: "I was registered to go with the first
ship, but someone from Lithuania, good friend, took over my place, and I
had an argument with the man from the Joint Distribution [Committee],
he was responsible for that, and I talked to the American functionary, the
military office, there, and he says you probably know why it is. I say, I know,
why don't you tell me; I'd better not talk about that." Eli suspected bribery
or some kind of influence peddling, and the official's response to his question suggests that he may have been right. When I received a copy of my
father's HIAS immigration file, I understood even more fully the reasons
for his frustration.[5] In Dachau, my father was prisoner number 81993. In

4. In the NYPL interview he explains further: "I love Israel. I had a Jewish education.
I love Israel but when I was thinking to go to Israel, I had the bitter taste of our own
Jews . . . whether they sent to death their own people . . . they discriminated . . .
they were taking away their food . . . they had parties in the ghetto . . . weddings . . .
wine . . . cigarettes . . . everything, while everybody was miserable . . . and I was sore
at them" (Rochelson, NYPL interview 33).

5. I am grateful to Gunnar Berg, archivist at the YIVO Institute, for duplicating this
file and sending it to me even before I visited the YIVO archives. The complete file
number is RG 246.2, USNA-HIAS Case File #B-10983.

the substantial paperwork that documents his departure from Europe and his first year of acclimation to American life, he is case number B-10983. His address as of April 18, 1946, was an emigration center in Munich, and he remained there until his departure in early June, nearly two months later, away from meaningful work and relationships and uncertain whether his brother in New York was getting through to the proper authorities. He had surely had enough of being treated as a number, whether as a prisoner or a "case."

His arrival in 1946 made Eli one of the earlier postwar immigrants to the United States. Having a brother in New York might have helped, and so might his status as a physician (see Kobrin 108). But since at least the autumn of 1945 he had been seeking his American brother's financial sponsorship without knowing how that was progressing, while Dave was waging his own battle with the emigration bureaucracy. In December, Eli sent a letter to Dave via the brother of another survivor in Landsberg, Bernard Wollen of Syracuse, New York. The HIAS file at YIVO contains an English translation of the Yiddish, produced by a translation service in New York City. A note attached reads, in part, "My brother [in Landsberg] informs me that your brother has been worrying very much at your failure to get news over to him." Eli wrote that he had not heard from Dave since November 14, 1945, "nor did I get the letters you say you sent me through the 'Joint'"—and if Dave said he had sent them, I have no doubt that he had. Eli adds, "As regards my wife, I suppose we can have no hopes (that she is alive) since you would have heard from her. If you fail (or delay) to file your papers for me with the Consulate, there is danger that the quota might be soon filled by the others and I will then have to wait for another quota."

Another typewritten letter, from someone at a "Location Service Unit," presumably of HIAS or the National Refugee Service, accompanies the forwarded, translated letter. It is dated February 6, 1946, more than a month after Eli wrote. A search form completed by this official reveals frustration on the American side. Here my father is "Eli Robinson, B6788"; the agency had apparently given him his brother's changed surname.[6] A penciled note at the bottom of the page reads, "Mrs. Robinson said that her husband is subject's brother, and that they are anxious to get in touch with subject but have difficulty with the mail situation. Through HIAS, they have been trying to get subject to this country, but have been informed that they must wait for an American Consulate to open in Germany."

Confusion abounded as the National Refugee Service, which took on Eli's case, believed that needed affidavits had been sent to Paris when, in fact, Dave had sent them to the consulate in Munich.[7] "Would not the fact that he has been moved from the Landsberg Hospital, where he was working, to the Emigration Center in Munich with registration number mentioned above, justify my belief that the visa and all papers are ready at the Munich Consulate, and that it is just a matter of a month or so before he will sail?" wrote Ida in a handwritten letter signed by Dave. On June 8 they sent a check for $162 to cover Eli's passage; at this point his NRS case number was 36836 and he had already set sail on the *Marine Flasher*, a repurposed troopship, on June 6 (figure 44). Bernard Wollen's brother had arrived on the same ship on May 20, presumably on the voyage Eli had intended to take.[8]

---

6. Dave never felt comfortable with the name of Robinson, and when Eli, on arrival, offered to change his to match, Dave advised him not to. Only the pronunciation of Rochelson changed in America, with the *kh* sound of the *ch* becoming softened to an easier *sh* or *ch* (as in *shin* or *chin*) before I was born. My father at some point also changed the European Ilija to Eli. Confusion at the National Refugee Service may have been exacerbated by the fact that Eli ended up with two files, one as Ilija Rochelson and another as Eli Robinson. An internal memorandum of June 24, after Eli had arrived in the United States, requests that the two sets of materials be combined in the Ilja [sic] Rochelson file.

7. This correspondence is in the USNA-HIAS case file #B-10983 housed at the YIVO Institute, and includes letters back and forth on May 22 (from the NRS) and May 26 (from David Robinson). This letter also indicates that Eli's address on April 18 was the emigration center in Munich.

8. The bureaucratic difficulties and misunderstandings that survivors encountered in the United States, which Beth B. Cohen recounts powerfully in "Face to Face," clearly began even while the survivors were in Europe, trying to get out.

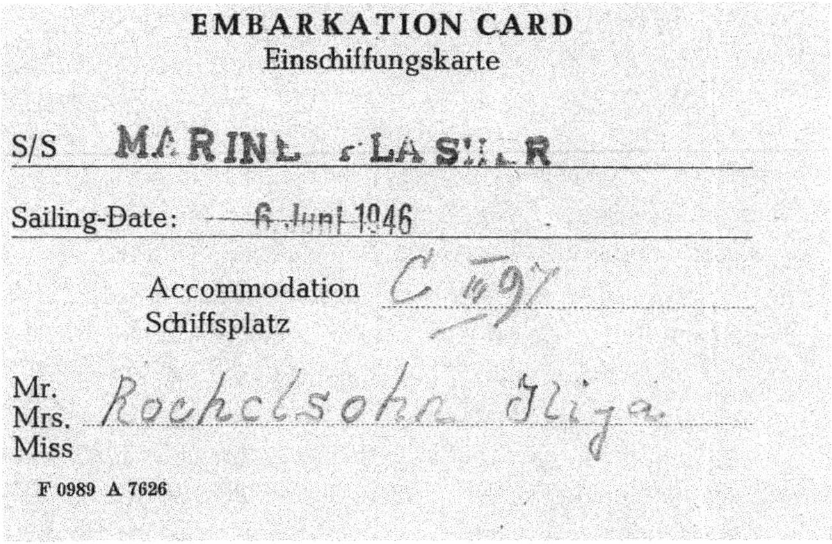

EMBARKATION CARD
Einschiffungskarte

S/S   MARINE FLASHER

Sailing-Date: ─── 6. Juni 1946

Accommodation *C 497*
Schiffsplatz

Mr.
Mrs. *Rochelsohn Elija*
Miss

F 0989 A 7626

Figure 44. *Marine Flasher* embarkation card. Family collection.

Eli arrived in New York, at last, on June 18, and his account of the journey is poignant:[9]

> The boat trip was good, we were happy, we were having two or three tiers bunk; that was [a] military ship. All [the passengers were] former inmates of concentration camps. Yes, it was crowded. On the boat there was plenty of food. The Jewish organization from New York gave $10 to each and we bought cigarettes and all other things, and we were very, very happy. We came in about five or six days,[10] in the morning, and we were

---

9. The *Marine Flasher*, a US troopship that brought troops from Asia to San Francisco after V-J Day, became a transport for Holocaust survivors via Bremen in the late spring of 1946. The ship traversed the route from Bremen to New York until September 1949 ("The Story of the S. S. Marine Flasher"). A survivor I talked with briefly, who arrived as a teenager (and whose name, alas, I do not recall), told me that the bunks were still the hammocks used by soldiers or sailors, and they swayed back and forth all night.

10. In fact, it was twelve days, since according to the ship's manifest it set sail on June 6. That Eli remembered it as a much shorter journey is noteworthy. The commuter boats mentioned later in the account must have been the Staten Island ferry.

awakened by screams; we see the Statue of Liberty. But they didn't go in, into the port, into the pier, until the sun came out. [On seeing the Statue of Liberty,] Oh, I was very excited. Then we saw a lot of people going to work, on little boats, going to work—I don't know: they do it now, too? There are a lot of people going to work and they were waving to us. Then we came in when the sun came out already; we came back, we saw this Statue of Liberty, we were excited, happy, and then I was met by my brother Dave, and I stayed with Dave for about one month, and then I, without knowledge of English, I took a job as an intern—and Dave was in America, I was corresponding with him, and I was very happy, of course he recognized me, and I recognized him.[11] As a matter of fact, he went into the ship to meet me, because he was working for the merchant marine, and after they bawled him out; he has no right to go in, even if he was working in the merchant marine.

Dave and Ida helped Eli get settled in Brooklyn. He lived with them at 12 Crown Street, and they supported him until he began his internship at Israel Zion Hospital on August 1; as an intern he lived on hospital grounds.[12] An early letter, written to Dr. Nabriski in July 1946, gives a glimpse of Eli's first impressions of the United States. His colleague had written from Paris, where he stayed for three months on the way to his future home in Palestine. Eli replied, in part,

[i]f Paris looks, after a couple of wars, as peaceful as it does before the wars, then you can imagine how New York looks. Life standards here are extremely high. Most people live very well. People think that the unemployment rate in New York is high. This isn't true; the people who don't have a job are ones that don't want to work. The same that we don't understand Americans in Germany is the same way they don't understand us here.[13]

11. They had seen each other only fourteen years earlier, in 1931, when life was very different.
12. Israel Zion (now Maimonides Medical Center) was located in the Borough Park neighborhood of Brooklyn. It became Maimonides Hospital in 1947.
13. Translated from Russian by Olga Skarlat. Copy of letter in family collection.

The United Services for New Americans (USNA)—a Jewish organization with an intentionally non-Jewish name (B. Cohen 138)—paid $225 for Eli's dental care, after he assured them that neither his own earnings as an intern nor his sister-in-law's teacher's salary (on which, he said, she and his brother largely depended) was enough for the reconstructive work and dentures that he needed after imprisonment. His efforts to find a suitable dentist are recounted in detail in a three-page, single-spaced typed USNA report, in which I read with both fascination and sadness about the origin of the false teeth that I had often glimpsed in their glass. I had always assumed that my father lost nearly all his teeth in the camps, but the USNA report documents disagreements among dentists, one of whom removed eight of my father's teeth and another who believed he might have saved them. They left Eli exasperated.

The USNA report also gives a general summary of Eli's situation after a year in America. A section dated May 22, 1947, reads as follows:

> He is finishing his internship in 2 months. According to Israel Zion he has done exceedingly well. Also according to indications he seems to have passed his English examinations.[14] Mrs. Zahm [the interviewer who received and transmitted this information] said that she had been planning with Dr. R. for his future. . . . It was decided that he should be permitted to study uninterrupted until October so that he can take the N. Y. State medical examinations then. There is some hope that once he has passed [these] it will be possible to refer him to South Dakota, which is about the only State in the Union at present considering immigrant doctors.

Once again, Jewish doctors were being sent to the provinces.[15] But as Eli's narrative makes clear, he did not go from Brooklyn to South Dakota. He

---

14. Eli's notes on an application form suggest that he intended to take the exam on May 20, 1947. However, a document of September 25 indicates that he actually passed it on September 13, and his testimony makes clear that he passed on this second attempt.

15. I am grateful to my brother Burt for making this connection between Mottel's options in prewar Lithuania and postwar life in the United States.

went instead to the Casualty Hospital in Washington, DC. His accounts of life there and at Israel Zion demonstrate that suffering the nearly unimaginable hardships of a Nazi concentration camp does not make one immune to smaller discomforts:

> I went to Maimonides Hospital [then known as Israel Zion] for a year internship, $35 a month, with a lousy room with bats at night. . . . [F]ood was OK, but the room was terrible, with bats, and I worked all year; at the same time I studied English, I went to a tutor, I had to pass my examination in English and then pass my—after I passed the examination in English I was permitted to take the State Boards. The first of July, 1948, I got my [initial] license to practice medicine, after [i.e., later] it took me eight months to take the State Boards.
>
> After Maimonides, I took a job in Washington in the Casualty Hospital; I worked for a few months from seven in the morning, [to] seven at night. They put me in a room in the attic. At that time there were no air conditioning and I was simply suffocating, in spite of the fan. They asked me to stay, they said they would give me every week to go to New York, for the money, for the railroad, but I said no because I had commitments with the Swedish Hospital [of Brooklyn]. I went as a resident to the Swedish Hospital and after that I decided to have some experience in lung diseases and I went for a year in Brooklyn Thoracic Hospital, where I worked the whole year in pulmonary tuberculosis.[16]

Among the items in Eli's personal archive is a handwritten note dated December 1, 1946, probably a draft, to Mr. Gillis, 310 Riverside Drive in Manhattan, inquiring about lessons in English to prepare for the

---

16. The Eastern Dispensary and Casualty Hospital in Washington was founded in the late nineteenth century to care for indigent patients. It changed location in 1905 and expanded throughout the years; it was significantly modernized in the late 1950s. After several name changes, it is now known as Specialty Hospital-Capitol Hill ("Lost Capitol Hill"). The Swedish Hospital of Brooklyn, founded in 1906, closed in 1975. In 1957 the Brooklyn Thoracic Hospital merged into the Brooklyn Hospital Center.

required exam. In the NYPL interview he mentions that many refugees went to a tutor in Manhattan, and that he passed the English exam on his second try (Rochelson, NYPL interview 37; see figure 45). Ida mentioned in her 1931 travel diary that Eli spoke some English, but he had probably learned a little to prepare for their visit. In a form that he filled out by hand for the State Education Department (a copy of which he saved), Eli wrote that he had had contact with English-speaking people at the DP hospital in Landsberg, and that he currently undertook to improve his English by speaking only English with his colleagues and personnel at Israel Zion hospital, writing case histories, attending his English classes six hours a week, listening to the radio daily, and reading the *New York*

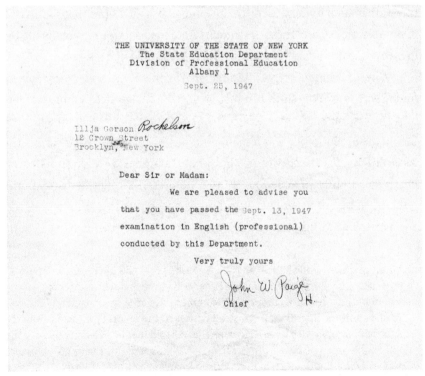

Figure 45. Letter notifying Eli that he had passed the English exam necessary for him to take the New York State medical examinations. Family collection.

Times daily. For as long as I knew him, Eli's written and spoken English were excellent.[17]

Eli's determination and perseverance (or, as he called it, stubbornness) are illustrated nowhere more clearly than in his ultimately successful effort to reestablish his medical credentials and status as a physician. He documented the process in a file of typed pages, letters, official documents, and photocopies in a grey heavy paper folder, fastened inside with a metal clip. A neatly printed label on the cover indicates his name (DR. ROCHELSON, ILIJA G.) and his address and phone number at the home of his brother at 12 Crown Street, Brooklyn. In the lower left corner is another label, a small strip of orange paper upon which is typed, ORIGINAL DOCUMENTS. Indeed, when I found this folder in the bottom drawer of a wardrobe in my mother's bedroom, decades after my father's death, it was accompanied by three other such folders, identical in content, but all, as the 1940s term had it, photostatic copies. These documents were the basis for reestablishing his identity and profession as a physician; Eli took no chances.

When I found the grey binder, it was inside a light green manila folder with a brown cloth binding strip, which also held additional letters, the responses to materials Eli had submitted to a variety of agencies. Inside the green folder was a manila folder; its file name edge carries the carefully printed inked words, "Personal Data Sheets," and, on its cover, neatly but lightly penciled and underlined, in Eli's handwriting, is the phrase "To be taken care of." Burt and I believe that this simple note was an instruction to his wife and children that these documents were to be

---

17. Given my own professional career in English, I find the document in figure 45 especially poignant. I also recall my father telling me that when he took his medical exam he misread a question asking him to describe the circulation of blood to and from the intestines and instead described the blood flow to and from the stomach (possibly vice versa). However, he was told that he had done such a good job on the organ he discussed that they passed him anyway. I have no documentary evidence of this story, but it occurred to me many times as I graded my own students' work, and I may have at least once, as a result, given partial credit for a similar sort of mistake.

cared for and preserved. Together they attest to the labyrinthine process of establishing credentials after the violent disruption of the Holocaust and the more insidious roadblocks of the Cold War. The typewritten list at the start of the binder (appendix E) begins with a simple yet chilling sentence explaining the need for all that follows: "While in the concentration camp at Dachau (Germany)—see item 5 below—all original documents including the diploma of Doctor of Medicine were taken away by the Germans and destroyed." The list that follows includes testimonies of consular officials and Lithuanian professors tracked down in the United States; affidavits of colleagues in the Landsberg DP camp, testifying to Eli's medical work not only at Hospital 2014 but in the Kovno ghetto and Dachau; and certifications by the American military government in occupied Germany, including an ID card with a photograph and his former prisoner number, and a curfew pass allowing him greater freedom because he was a physician (figure 46). He also submitted a detailed, notarized affidavit, signed by his medical school classmates Drs. Simon Brandwein and Kazys Vileisis, as well as their professor, Dr. Jurgis Zilinskas, attesting to the accuracy of Eli's list of ten semesters' worth of courses, labs, and examinations taken at the University of Vytautas the Great. Another page of the affidavit, signed by Dr. Samuel Salman Griliches (Joseph Griliches's father) and Dr. Brandwein, attests to Eli's graduation from the "Russian Gymnasium of the Teachers' Association" after completing a ten-year course of study.

An unbound letter from the US State Department, dated May 28, 1948, makes clear why the file also contains pages copied from the 1940 volume of *Medicina*, "the official medical journal of Kaunas," which lists Eli among those awarded the medical degree. Apparently he had asked the State Department's help in obtaining a copy of his diploma from Lithuania. A department official replied that the US embassy in Moscow had been unsuccessful in that task, and that, because

the Government of the United States has no diplomatic or consular officers in Lithuania. . . . it is suggested that you again endeavor to communicate

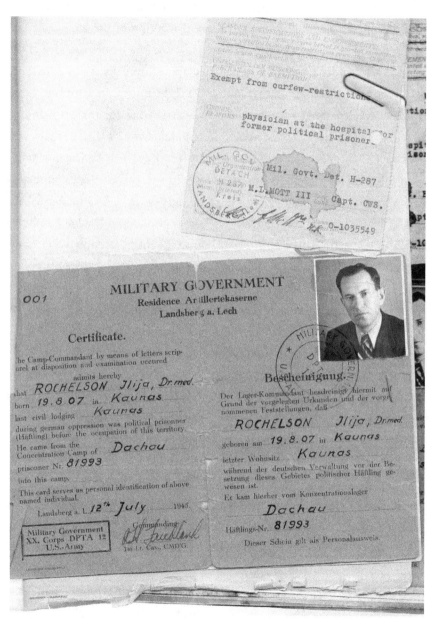

Figure 46. Identification card and curfew permit for Eli G. Rochelson at the Landsberg DP camp, Hospital 2014. Family collection.

directly or through an attorney with the person in Lithuania who would
certify to such a document, have that person or attorney forward the document to the Soviet Ministry of Foreign Affairs at Moscow with a view to
obtaining its seal and signature, and submit the document in turn to the
American Embassy at Moscow for authentification [—which, the official
hastened to add, was] not to be construed as involving a recognition by this
Government of the right of the Soviet Government to exercise sovereign
authority in Lithuania.

Copies of additional letters in Eli's files, in Lithuanian and in Russian, indicate that he may well have attempted to make the suggested inquiries. In
the end, however, he did not become enmeshed in Cold War bureaucracies and the politics of US-Soviet relations. He instead went to the library
of the New York Academy of Medicine, which collected the yearbooks
and journals of medical schools throughout the world. There he found the
page with a paragraph of names, one of them his, listed as having earned
the *Med. gydytojo diploma*: diploma of doctor of medicine. He had a copy
made at the library, signed by the librarian, and included it in his file.

The documentation he submitted allowed Eli to obtain credit for his
degree, and, as explained, after passing the state examination in English
he was permitted to take the medical licensing exam. It took eight months
of effort before he received his New York State medical license on July 1,
1948, and began the internship that was the start of his American medical
career. Yet one achievement eluded him, for a time. A letter from the Chicago headquarters of the American Medical Association, dated April 7,
1949, reads as follows:

Our records indicate that you are a member in good standing of your con-
stituent medical association and you are eligible for Fellowship in the American Medical Association with one exception.

Since you are a graduate of a foreign medical school it will be necessary
for you to furnish the Council on Medical Education and Hospitals with a
photostatic copy of your Diploma of Medicine and a certified translation.

When the forms referred to above are received, we will be glad to act on your request for Fellowship.

They must have missed the part about how "in the concentration camp at Dachau (Germany) . . . the diploma [was] taken away by the Germans and destroyed." Rebecca Kobrin has documented the intransigence of the AMA in recognizing the credentials of Jewish physician immigrants; Eli's was far from the only case (Kobrin 109). He persisted, however, and eventually obtained AMA membership.

He had somewhat different frustrations in trying to gain acceptance as a fellow in the American College of Chest Physicians (ACCP). In early June 1959, when I was eight years old and in the third grade, my family spent a week in Atlantic City, where my father, we were told, would be attending a convention. I remember the trip with great vividness, both because it was so much fun and because I missed what was predicted to be an especially exciting class trip in order to go. Lever House, one of the first glass and steel skyscrapers in Manhattan, had opened its doors to school groups, and my class planned its visit there long in advance. Paintings of ours, we were told or we imagined, would be exhibited in the building's big new windows. I regretted missing something so special, but my mother, who had been to Atlantic City before, assured me that I would love it, and I did. We stayed in the large and luxurious Ambassador Hotel, ate in a restaurant where the same flirty waitress served us each day, and shopped in souvenir stores full of glitter and color and saltwater taffy. I read *Anne of Green Gables*, my most beloved of the books Aunt Ida gave me from her library. What I did not know until recently, however, when I found the preserved correspondence, was that my father had taken his oral exam for the fellowship at that convention, and he had failed.

In August 1959, after receiving notice that he had failed both the written and oral tests, Eli telephoned and then sent a detailed letter of protest to Dr. Coleman B. Rabin. Dr. Rabin would serve as president of the ACCP in 1968–69; a memorial tribute in the *American Journal of Industrial Medicine* praises him as a consummate researcher, teacher, and clinician, a doctor who would never accept the word "retired" as a patient's profession and whose skill at hands-on examination often located problems or led to diagnoses of conditions that were invisible to X-rays, the high technology of his time (Teirstein 2). Eli contacted him because of a position he held at the ACCP, but it is possible, too, that the name Coleman Rabin (although his nickname, according to the memorial, was Kelly) signified a Jewish colleague. After summarizing in detail his training and experience in treating diseases of the chest since coming to America, as well as assurances given him during the oral exam, Eli petitioned Dr. Rabin to waive the requirement. His reason expressed considerable bitterness: "I cannot again face oral examiners who might not like the tilt of my nose or the roll of my 'r'" (letter in family collection).

Eventually Eli retook the exams, and he became a fellow of the association. I have no idea what, if any, material benefit he gained from being a fellow and appending the letters FACCP to his business card. But he persisted until he achieved that distinction. One of the many things the Holocaust took from my father was the ability to be a successful professional in the country where he had received his education and developed his roots. In Brooklyn he established his office in an impoverished area, in part because he was tired of middle-class Jewish patients second-guessing his opinions because of his accent. He knew that he was at least as good as his American-born colleagues, if not better than some, and he resented that he was often assumed to be inferior because of his foreign background. Eli frequently spoke of a Kovno professor who had suggested to him that he try to become a professor of medicine in Moscow. At that time he chose not to disrupt his life by moving, and yet, in the end, his life was disrupted even more. Eli knew that he was an intellectual as well as a physician, and he wanted that to be certified, too. Hence the stubbornness, as he would have put it, with which he pursued the fellowship until it was finally his in August 1961.

The documentation so persistently sought and so necessary to satisfy various bureaucracies tells a poignant human story. A letter from

Dr. Nabriski, head of the hospital at the Landsberg Camp and himself a Holocaust survivor, attests on letterhead of the Hospital for Former Political Prisoners (D. P. Hospital 2014) that "Doctor Ilija Rochelson has been working in our hospital since its foundation . . . as Head of Dispensary and assistant Chief of the hospital." In a more personal way, he adds,

> Just after his liberation from the concentration camp Dr. Rochelson used his whole energy in establishing of the hospital and his services in this matter were of great value.
>
> By his medical knowledge as well as by his constant helpfulness, human and friendly relation to the personnel and patients Dr. Rochelson has won the love and the respect of all his collaborators and patients.
>
> The hospital is very sorry for the going away of Dr. Rochelson . . . because of his departure for America and wishes him much happiness and success in his future life.

The letter is cosigned by Lt. B. Streim, a US Army medical officer, as well as by W. J. Korn, a deputy director of the UNRRA team that supervised the hospital, who "confirm[ed] . . . the facts stated herein," and added "that Dr. Rochelson has also proved to be of greatest integrity." A similar document from the American Joint Distribution Committee is cosigned by a captain of the Quartermaster Corps. Much has been and is still being written about the lives of Jewish concentration camp survivors in postwar Germany and then in the United States. Eli G. Rochelson's personal archive, which the careful copying and binding of his medical documentation file demonstrates he intended to maintain as a historical record, illustrates both the bureaucratic hurdles that survivors had to transcend and the warm and nurturing professional and personal relationships they forged, which helped keep them going. It is also a testament to that "stubbornness" that never allowed Eli, himself, to desist when he knew there was something he needed to achieve. That stubbornness sometimes showed itself as righteous anger, as in the letter to the American College of Chest Physicians implying bias in the oral exam, and in the last sentence of his 1946 article in *Der Tog*, in which he follows a description of the 1941 Kovno ghetto Great Action with an excoriation of the dubious "justice" that allowed survivors still, five years after the war ended, to languish in displaced persons camps (see appendix D).

9

A New Marriage and Family

FOR ELI, THE meaningful work of medicine and the restoration of his professional identity helped him to look forward, beyond the almost incomprehensible sadness of what he had lost. However, work alone was not enough. In 1948, his residency at the Swedish Hospital of Brooklyn brought him more than additional training and experience. On Kol Nidrei night, the eve and the start of the solemn holiday of Yom Kippur, he was listening to the religious service on the radio in his room. He had been promised that he would not be disturbed but told he needed to stay on campus in case of emergency. Meanwhile, Masha Friedman, an elderly and religiously observant immigrant woman, had left dinner for her daughter Pearl to eat when she came home from work, and they planned to meet at the synagogue close to their apartment in Brooklyn. While the older woman was waiting in front of the shul, boys on bicycles or roller skates somehow knocked her down, and by the time her daughter arrived, she was extremely upset—not so much at the blood pouring from her head wound but at having to go to the hospital in an ambulance on a holy day, when riding in a vehicle is forbidden except to save a life.

That turned out to be Eli's emergency. He was not thrilled to be called away, but he was told he was the only Yiddish-speaking doctor available, and this hysterical woman spoke no other language. Eli recounted the story that would become famous among our family and friends:

When I was listening over the radio [to the broadcast] in Temple Emanu-El, the Yom Kippur services—they told me to come down, and there is an old lady who fell down and busted her head. I came down, was an old, nice Jewish lady, and I talked to her in Jewish; Oh, she says, wonderful, you talk in Jewish. I want to give her a needle for anesthesia, she says, No, if you talk to me in Jewish, I don't need anything, and sure enough I put in about sixteen stitches, did a good plastic job, and then she was admitted in the hospital for further observation, skull X-rays, and observation. And then I met Pearl, a young healthy wholesome-looking farmer's daughter, that's my usual taste, but I didn't talk to her. [At some point] I mixed up her with [her older sister] Betty.[1] Then I talked to my patient, Mrs. Friedman; I say, Look, Who is this nice lady? I would like to go out with her. She says, Oh, no, she is married, she has children, and I say, That's so? She says, Don't worry, I have another daughter for you. OK, I would like to see her. And then I said to Mommy [because it was Pearl, later our mother], I got in touch with her; I saw her once in an elevator in a beret, I saw her in an elevator and I liked her: the pink cheeks with the nice hat, and I wanted.

The next part did not become family lore, although perhaps it should:

Then, she says, No, I have a date; I cannot go out with you. And I got so mad, I says, OK—I didn't tell it to her, but, so you want to go out with somebody else, OK with me. And I didn't intend to even to talk to her because she couldn't break a date with another fellow, you know. To make the story short, somehow we were talking, talking, till she got me in her net and I said, OK, we'll get married, what's the sense. I don't regret.

Dad describes his marriage jokingly and sardonically, and I hear Burt's laughter in the background. In the NYPL interview, Marsha Rozenblit asked my father if he felt having an American wife was helpful to him in adapting to America. The transcript records, "It's a good help. An American wife is a good help. Pearl was a help. Pearl was instrumental in times

---

1. He had seen Betty, too, and asked her mother about her.

of depression or indecisiveness, I would say . . . and aggravation. . . . You cannot go life where everything is roses. . . . She was always ahead and straightened me out. And she straightened me out in relationship with other people because sometimes I get militant and talk back. . . . And I have a habit like that. I did it in Europe, I did it in the medical college. I did it with some professors" (Rochelson, NYPL interview 77).

Before, Ida had begun setting up dates for him with her friends. But Ida was fifty-three years old in 1946, and Eli only thirty-nine. To judge from the descriptions he gave us in later years, the women she chose were not appropriate for a man who still felt young, regardless of what he had been through. While Pearl was not literally a farmer's daughter (Max Friedman worked in the New York garment district), she had the bright smile and rosy cheeks that won her future husband's heart (figure 47). She was the youngest by ten years of her immigrant parents' four children, and the only

Figure 47. Pearl Friedman, 1940s. Family collection.

one who was born in America. She always had an optimistic personality. She was outgoing, smart, and had many good friends. Eli sensed that she would bring new life to his spirit, as well as new children to their new home.

The Kol Nidrei night on which Eli met Pearl was October 12, 1948, two years to the day before my birth. They were married on April 29, 1949, a day that happened to be the anniversary of the liberation of Dachau, but it may have been chosen, instead, because my maternal grandfather was at that time dying of cancer, and they wanted to be married while he was still alive. As it happened, however, he died six days before their wedding ceremony, which took place in the apartment where my mother lived with her parents, right after the *shiva* period of mourning was over. My parents honeymooned, briefly, at a resort favored by Holocaust survivors, probably in the Catskills (figure 48).

Until her death in 2010, Pearl saved romantic greeting cards that Eli had sent her in the early years of their courtship and marriage, as well as a

Figure 48. Eli and Pearl Rochelson on their two-day honeymoon, late April 1949. Family collection.

string of faux pearls, one of Eli's first gifts, with a note promising that one day he would give her real ones.[2] The lovingly preserved cards and notes show that Eli was a true romantic, but they also show that the relationship was complicated. On April 10, 1949, a few weeks before their wedding, Eli gave a short poem to Pearl, in which he called her "my darling,/who gave me sense in life." The words *sense* and *sensible* come up often in his notes, as if to explain to Pearl that she helped him make sense of his life, after the struggles and losses of the preceding years.[3] In a long, beautifully handwritten note, in clear and graceful English, Eli wrote to Pearl on their wedding day:

> Yes, my dear, I'm marrying you today. And I'm happy. . . .
>
> Pearl, I waited, I hoped and I prayed. Is there anywhere a person who will understand me, who will love sincerely, who will give the warmth and the sensible understanding which I needed so much.
>
> I lost my hope. I walked through life indifferent and disappointed. There were no feelings in me, no satisfaction in work, no happiness in life. And after you came, my dear. . . . I felt a ray of hope, a feeling that maybe you are the one who will bring me sense and contents in life. The more I saw you the more I felt that you are the one I desired.

When I read these words, feeling their power, I wished that I could talk about them with my parents, now both gone. But I was not prepared for the next and final paragraph:

---

2. I have no idea what happened to notes that Pearl might have written to Eli. Like him, she was an excellent writer, and she enjoyed writing clever poems to family and friends. I still have the faux pearls, along with the brown velvet beret Pearl wore that Kol Nidrei night.

3. This word use was not unique to Eli, among survivors. Beth Cohen quotes a young man who resettled in Denver, as saying, "I don't seem to see a sense in life and little by little I lose the courage to live and that worries me" (152).

> I beg you give me the opportunity to love you, don't tell me
> that I have no understanding. . . . It is not true. Give me
> love and happiness and I'll return to you the same. Let's our
> motto be "we have to work to live" for our mutual happiness.

How could someone, on his wedding day, still be asking his soon-to-be wife to let him love her? How could she, apparently not long before the wedding, have told him he had "no understanding"? Pearl and her sisters, in later years, talked about how they "got up from *shiva*, walked around the block, and then Pearl and Eli got married." It could not have been easy for Pearl to get married less than a week after her beloved father's death. Perhaps, when Eli expressed joy at the coming marriage, she accused him of not understanding how she felt, although if anyone understood grief it was he. Again, this is all speculation. I don't know. But whatever the immediate situation, it could not have been easy for people with such different pasts to join their lives together. In the end they did work hard for their mutual happiness. They were married just short of thirty-five years when Eli died on February 15, 1984.

They had their share of arguments, of course. Despite our parents' undeniable seriousness and dignity, Burt and I have discussed how we each often saw them as Lucy and Ricky Ricardo from the *I Love Lucy* television show—Mom the assertive and outspoken American wife, Dad, the successful professional who yet could seem stymied and defeated as he strove to make his case in accented English. Like Lucy, too, my mother may have felt somewhat frustrated, after my birth, that her arena of action was circumscribed. Although she enjoyed being a mother as well as a doctor's wife, and she helped her husband with office paperwork—sitting opposite him in his study long after the children had gone to bed—she had had a fulfilling and independent career as a bookkeeper for seventeen years (figure 49). Marriage had to be a significant change.[4]

---

4. In 2009 I learned something important about my mother's connection to my father's first wife. My daughter, then aged twenty-one, decided to change her given

Figure 49. Pearl at her desk in the New York office of Robbins Mills, where she worked from 1942 to 1950. Family collection.

Yet Pearl and Eli created a happy and mutually satisfying life together. In addition to providing him with love, children, and a warm, nurturing home, Pearl brought Eli a large extended family that had originated in a town not far from Kovno[5] and spoke the same dialect of Yiddish. They embraced my father warmly, and he was very close to my grandmother (whose head he had stitched, and who lived with us until she died in 1962), as well as to my maternal aunts and uncles, who lived nearby and whom for years we saw daily. Just as Eli became part of Pearl's family, she, in turn, became part of his. She made sure that we had a close relationship not only with Dave and Ida but also with Eli's extended family in Oklahoma, with several of whom

name to Serafima, to honor the memory of someone whom she felt was part of our family but still had no namesake. I was afraid to tell my mother, thinking it might arouse uncomfortable feelings. But it was the very opposite. Tearfully, my mother explained that she was glad young Serafima had chosen that name because she, Pearl, had often felt guilty that she had enjoyed being my father's wife when the first Serafima had suffered such a horrible death. She was happy, now, that Serafima finally "had a name," and her words were extremely meaningful to all of us.

5. Dolhinov (or Dolginovo), Belarus.

I remain in touch and who continued to visit my mother until her death, whenever they were in New York. I have fond memories of a trip by train from New York to Tulsa, complete with Pullman sleeper, dining cars, and glass-topped observation cars, on Thanksgiving weekend 1960. Even at that time, I knew that I was experiencing an important part of American culture on those trains (although I was unaware of how soon they would become part of the nation's past). Perhaps equally impressive and surprising, however, was getting to meet a huge extended family on my father's side, people who thought I looked like him (in contrast to my New York family, who said I was the image of my mother), and who met for Thanksgiving dinner in an enormous ballroom at the Mayo Hotel. For years—at my mother's encouragement—I had written a poem that we sent to Tulsa, to be read at this annual event. In 1960 I had the opportunity to read my own poem aloud. Additionally, on that warm Oklahoma weekend late in autumn, I first encountered the suburban lifestyle of ranch homes and streets with only minimal sidewalks, although the blue Naugahyde sofas in cousins Lou and Susan Fenster's home were similar to the yellow ones in mine. Thus I came to know middle America through my European-born father.

Dad established a private medical practice, and he worked as a physician in internal medicine with a subspecialty in diseases of the chest. Although obstacles I have discussed may have prevented his American relatives from bringing Eli and his family to the United States before the war, they helped him substantially once he arrived in 1946. The man I knew as the patriarch of the Tulsa branch, Maurice Sanditen—who with two of his brothers, Herman and Samuel, founded the Oklahoma Tire and Supply Company (Otasco)— gave Eli $2,500 to purchase the most up-to-date medical equipment. The correspondence between them is touching in its reflection of Maurice's sincere generosity and my father's gratitude, as well as poignant in Maurice's offer of a vacation stay at the home and on the yacht of a wealthy business associate in Ohio. The gap in experience and wealth between the cousins at this time was so large as to make me wonder how much Maurice actually recognized the extent of the disparity, and yet Eli seemed grateful for the generous invitation. He apparently tried to find a way to accept, although in the end the visit did not take place. He later expressed his thanks movingly, too, in a letter to a cousin in Wichita, Jacob H. Bloch (figure 50):

> It is almost three years since I came to the United States and I am beginning to realize the miracle of man.
>
> In the early days . . . I suffered a period of frustration and sadness for my harried past and heavy personal losses, but I have found that time and the warmth and interest of my family are wonderful healers. . . .
>
> Now I am ready to open my office and begin to practice, and thank God again for the concern my family showed. My cousins from Tulsa gave us a very gracious and handsome start and now you, whom we didn't even notify of our marriage or office, sent us such a generous gift and warmly sincere note.

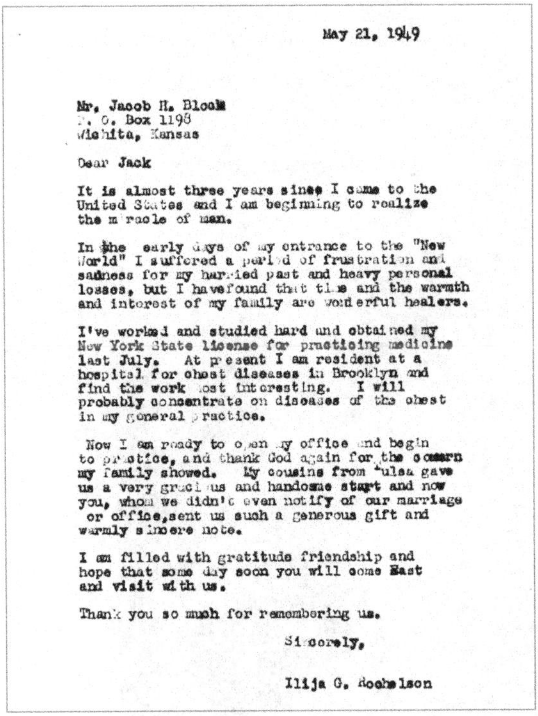

May 21, 1949

Mr. Jacob H. Bloch
P. O. Box 1198
Wichita, Kansas

Dear Jack

It is almost three years since I came to the United States and I am beginning to realize the miracle of man.

In the early days of my entrance to the "New World" I suffered a period of frustration and sadness for my harried past and heavy personal losses, but I havefound that time and the warmth and interest of my family are wonderful healers.

I've worked and studied hard and obtained my New York State license for practicing medicine last July. At present I am resident at a hospital for chest diseases in Brooklyn and find the work most interesting. I will probably concentrate on diseases of the chest in my general practice.

Now I am ready to open my office and begin to practice, and thank God again for the concern my family showed. My cousins from Tulsa gave us a very gracious and handosme start and now you, whom we didn't even notify of our marriage or office, sent us such a generous gift and warmly sincere note.

I am filled with gratitude friendship and hope that some day soon you will come East and visit with us.

Thank you so much for remembering us.

Sincerely,

Ilija G. Rochelson

Figure 50. "The Miracle of Man." Copy of letter sent to cousin Jacob H. Bloch, May 21, 1949. Family collection.

With such financial assistance, Eli began his private practice in our street-level apartment at 542 Parkside Avenue in Brooklyn. In 1955 we moved to a house in the Midwood area, and Eli purchased a building, to which he moved his office, on Marcy Avenue in Williamsburg on the edge of the Bedford-Stuyvesant neighborhood (figures 51, 52, and 53). The Jews of Midwood in the 1950s and '60s were most likely to be Conservative, Reform, or of no affiliation, whereas at the time of this writing the area has a large Orthodox population. And unlike much of Williamsburg today, the area surrounding where Eli's office stood is still not gentrified or trendy; his patients were predominantly low-income Puerto Ricans and African Americans. It was part of Eli's character to want to help the disadvantaged and the poor, but, as mentioned, he had also become frustrated with American-born Jewish patients who distrusted his expertise because he was a refugee. He was devoted to his patients in Williamsburg, and I remember how proudly he told me, once, that he had signed a medical form for a young woman in his practice who was about to attend my own alma mater, Barnard College. At one point he developed plans for a

Figure 51. Eli at his desk in the first office of his private practice, at 542 Parkside Avenue, Brooklyn, August 1951. The framed document above the desk is his license to practice medicine in New York State. Family collection.

Figure 52. Eli and Pearl Rochelson in front of their home at 817 East 17th Street, Brooklyn, in 1974. Family collection.

Figure 53. 493 Marcy Avenue, the building that housed Eli Rochelson's medical office from 1955 to 1984. Photograph by Burt Rochelson, 2016. Family collection.

community center in his office neighborhood, and he was disappointed that it was never built.

In addition to his primary practice, he was one of the survivor physicians employed by the German consulate to examine Jewish Holocaust survivors applying for restitution for medical conditions and disabilities. The German government knew that survivors were reluctant to be examined by German doctors, and that part of Eli's job was victim advocacy. Whether he felt any ambivalence working for the German government, I don't know, but he took his role as patient advocate seriously. I remember with affection a few of the consular officials my parents came to know well. Ilse Kaminski once gave us as gifts goblets of dark red Bohemian crystal, one each to me and to my parents, each slightly different from the other. For many years I have used mine as the Elijah's cup at our family seders, seeing it as a symbol of peace and reconciliation. Now that I have my mother's, too, it is our Miriam's cup.

Our family's religious practice was like that of many Jews in Brooklyn in those years. We kept kosher at home, but not outside. While my Bubby was alive, we attended holiday services at a small Orthodox synagogue, which I suspect my father enjoyed for its evocation of the shuls of his youth. As Burt neared bar mitzvah age, however, we joined a large Conservative synagogue. Because my parents, having been brought up in East European Jewish traditions, thought bat mitzvah was something of a fad, I attended religious school at a Reform temple, which did not require bat mitzvah, and was I confirmed on Shavuot 1964. My father presided at large family seders, where the men gravitated to one end of the table, the women to the other, and which I looked forward to all year long. Because of my grandmother's presence, even more than my father's, Yiddish language pervaded my childhood home, and I understand spoken Yiddish well. It was a rich Jewish life, eclectic and meaningful.

Although Dad worked long hours when I was a child, returning home often at around 9:00 p.m. to what I always envisioned as a time of warm intimacy with my mother, eventually he was able to be home for family dinners, and he was always available to sit and talk with his children in his study. As a doctor, he especially enjoyed helping us with science projects.

I recall how he explained to me the meaning of the blue and red blood in diagrams of the heart, and I still own a wooden model of the lungs that he gave me when I was a child; it is in the room where my grandchildren sleep when they visit. I have fond memories of Saturday nights, watching the Jackie Gleason show on our family television, sitting on my father's lap in a living room full of aunts and uncles. When I was very young Dad taught me to play chess, and we often played together. I never developed a sense of strategy, but I loved the game, especially our games. New Year's Eve was a special occasion in our house, when our parents' friends came, all dressed up, and danced to the music of Guy Lombardo and his orchestra in our living room. My cousins and I would play games on the stairs, and we invented our own master of ceremonies, "Man Sombrero." It felt like a magical night, and I sensed that it was for my parents, too. For me, it represented an adult sophistication, which somehow I knew was also European. I loved watching my elegant parents dance and look so happy.

On Sundays our family either visited Aunt Ida and Uncle Dave in Queens (they had moved from Crown Street) or we spent the afternoon at a museum or some kind of performance; Dad loved the Moiseyev dancers and Mom the Museum of Modern Art,[6] and I enjoyed going to both, multiple times. We went to concerts of Russian and Yiddish music, and at least one Chekhov play—I remember *Three Sisters*—at which Dad listened to the Russian while the rest of us used headphones for simultaneous translation. Late afternoons on Sundays, especially in summer, Mom's extensive extended family would drop by, and we'd gather for a dairy meal of herring and bagels in the dining room. Sometimes the families of friends from Kovno would visit, or we would visit them, although I never got to know any of their children well. Only recently, as I've gone to meetings of Assistance to Lithuanian Jews, have I become reacquainted with Sharon Silber, whose mother I was speaking to when Nissan Krakinowski recognized my name, as well as Bella Pace, Cindy Perry, and their siblings. At the 2014 meeting

---

6. I remember going to the Brooklyn Museum often with my mother, too, although not as a family. Mom had a special affection for that museum, as I did, and when she was sixty she became a docent there.

we began to organize a gathering of the Kovno descendants, nearly all of us American-born and all now in (at youngest) late middle age. The next January a group of ten or twelve of us, including Burt, met at a restaurant on the Upper West Side of Manhattan and talked for hours.[7] More recently we had dinner at an outdoor restaurant near Fort Tryon Park. I like to think of us as the Kovno kids, reconstructing in our own way those long-ago bonds.

In summers when we were children, Pearl and Eli took our family on two-week vacations to Lake Mahopac, north of Westchester County, and other locations not too far from New York City (figure 54). Eli enjoyed swimming in the ocean, which he lovingly called "the sea," at beaches closer to our home. His favorite stroke was the side stroke, which he referred to as "swimming like a frog." In later years we went to Bermuda, Israel, and Europe; and in Paris and Italy, in 1972, Eli reunited with his cousins Riva and Genya (figures 55a and 55b). I vividly remember a conversation at a Paris restaurant, carried on among all of us in English, Yiddish, French, and Russian.

Figure 54. Family vacation, early 1960s; left to right. Pearl, Eli, Burt, Meri-Jane. Family collection.

---

7. We were sons and daughters of Drs. Pace, Perry, Rochelson, Silber, and Rosenstein, the last a female physician who had graduated medical school with the others but who had stayed in the Soviet Union and eventually emigrated to Israel. Several of us got to know her daughter, Paulina, who now lives in the United States, at a meeting of Assistance to Lithuanian Jews.

Figure 55a. Pearl and Eli with Riva and Max Kané-Kahan, Paris, 1972. Photograph by author. Family collection.

Figure 55b. Pearl and Eli with Genya Lubovsky, Abano, Italy, 1972. Photograph by author. Family collection.

Our trip to Israel in 1968 was especially significant. Although Eli had not wanted to emigrate to Palestine after the war, his admiration for the State of Israel was enduring, and in 1968, just one year after the Six-Day War, we joined our Fenster and Minsky cousins from Tulsa in a bus tour on which we took up most of the bus. Israel's spirit was optimistic, and it was exciting to feel that we were among the first Jews in many years to pray at the Western Wall. I remember visiting the Knesset, the John F. Kennedy Forest, the Israel Museum, and similar places in a 1960s tour geared to Americans, as well as the Cave of Machpelah, near Hebron, and locations of Christian interest both in Jewish Jerusalem and the newly accessible West Bank. We were unaware of political contentions that even then must have surrounded those areas. I remember taking off my shoes to visit the Dome of the Rock and the Al-Aqsa Mosque, touching the rock itself and learning about Islamic calligraphy.

But Israel was also a personal journey, a time for my father to reconnect with friends from the past and for his family and those friends to meet each other. I have mentioned our visit to Masha and her family; they lived in Binyamina, then a small, rural place. It was also the first time that my father would see his relatives in Hadera, the children of his aunt Minne Kanter's son Uri, and the first time since the 1930s that he saw the companions of his youth, Joseph and Chana Kushner. I visited the Kanter family again in 1974, when I spent the summer in Israel studying Hebrew at the Hebrew University of Jerusalem. In later years I forgot the daughters' married names and we lost touch, and even the resources of the internet have not (yet) been able to reconnect us. But Joseph and Chana and their family became my lifelong friends. I visited them on every Israel trip and, now that Joseph and Chana have died, I visit their children, grandchildren, and small great-grandchildren and connect with their day-to-day lives via Facebook and e-mail. Nurit Nahmani, with whom I saw Lithuania in 2003, is Joseph and Chana's daughter. We had met Ruth and Mota (Mordechai), Joseph's niece and her husband, a few years before our 1968 trip, when

Mota, a highway engineer, was working with a company in New York. My mother became something of a mother-away-from-home to this young couple during their US stay, and I looked up to them as older, wiser siblings. When I visited Israel on my own, Ruth Blank took on that semimaternal role with me.[8]

In 1968, the meeting between Eli and Joseph was emotional and unforgettable. They embraced repeatedly, each saying, I can't believe it. Joseph told me, years later, that after the war he awaited word from family and friends in Europe, and heard from no one. Then, at some point after the liberation, a letter arrived addressed to "Joseph Kushner / Advocat / Haifa," and it was from my father. When Joseph had made aliyah, he intended to go to law school, and Eli was unaware that he had changed his mind and become an accountant. But there was another Joseph Kushner in Haifa who was a judge. He knew the Joseph whom Eli was looking for, and he forwarded the letter. Joseph told me that when he read it he was overwhelmed with emotion. Of all the people he had known in Europe, his friend Eli was the only one to survive. They immediately continued to correspond, exchanging photographs of their children throughout the years, finally sharing those hugs in Haifa. They had one more visit, when Joseph and Chana toured the United States in 1980 or '81. After my father died, my mother gave me a belt of his to give to Joseph on my next visit, in 1986.

In the fall of 1969, soon after I had transferred to Barnard and was living in Manhattan, my parents called me with exciting news. My father had received a letter from his brother in Russia. The Cold War was still in a very icy stage, and Misha had written to him through Polya Meerovich, my father's sister-in-law, who had survived the war in Russia, returned to Lithuania, and kept up a regular correspondence with Eli until his death.

---

8. When Ruth died of breast cancer in 1991, in her very early fifties, I lost a dear friend, but Mota and their children are still my cousins. Nurit's husband, Yakov, and her brother, Eli, are also now gone, having died in their early sixties and seventies. I felt these all as losses of family.

Misha's letters did not disclose where he was living; they arrived in envelopes written by Polya with her return address. As Eli explained, his brother had been a decorated functionary of the Communist Party, a bureaucrat likely living "in a dacha in Sochi," and thus someone with a great deal to lose, should it become known that he was in touch with a brother in the United States. Indeed, the last previous correspondence my father had received from Misha had come when he learned that Eli had decided to go to the United States after the war, and Misha told him he was making a terrible mistake. The ostensible reason for this new letter was to let Eli know that he had arranged to have their father's grave moved to the new Jewish cemetery in Kaunas. Apparently the old Jewish cemetery was to be destroyed, and families (if they could be found) were given the opportunity to relocate the graves. Enclosed in the letter was a small photograph of my grandfather's grave and the assurance that it was safe in its new location (figure 56). Of course, it was the beginning of a much more intimate correspondence. In subsequent letters my father and uncle exchanged pictures

Figure 56. The gravestone of Bere-Mikhel Rochelson (inscribed with his Hebrew name, Dov-Mikhel b"r Eli'Gershon), as sent in a photograph to Eli by his brother Misha in 1969. Family collection.

of their families. I learned that Misha was married and had two daughters, both of whom were in middle age at that time and had remained single. Eli and Misha wrote to each other until 1974, when Misha died of cancer. When we learned of his disease we felt that there was a deeper reason for his initial contact than simply information about the gravestone.

During the five years of their contact, I asked my father many times why we didn't travel to the Soviet Union so that the two of them could reunite. He cited his brother's fears, apparent in the secretive way he sent his letters, and he seemed to have no idea where his brother lived. He also mentioned his own fears; as he described, he was told he could be in serious trouble if he ever decided to go to the Soviet Union, having changed his mind and gone to the United States after the war. Even if all those fears could be surmounted (and, clearly, they would not be), our family's impression was that Soviet travel regulations would have made a personal visit impossible as well as risky. We never made such a trip.

When I visited Lithuania in 2003, however, I brought the photograph of the gravestone with me. My husband, Joel, and I were traveling with Nurit and Yakov Nahmani, Joseph Kushner's daughter and son-in-law, who had been trying to convince us for years to make the trip together. Since they were Israelis, when we visited the cemetery they read the Hebrew on the gravestones easily, and while I struggled to make out inscriptions letter by letter, they both suddenly called out, here it is! I walked quickly to where they were standing and I saw the stone, exactly as it appeared in the photograph. I broke down and cried, a reaction I hadn't expected, and I started talking to my grandfather in a Yiddish that came back to me from having heard it in my childhood home, but which I had hardly ever produced in speech. "I am your grandchild. This is my husband. We have two children. . . ." The words poured out amidst my tears. I found pebbles to place on the stone in the traditional sign of a visit to a grave in a Jewish cemetery, just as I might put pebbles on the graves of my maternal grandparents in Elmont, New York. It was such a homely and simple gesture, yet one that in my wildest dreams I had never imagined being able to do. Joel,

Nurit, and Yakov added pebbles of their own. Suddenly my grandfather's monument, which had remained unvisited for at least thirty years, if not sixty, looked like the graves of people whose families paid regular visits. His granddaughter had come, from the other side of the world. Nurit and Yakov later visited the old Jewish cemetery, which had not, in fact, been replaced with a highway or apartment blocks or anything else. But the site was in terrible condition and the remaining gravestones were tumbled and vandalized. The new cemetery was well maintained, but there was no signage to mark it or to direct visitors to it. We had found it only because a kind woman we met in a gas station brought us to local businesspeople who pointed the way. When we left, Yakov took out his ballpoint pen and drew a small Star of David on the nondescript cemetery gate.

~

Eli practiced medicine until shortly before his death. He was seventy-six years old, and his last year witnessed the birth of two grandsons, something he told us he had never expected to see. Yet, in the months leading to his death, the importance he placed on his professional identity led to considerable sadness. Although he had suffered more than one transient ischemic attack (TIA, or mini-stroke), he did not want to give up his medical practice. When illness finally forced him to do so, I remember hearing him say, "If I am not a doctor, I am nothing." I recognized right away that it was untrue, but I also saw in it a reflection of the trauma he had survived and the means by which, emotionally and practically, he had survived it. Work was, in part, a way of displacing painful memories, but also a justification for his survival when so many others, especially his wife and child, had perished.

Some years before he died, however, Eli reflected upon his life in a way that I had not expected, and gave me an emotional gift for which I remain grateful. We were standing outside somewhere; I remember it as an airport but I can't be sure. My Aunt Mae, my mother's eldest sister, had been speaking about her son, who had died of a heart attack years earlier at age thirty-seven.

Dad had been especially close to this nephew, who was close to the age that Borya would have been, who was a doctor, and who even had a similar name. Barry's death had been a shock to the whole family, and although my aunt continued her life with great strength, surviving another fourteen years and taking pleasure in her grandchildren and all the family that remained, there was a sadness about her that never fully disappeared—indeed, not unlike my father's sadness. But at that airport, or wherever it was, Eli looked at her as she walked away from us and he said to me (as had been said to him), you have to be rational about these things. There is nothing that can be done, and you have to go on. He added: When I die, I don't want you to grieve too much. I thought I would die many times in the past, and I never expected to live this long. Those words, which I paraphrase after many years, helped me to deal with my father's death when it came, and in those words, too, he gave me permission to be happy. Whether he said it or not, or maybe it was in the way he spoke, I knew that he meant his life had turned out better than he had expected, as well as longer. He thus reassured me that I—and my mother, my brother, all the rest of us Americans—had given him a second life that he enjoyed and that had meaning, despite his having lost that first life that always seemed to be in the background. I did not have to grieve too much for his death, or for his past. I was not Borya, but I was his child, and I deserved to go forward and live my life.

He died on February 15, 1984, in the intensive care unit of Interfaith Medical Center, in the building that had been the Jewish Hospital of Brooklyn, the hospital with which he was primarily affiliated from the 1950s to very shortly before his death. The Jewish Hospital had merged with St. John's; hence, Interfaith. In March and May of the previous year, Burt's son David and my son Daniel were born. A few months earlier, Eli was advised to undergo gall bladder surgery, but he told his physician he wanted to wait until after the births; he wanted to live to see the babies, and he did. He was a grandfather. However, other medical problems developed. During the autumn when David and Danny were not quite toddlers, Eli underwent successful surgery to remove plaque from his carotid artery, but by late January his condition was serious and he was admitted to the hospital. I received a call from New York and flew north right away. I saw my father and I spoke to him. He recognized me, and when I said, "I love you, Dad," he smiled at me and squeezed my hand. I told him about what eight-month-old Danny was doing: standing up, smiling, probably starting to vocalize a bit. It was a conversation, although I don't remember what, specifically, he said or asked me. I was grateful for the smile and squeeze of the hand, and maybe even the voice that said, "I love you, too." That night Dad had a massive cerebral hemorrhage and went into a coma.

Interfaith Medical Center is located between Bedford-Stuyvesant and Crown Heights. In 1984 it still had the old-fashioned intensive care unit, with multiple beds in a large room and virtually no privacy for patients. Families could visit for ten minutes out of each hour; the rest of the time we sat on molded plastic chairs opposite the elevators. My mother, brother, and I at various times shared those chairs with families of young men being treated for gunshot wounds. I realized that their deaths, if they occurred, would be more tragic than my father's at age seventy-six, but of course that didn't help. We all tried to make comforting small talk. We were all devastated.

My father had many visitors, members of the family and those who were like family, such as Noemi Marquez Mesquita, who had been his office assistant for three decades. We all spoke to him and hoped he heard us, although his coma was deep. We learned from Eli's medical record that on the night of the cerebral hemorrhage a nurse recorded that he was speaking incoherently, asking for "a club soda." Burt, our mother, and I knew that this was not incoherent at all. Eli drank club soda, not water. He was simply thirsty, and apparently no one responded to his request. At another point he referred to the ICU attendants as "Nazis." This did not surprise us.

After about ten days, I went home to Florida. Danny had been in New York with me, staying with a different friend or family member every day. Nursing him at night gave me comfort, although I felt that it was wrong to have him continue this way indefinitely. (He is now, as an adult, easygoing and resilient; whether he had those qualities from birth or developed them in part through this experience I don't know.) I also realized that I myself was beginning to hope for my father's death, so that this miserable waiting could end. My mother agreed that Danny and I should return home. We went to a crafts fair with Joel over the weekend, and I was able to relax a bit. I'm sure I pretended that my father would get well and all would be back to normal, although I never sent the Valentine card ("to Grandma and Grandpa") that I had bought and still have. Early on Wednesday morning, Burt called me. Dad had died overnight, and no one from the family was with him. I hope that our love, at the end and all through the life we shared, somehow sustained him through those last days. I flew to New York immediately, and Joel and Danny joined me soon after. The funeral was the next day, and the chapel was filled.

My father had given me the greatest compliment of all when he saw my bound dissertation and turned the pages of its bibliography, recognizing the amount of effort it took and praising me for what I had done. In every subsequent achievement of my academic career, I have sensed him by my side, inspiring me and cheering me on. Listening to his voice in the recorded interview, I was brought back not just to the history of his life but to the life we shared together and to the more extended time I wish we had had. Completing this book now, more than thirty years after I spoke to him last, I miss him again and at the same time feel his presence. I also feel grateful that I inherited his stubbornness (figure 57).

Figure 57. Eli G. Rochelson, MD. A professional photograph taken sometime in the 1970s. Family collection.

Epilogue

Searching for Borya

I was an inmate of the Dachau Concentration Camp, brought from Lithuania in July 1944 and liberated by the American army April 29, 1945. My prisoner's number was 81993. With me, was my son, Boris, 10 yrs. old at that time, prisoner's number 81992 or 81994, who was removed from the camp after two weeks—his fate unknown.

Any information you might be able to give me as to the whereabouts or fate of my son would be greatly appreciated. Other sources I had tried had been fruitless, but my efforts are ceaseless.

—Opening paragraphs of a letter from Ilija G. Rochelson (my father) to the International Tracing Service, Arolsen, Germany, June 10, 1950

AS ELI'S NARRATIVE records, in late November 1944 some prisoners from Auschwitz had been sent to Dachau and they told him that his son was alive, that he was playing chess, and that he had asked them to send his regards. After the liberation he learned that his son had been killed when he contracted measles. He told us that he always said Kaddish for his son on the second day of Rosh Hashanah because, after the war, a group of survivors had gotten together and agreed that this would be when they would observe the *Yahrzeit* of relatives whose dates of death were unknown, since they would certainly be in synagogue on that day. I found this an extraordinarily moving example of faith and devotion to Judaism after the worst imaginable tragedy, and I repeated the inspiring story often. Later, however, I gained information that suggested another reason for the Rosh Hashanah Kaddish.

For a number of years I have subscribed to the LitvakSIG interest group and listserv, now affiliated with JewishGen.com. It has helped me with my research, satisfied my curiosity, and raised new and unexpected questions on numerous occasions, but most astonishing to me was what happened when I responded to a request for replies from child survivors of the Kovno ghetto. Seeing that request, I replied that I was born after the Holocaust ended, but that my first brother had lived in the ghetto as a child. The person posting the message put me in touch with Shalom Eilati, who was at that time awaiting English-language publication of his extraordinary memoir, *Crossing the River*. Reading his book put me in touch with aspects of my brother's experience that I could not have known in any other way, and conversing with him, both in person and via e-mail, has given me valuable insights into the experience of child survivors. He has become a treasured friend. But what Shalom wrote to me in response to my first message told me more about my brother's last months than I had ever imagined might be known.

From Eli's accounts, even though he spoke of a children's selection, I had pictured Borya leaving Dachau on his own—in a small group, perhaps, but essentially unique and not necessarily knowing the other children. (Similarly, I had never thought in terms of larger populations when I learned that my father had been sent to Dachau and his wife to Stutthof, but when I visited Kaunas I learned that those were the common destinations for Kovno's Jewish men and women when the ghetto was liquidated.) What Shalom told me was that my brother was one of a distinct group, now well known in the literature of victims and survivors as the 131 Boys of Kovno. He directed me to a website connected to Lochamei Ha-Ghettaot, the Ghetto Fighters' House Museum in Israel, which has a memorial to those of the 131 who were killed in the Shoah, and there I found my brother's name, Boris Rochelson, next to a small rose and the false date of birth his parents had given to the Nazis in an effort to save his life. This list of names and recorded birthdates is now on a different website,[1] but the story

---

1. The story and the names and dates (without the memorial graphics) may be found in "The 131 Boys of Kovno." My brother's birth date is listed as October 9, 1930,

of the 131 remains on the pages of the Ghetto Fighters kibbutz. It tells how the boys remained with their fathers when their mothers were taken off the train at Stutthof, and how they were sent to Auschwitz in a children's selection at the end of July 1944. It also tells how 90 of the boys were killed in a series of mass selections on Rosh Hashanah and Yom Kippur just a few months later. So Borya's *Yahrzeit* may in fact be the second day of Rosh Hashanah, and, as my mother confirmed to me much later, she believed our father knew that. Perhaps he did not want his living children to associate a happy holiday with such a sad event.

I learned details of one of those Auschwitz selections from someone who survived it, Rabbi Laszlo Berkowits, author of *The Boy Who Lost His Birthday*, and the father of my synagogue rabbi's wife, Deborah Litwak. Rabbi Berkowits was older than Borya, a teenager of about sixteen, and so he passed the tests of height and physical maturity that served as a selection. When Rabbi Berkowits spoke to our congregation I asked him, afterward, if he had known my brother, repeating the question I had asked obsessively in synagogues during my visit to Lithuania, hoping again for an affirmative answer. But, like everyone else I had asked, Rabbi Berkowits told me, no, he had not, and he then said something that had never occurred to me before. He said that Auschwitz was a camp of adolescents, and there were thousands of them; those much older and younger were sent to the gas chambers right away. I tried to picture that horrific summer camp, comforted minimally by the knowledge that none of those children was truly alone, even though, in essence, each one was.

I have heard the stories of the High Holy Day selections many times since then. Shalom Eilati directed me to the Greene and Kumar compilation, *Witness*, in which "Arnold C." records the story of the 131 boys.[2] In the summer of 2013 I had the privilege of meeting in Israel with Moshe

---

when in fact it was October 19, 1934. The earlier birthdate appears in Nazi records, and therefore in the records of the International Tracing Service.

2. In fact, as all the survivors point out, there were only 129 boys who arrived at Auschwitz-Birkenau. Two had jumped from the train as it traveled through Poland. See Eilati

Kravetz, the survivor who was instrumental in establishing the story of the 131 boys at Kibbutz Lochamei Ha-Ghettaot and creating the memorial there to the ninety or more who were murdered by the Nazis. Moshe had earlier told his story to Kenneth Waltzer, whose paper on the "Kovno Boys" I reread before our interview to refamiliarize myself with the basics Waltzer had recorded. Speaking in Hebrew, with my friend Nurit Nahmani translating,[3] Moshe filled in details of his experience. He explained that he did not know or did not remember Borya, but he hoped that by conveying to me the feelings he had had I might have some sense of what my brother had gone through. The experience of listening to his account was emotionally draining; I was glad I had recorded it, because it was a long time before I could bring myself to listen to the recording and hear the details again, some as if for the first time. In that afternoon in Haifa, in my friend's living room, I heard the story twice, first in the Hebrew that I could only imperfectly make out, and then in Nurit's near-simultaneous translation. Moshe spoke of the fear and quiet confusion of the boys in the railway car from the camp near Dachau to Auschwitz-Birkenau, boys who had suddenly been separated from their last remaining parents. These boys had witnessed horrors and would witness more, but now there was the additional grief of separation and the feeling of being on their own, or, more accurately, only with each other.

Several of the testimonies generously streamed by the United States Holocaust Memorial Museum tell the story of the first selection, when Mengele (as some of the men remember) came to the barracks and took down the numbers tattooed on the arms of the boys who seemed younger or smaller, as they stood in the *appelplatz*—as Lurie remembered, completely undressed, or, as Moshe put it, without shirts, without eyeglasses, half naked. Because I received Moshe's words in my friend's translation, I

134, Greene and Kumar 112. "Arnold C." is Arnold Clevs, whose recorded testimony I listened to later at the USHMM. Evidence suggests that Borya's number was B-2874.

3. Nurit, who traveled with me to Lithuania in 2003, is herself an academic with Kovno roots, now retired from the social work faculty of the University of Haifa.

cannot quote them directly. But my transcription of the translated words tells the story:

> It was not a secret; everyone saw the crematoria and they knew the pro-cedure. He called some of the boys aside and a clerk wrote their numbers down. . . . Mengele took out sixty boys. All of them went back to the barrack but he wrote down their numbers. The boys who would live were next to the boys who would die; in the same bed there was one alive, one who was dead already. They didn't talk about it. They didn't say anything. In the morning, it was silent.

Moshe told me that others in their group, who meet periodically, remember that the boys cried during that night. What Moshe remembers is that it was quiet "like the grave," and that in the morning the boys whose numbers had been taken were told by an officer to get up and leave the barrack, and they left quietly, "in an automatic way, even."

I have heard categorically from Shalom Eilati, Moshe Kravetz, and Sol Lurie[4] that Borya could not have had measles and could not have been shot, that all of the 131 who were killed in Auschwitz were killed in the gas chambers and cremated. Eventually I realized that the word Eli used to describe his son's killing was "liquidated"; it was I who had interpreted that as "shot." But I continued to seek evidence that measles might have played a role, that what my father had so clearly been told might in fact have happened. Shalom Eilati, early on, had told me about the *Auschwitz Chron-icle*, a compilation of events at Auschwitz, day by day, edited by Danuta Czech from a wide variety of testimonies and other documentary evidence. When I looked for it in my university library—expecting to have to order it through interlibrary loan—there I found it, right on the shelf, on my cam-pus. I discovered in its pages how on August 1, 1944, the transport of boys from Kovno, via Dachau, arrived at the camp, and that some were sent to

---

4. After I heard Sol Lurie's testimony on the USHMM website, I used the internet to find his address and sent him a letter. He telephoned me as soon as he received it, and we had a good long conversation.

an infirmary. At this early point in my research, I thought that if my brother was one of that group, perhaps it was because he had contracted measles. But then no one at Auschwitz would have seen him playing chess, or have reported anything about him to his father. Ralph Codikow's testimony on the USHMM website reports that when the Kovno boys arrived they were placed in quarantine for a few days in Birkenau lager A, but they were later transferred to lager B and then D, both locations from which selections took place.[5] However, Codikow also reports that there was in fact measles at Birkenau and among the Kovno boys—a point substantiated in an online printed testimony by Moshe Kravetz. Reporting on selections in the fall of 1944, Moshe comments on his own comparative good fortune:

> It is enough for me to state that out of the 129 children who went into the camp, only about thirty children remained after the selection. After passing through the selection with a lot of luck and a bit of resourcefulness, I managed to have the measles and also to survive that. You must know that in Birkenau measles could definitely have been a fatal disease, either because of our poor physical condition, or because the sick bay was frequently "evacuated." I was sent to another camp. ("Moshe Kravetz Story")

---

5. Moshe Kravetz, on reading this section in manuscript, disputes that the boys were ever in Lager B. He recollects that they were sent to quarantine in Lager A, which was where both selections took place (e-mail to author, November 22, 2014). He adds that the Kovno boys were in Birkenau from August 1, 1944, through January 23, 1945, but that he left the group at some point in mid-November and knows the later stories only from his friends' testimonies. The various testimonies I listened to at the USHMM also differ on the letters and numbers of the camps in Birkenau to which the boys were sent, but they agree on the basics. Danuta Czech's *Auschwitz Chronicle* indicates that the boys were sent to Men's Quarantine Camp B-IIa (Birkenau) on arrival on August 1, and were still there as of August 7 (676, 681). This is the last time the *Chronicle* mentions the Kovno boys specifically until it describes the September 18 Rosh Hashanah selection: "65 boys from Kaunas in the men's prisoners' infirmary, Camp B-IIf, who were delivered to the camp on August 1, are selected. They are killed the same day in the gas chambers" (713). This record contradicts the reports of survivors among the boys who state clearly that the selection was made the day before the murders. The Yom Kippur selection mentioned by survivors is not recorded in the *Auschwitz Chronicle*.

Ralph Codikow recalled that, in Birkenau, five to ten of the boys contracted measles, and that while they stayed in the hospital they were treated by a kind and understanding French Jewish doctor who saved their lives. He remembered the doctor running back and forth trying to declare the children well and no longer contagious. He succeeded, and they were able to be evacuated in November 1944 for farm work, along with Moshe Kravetz and presumably other young survivors. According to internet records, Ralph Codikow died in 1995, before I began the research for this book. I was thus not able to ask him, as I have asked others, whether or not he knew my brother. However, there is a big difference between five and ten boys, and, as every child survivor I have spoken to confirms, the situation of trauma interfered with remembering details. Ralph Codikow said that all the sick boys went on to work on the farm. But perhaps one or more of them did not survive; perhaps they were "evacuated" in the murderous way that Moshe Kravetz mentions. This might have been Borya's fate. In the end, of course, it doesn't matter. But since Eli reported the measles story in two separate testimonies, I can't entirely let it go.

Before I knew anything about my first brother's death, and even after I thought I knew the story about the measles, I would search for the name Boris Rochelson, or anything like it, in every telephone book in every out-of-town hotel I visited. I learned later that my brother Burt would do the same. After all, each of us reasoned to ourselves, many people who survived the Holocaust found their relatives only years later, and reunions were still occurring. Just maybe, we thought, our brother was out there. My research confirms that he was not. But what I did not know until recently is that someone else was searching in agony for him, besides his father, when I was a child. Mariya Meerovich's letters tell a tale of survivorship in some ways much sadder than Eli's.

If I had thought about it, I would have noticed that my father mentioned in his testimony that his brother-in-law Misha Meerovich had made that last train to Moscow with his wife (Polya) and his mother, and that they survived the war. I knew that Polya had settled in Vilnius afterward, since that was where her letters were postmarked, and when I studied Russian in college I read a few of them. The fact that my father's mother-in-law—his son's grandmother—had also survived, never made it to my consciousness. Even when I saw the photograph marked on the back "Borya with his bubbies" (figure 4), I thought to myself that all of them had been killed. That changed in very recent years when I found some Russian letters that were signed not by Polya but by "Mariya Moiseevna." At some point I remembered the names on the copies of vital records that I had obtained in Lithuania: Serafima's mother's name was Mariya, and Moiseevna would have been her patronymic. But although I received translations of the Russian letters first, Mariya's postwar story is best told beginning with the earliest communication I have, a Yiddish postcard signed "M. M. Meerovich."

I found the postcard extremely difficult to read, even though I can make out Yiddish when it is clearly written, and this message was necessarily short. Two Yiddish-speakers to whom Burt and I showed it could not make out the writing, and I realized that it was the Yiddish of someone more used to writing in Russian, so that the letters and spelling must have been fairly nonstandard. Finally Rivka Schiller translated what turned out to be an early inquiry to my Uncle Dave in Brooklyn. It is dated May 23, 1946, and it bears multiple postmarks from both Vilnius and New York, the latter dated two months later. But if censors had had their eyes on the content, it was unlikely they could have read it.

The message expresses urgency but also hope:

> Very Esteemed Mr. Robinson!
>
> Please oblige me by informing me what you know concerning your brother, Dr. Iliya Rochelson. I am searching for him all the time—where [are] Iliya, Sima, and my only grandchild, Boretzken. . . . I am asking you greatly, send me his address. This is Iliya's dear mother writing you. My son and I are alive. Your brother Moishe and his family are also

> alive. He is now living in Simferopol. . . . Heartfelt greetings
> to you—from my son and me.

Simferopol is in the Crimea, in southern Ukraine. When Eli spoke of his Russian brother's "dacha in Sochi," he must have known of this; both are in southern Russia or Ukraine, near the Black Sea. Of course it was his mother-in-law writing, not his mother. Mariya Meerovich may have been expressing the closeness she felt—that she was like a mother to Eli—as well as her desperation. By the time Mariya sent the card, the war had been over for more than a year. By the time it arrived in New York, Eli would have been there just over a month. He himself may have replied to it, and I can only try to imagine the difficulty that would have entailed, as well as the sadness and grief on both sides.

The two Russian letters I have are dated fifteen years later, in 1961. Olga Skarlat's translations reveal a woman distraught with grief, alternately angry at Eli for ignoring her and, later, grateful for the gifts he sent her. In the earlier letter, Mariya asks about Eli's and Dave's health, and complains about not hearing from him and her own weariness with life. But she also reveals how she is haunted by the memory of her daughter and grandson:

> You know, every day I am hoping to meet him. I am looking for him every-where on the streets. I think the Nazis killed him. He was by himself; he was running and shouting: "Father (papa), save me." Do you think it could happen to him?
>
> . . . I am hoping that one day Borya and Zina will open my door. I can't sleep. I am constantly thinking about him, but the Nazis must have burned him in the oven right away.
>
> Sima died from starvation. Every time I see her friends, I do not feel well. Maybe I just have to get used to it.[6]

---

6. Translated by Olga Skarlat. Although Sima was Serafima's Yiddish name, the name in the letter is clearly Zina and not Sima. Mariya was distraught when she wrote, and perhaps that accounts for the mistake.

Just as it never occurred to me that Sima's mother had survived, so it never crossed my mind that friends of hers might have lived, too, and, like so many others, had gone to Vilnius.

In the next letter, not long after, Mariya seems to be in a better mood. "It seems like you have not forgotten about me. Thank you for the wonderful presents, my dear." As I read about the clothing and bedcover she had asked for, I remembered going with my parents, once, to a storefront that shipped goods to the Soviet Union. They had to be new, and they were usually soft goods like these, or even just bolts of new fabric. I think of that place when I pass similar stores in Miami, offering to ship goods to the Caribbean. In any event, I assumed that we were sending things to Polya, or to the families of my father's cousins, Leiye and Feyge, who had also survived the Holocaust in Russia and had returned to Lithuania. At least some of those items, of course, went to Borya's grandmother.

In her own letters, Polya reported on her mother-in-law's increasingly fragile condition, physically and mentally. In February 1963 she suffered a stroke, after a pleasant day on which she had received another parcel from Eli:

> She was happy as a baby to receive a kerchief. She has been wearing it all day long. She especially liked one of the dresses, and with little alteration, she would have been able to wear it in summer. She has been talking about you for [a] couple of days.

The stroke, however, left her sleepless and anxious; she shouted "that someone was waiting for her outside" and she called "for Misha and Borya."[7] Polya, who worked during the day, worried about her safety. Mariya died on March 4, 1963. On July 21 Polya expressed her own sadness in a letter to Eli, her own concerns that she had not heard from him. In later years,

---

7. Letter of February 4, 1963, translated from Russian by Olga Skarlat. Misha—Mariya's son, Serafima's brother, and Eli's friend and brother-in-law—had died seven years earlier, on March 6, 1956. I regret that I do not have the entire Russian correspondence.

however, as I was aware, they corresponded often; I have a colorful Russian New Year's card, with a cheerful greeting, that Polya sent to our family at the end of 1982. I can imagine now, however, the pain it must have caused my father to read, in particular, of his mother-in-law's distress. In one of her letters Mariya Moiseevna told him she forgave him; in another she asked for his forgiveness. Maybe she was just thinking of his failure to write. But Eli may have thought of other reasons for forgiveness, and I don't know if he ever fully forgave himself. Like many Holocaust survivors, he was an overprotective parent, determined never to lose another child.

The very dramatic grief of Mariya Moiseevna may have been in my father's mind when he spoke to me about dealing with loss in a "rational" way. Now all these people are gone. The JewishGen Online World Burial Registry records the burial sites of Marija, Mihail, and Paulina Meerovitch (spelled differently from the way I have come to know them, but clearly the same people) in Saltonishkiu Cemetery, Vilnius. Polya joined Misha and Mariya in late January 1988, almost exactly four years after Eli died. Everyone who knew Sima and Borya is now gone, as are all my aunts and uncles, the grandmother I knew, and both my parents. In the fragments of memory and text, archives and digitized recordings, still something of their stories remains.

Appendix A

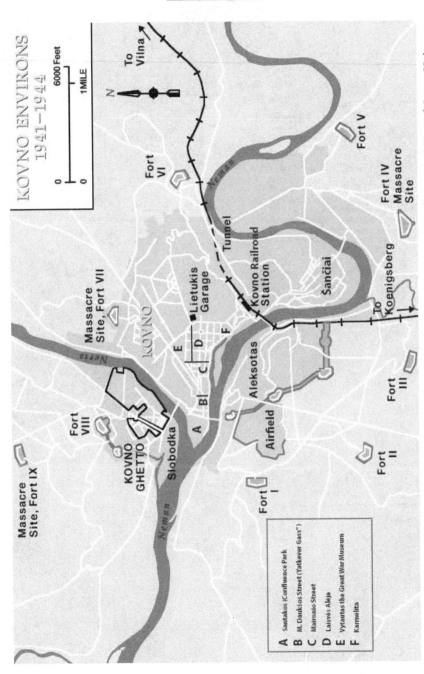

KOVNO ENVIRONS
1941–1944

N

0   6000 Feet
0   1MILE

To Vilna

Fort VI

Massacre Site, Fort VII

KOVNO

Tunnel

Lietukis Garage

Kovno Railroad Station

Fort V

Fort IV
Massacre Site

Koenigsberg

Šančiai

To Koenigsberg

Aleksotas

Airfield

Fort III

Fort II

Fort I

Massacre Site, Fort IX

Fort VIII

KOVNO GHETTO

Slobodka

Neman

Neris

A   B

C   D   E   F

A   Santakos (Confluence Park)
B   M. Daukšos Street ("Yatkever Gass")
C   Maironio Street
D   Laisvės Alėja
E   Vytautas the Great War Museum
F   Karmelita

Map of Kovno and Environs, 1941–1944. Adapted from "Kovno Environs, 1941–1944." Courtesy United States Holocaust Memorial Museum.

213

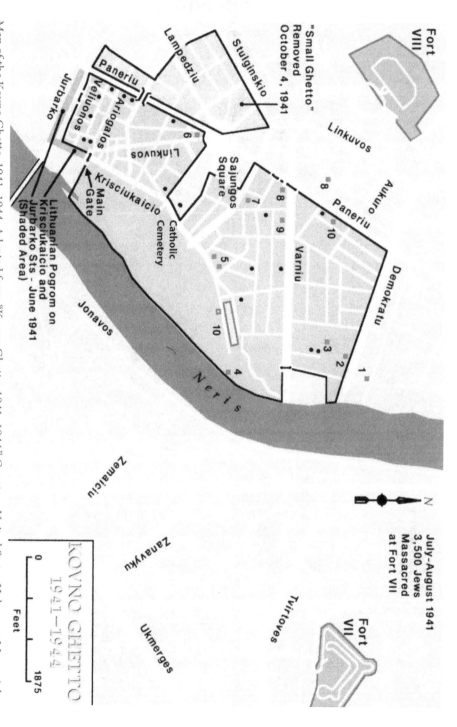

Map of the Kovno Ghetto, 1941–1944. Adapted from "Kovno Ghetto, 1941–1944." Courtesy United States Holocaust Memorial Museum.

Appendix B

Rochelson and Lubovsky Family Diagrams

EACH OF THESE diagrams focuses on families and individuals mentioned in *Eli's Story*. They are not intended as complete genealogies but rather as a means to help readers further understand relationships mentioned in the narrative. Family branches with many descendants (apart from Eli's) left Europe before the Holocaust, some at the end of the nineteenth century. Deaths of those murdered in the Holocaust are mentioned in the text, although not indicated in these lists. Only a few remarriages are indicated here, and surnames of living people are avoided. Major places of settlement before and after the Holocaust are listed in parentheses. Bold type indicates the names of progenitors of major family branches.

The Rochelson Family (Lithuania branch)

MOSHE ITSYK ROCHELSON (POSSIBLY MIKHELSON) M. MURAVSKY ?

Son, Ilija Gershon Rochelson (b. ca. 1830) m. Devorah/Dvera

Daughter Yachle m. Rabbi Shmuel Rabinowitz (Chicago and other parts of the American Midwest)

Children, grandchildren, great-grandchildren

Daughter Chaye m. Louis Bloch (Chicago and other parts of the American Midwest)

Son Bernard (Ben) Bloch

Children, grandchildren, great-grandchildren

Son Jacob H. Bloch (recipient of letter in figure 50 and
grandfather of family genealogist Eric M. Bloch)
Children, grandchildren, great-grandchildren
Three additional children, plus grandchildren,
great-grandchildren

Daughter Yente m. ?
Two Daughters

**Daughter Dina m. Abraham Zanditen (Sanditen) (Tulsa,
Oklahoma)**
Daughter Rivka (Rifka/Rifke) m. Gershon Fenster
Daughter Rosalee m. Samuel Minsky
Two daughters
Son Louis m. Susan Fink
Three children, grandchildren
Son Irving m. Irene Turk
Three children, grandchildren, great-grandchildren
Son Herman m. Anne Sanditen (sister of Ida Sanditen
Robinson)
Son Edgar m. Isabel Raffkind
Four children, grandchildren
Son Ira m. Mary Kurtz
Two children, grandchildren
Herman m. Sadye Brenner
Son Maurice m. Myrtle Foster
One child, grandchildren, great-grandchildren
Maurice m. Charlien (Chic) Steel
Son Isadore Sanditen
Daughter Ida Sanditen
Daughter Jeanette m. Harry Mann

Children, grandchildren, great-grandchildren

Son Samuel m. Lillian Goldner

Children, grandchildren, great-grandchildren

Son William

Son Julius m. Mildred Taichert

Two daughters, including Sanditen family genealogist
Deana Sanditen Maloney

Children, grandchildren, great-grandchildren

Daughter Sybil

Son Ely m. Betty Lehman

Children, grandchildren, great-grandchildren

Daughter Sarah m. ? German/Herman

Daughter Feyge m. ? Cerisodas (Feyge survived in the
USSR, Lithuania)

Daughter Leiye m. Victor Kutnovsky

Son Lazar m. Alexandra Shushkova (USSR,
Lithuania)

Child (Misha?) and grandchild

Son Yakov m. Inna Bidner (Denver, Colorado)

Daughter Zhanna m. Patrick

Children

Daughter Taube (Taibe/Taibke) m. Michael Rudansky
(Israel)

Son

Daughter Minne m. Mendel Kanter

Son Shlomo (Shloimke)

Daughter Grunye

Daughter Paike

Son Uri m. Dobe (Israel)

Daughter Nechama m. ?

Son

Daughter Rivka m. ?

Son

Son Eli

Son Yankel/Yankele

Daughter Chana m. Jacob Rosen (Chicago and other parts of the American Midwest)

Children, grandchildren, great-grandchildren

Son Bere-Mikhel m. Henye Lubovsky

Daughter Chaya (Anna) m. Albert Arendt (Berlin)

Son David Jonah m. Ida Sanditen (New York)

Son Moshe (Maishe/Mikhail/Misha) Rochelson m. ? (Crimea)

Two daughters

Daughter Gitel (died in infancy or early childhood)

Son Mordechai (Mottel/Mottle/Motteh)

Son Avraham (Abraham) m. Rosa (Rose) Kagan/Kaganov

Daughter Sarah

Son Ilija Gershon (Eli Gershon) m. Serafima Meerovich

Son Boris (Borya/Bertchik/Borinka/Boretzken)

Ilija Gershon (Eli Gershon) m. Pearl Friedman (Brooklyn, New York)

Daughter Meri-Jane m. Joel

Son Daniel m. Sarah

Son Samuel

Son Karl

Daughter Serafima

Son Burton Lee m. Myra

Son David m. Ebonie

Son Jack

Son Ellis m. Emily

Son Jordan

Son Burton Lee m. Robyn

The Lubovsky Family

DAVID LUBOVSKY M. ?

Daughter Sarah m. Jacob (Yetzner) Esner (New York)

Son Abraham m. Sara

Children

Daughter Belle (Beile)

Daughter Pauline (Peshke)

Son Morris (Moishe) m. Anne Weinstein

Son Seymour m. Estelle Blum

Daughter Barbara

Son William (Bill) m. Sandra (Sandy)

Daughter Laura

Daughter Melissa

Daughter Sylvia m. Kenneth Strauss

Children

Daughter Betty (Ruth) m. Stanley Israel

Children

Son George (Louis) m. Lila

Children and grandchildren

Son David m. Ruth

Children and grandchildren

Daughter Dorothy

Daughter Natalie m. Aaron Cohen

Children and grandchildren

Daughter Harriet m. Donald Wilner

Children and grandchildren

Son Robert m. Dorothy?

Son Mordechai (Mordkhel) m. Chaya Zandberg

Daughter Essia (Esther) m. Mark Volosov (USSR)

Son Volodia m. ?

Daughter Marina, daughter of Volodia and his unnamed wife

Son David

Daughter Dora m. Ozhinsky

Children

Daughter Genya (Evgenya/Eugenie) (Berlin, then Nice and Paris)

Daughter Riva m. Max Kané-Kahan (Nice and Paris)

Daughter Jenny (Adrienne Eugenie) m. Rodolfo Pizzochero (Milan)

Son Pierre m. Roland

Daughter Henye m. Bere-Mikhel Rochelson

Daughter Chaya (Anna) m. Albert Arendt (Berlin)

Son David Jonah m. Ida Sanditen (New York)

Son Moshe (Maishe/Mikhail/Misha) Rochelson m. ? (Crimea)

Two daughters

Daughter Gitel (died in infancy or childhood)

Son Mordechai (Mottel/Mottle/Motteh)

Son Avraham (Abraham) m. Rosa (Rose) Kagan/Kaganov

Daughter Sarah

Son Ilija Gershon (Eli Gershon) m. Serafima Meerovich

Son Boris (Borya/Bertchik/Borinka/Boretzken)

Ilija Gershon (Eli Gershon) m. Pearl Friedman (Brooklyn, New York)

Daughter Meri-Jane m. Joel

Son Daniel m. Sarah

Son Samuel

Son Karl

Daughter Serafima
Son Burton Lee m. Myra
Son David m. Ebonie
Son Jack
Son Ellis m. Emily
Son Jordan
Son Burton Lee m. Robyn

Appendix C

Testimony on Medical Atrocities Submitted to the Nuremberg Trials by Dr. Eli G. Rochelson, 1946

I, the undersigned, Dr.   Rochelson, being duly sworn in, herewith declares the following facts, concerning atrocities and inhuman treatment by German Physicians in the Ghettos of Kovne, witnessed by me, to be true:

I. **Mid-September, 1941, Ghetto of Kovne:** The/hospital located in the section known as "Plein Ghetto", bearing the inscription "Danger -- Pest" (Seuche-Gefahr), was set on fire while the sick, the nurses and physicians were inside. In order to prevent any person to escape the blaze the hospital was surrounded by German soldiers, armed with machine guns. This act of arson was committed on orders of the Gestapo with the full knowledge and consent of the German medical authorities in Kaunas (Kovne).

II. Pregnancy in the Ghetto of Kovne was forbidden by the German medical authorities under the provision of capital punishment. This was the order of the German medical authorities. Epidemical diseases officially did not exist in the Ghetto. Jewish physicians, at the risk of their own lives, had to diagnose the case falsely in order to save the patients and themselves.

III. FATE OF LITHUANIAN JEWISH PHYSICIANS

A. For the least offense of German rules, physicians were sentenced and shot to death in both locations known as the small and large Ghettos.

B. To illustrate this, my colleague, Dr. Gerber, was shot for not having greeted a small time Lithuanian quisling.

C. Dr. Langman was publicly burned alive under the accusation that he tried to escape the Ghetto.

D. Dr. Randanski was beaten to death in the Camp known as "Fort No. 9".

E. Drs. Urbach and Kabaker were sent to the gas chambers on March 27, 1944 in the German general campaign known as "Old Folks and

Children's Action" (This action, in plain English, meant the murdering of sick, helpless old people, children and generally everyone in the Ghetto who couldn't be used for hard labor.)

F. All the time of the existence of the Ghetto, physicians were dragged to different camps in Lithuania and neighboring countries, where they were destroyed.

G. The inhuman conditions in the Camps and Ghettos led to the death of the following Lithuanian Jewish physicians: Dr. Vareter, Dr. Laserson, Dr. Elkes, Dr. Gerstein, Dr. Mueller, Dr. Fischer, Dr. Abramson and scores of others.

IV. Medical supplies to the Ghetto were allowed only in very limited quantities. It was up to the Ghetto itself to "create" its own *lubricate* *drugs* ~~medicines~~.

V. CONCENTRATION CAMP DACHAU

Physicians in this camp were treated most brutally and sent to do the most repugnant labor. When in February, 1944, I was caught doing my duty as a physician, helping my fellow inmates, I was publicly whipped in the most brutal manner.

VI. With the knowledge of the Chief Physician, Dr. Blanke, who held the title of Obersturmbahnfuehren, the inmates of the hospital barracks were beaten and treated with inhuman cruelty, i.e. at the ßdelousing process". The sick, who did not manage to get back into their clothes as quickly as they were ordered to, were beaten with whips and Dr. Blanke not only assisted, but actually took part in the beating. He himself made from time to time the selection of people to be sent to the extermination camps. In February, 1944, I witnessed in Dachau the following scene: All sick people were ordered out in the snow without shoes and stripped to the bone, with only a blanket covering everyone. Then Dr. Blanke appeared for medical inspection carrying a whip in his hand. He ordered all sick people to drop their blankets and started the medical visit. I could observe that scene from the barrack

where I was located. He deliberately stopped to inspect one man at a time
while the others were shivering naked in the cold frosty winter. Those
who
sick tried to ask for mercy were slapped with a whip in their faces.

After liberation, Dr. Blanke and his wife committed suicide by hanging
themselves. They left a five year old daughter.

Another example of medical atrocity is the fact that many of the
inmates were sent to work in wooden shoes without any other cover on their
feet. This was done deliberately in order to create quick and efficient
infections and diseases leading to death. Added to this Dr. Blanke has
ordered a diet of starvation for these hard working people without the
chance of warming up or getting any medical treatment.

Appendix D

Der Tog, October 28, 1946

Dr. E. Rochelson

English Translation by
Nissan Krakinowski and Rivka Schiller

Kovner Jews remember their Kedoshim today, on the fifth yahrzeit.

On the tragic day of October 28, 1941, 30,000 Jews from the Kovno ghetto were driven out of their homes.—11,000 martyrs—That is what is left of Lithuanian Jewry.

IT HAPPENED FIVE years ago in the Kovno ghetto. Still fresh in my memory is the burning of the Jewish hospital, when the Nazi murderers surrounded the hospital with machine guns and burned the sick ones, the nurses, the doctors, and the rest of the personnel. Yet fresh in my memory is the action in the small ghetto. Fresh are all the executions and shootings in the last months—and at once a new decree was declared; that all the ghetto's residents—around 30,000 Jews—gather together on the 28th of October, at 6:00 in the morning for registration purposes. Nobody would be let out on this day to go to work. Nobody dared stay at home. Sick, old, and children—all had to be at the assembly point. If somebody stayed at home, he would be shot. This is the way it sounded, the order from the Gestapo. We understood what this "registration" meant.

On the 28th of October, 1941, at 6:00 in the morning, following a sleepless night, people streamed to the assembly point in the ghetto. It was a dark, cold, and tragic (mournful) early morning. Screaming, crying, confused voices were heard amidst the shadows moving in the darkness.

In a very organized [manner] the German police came, [along with] the Lithuanian bandits and Gestapo leaders. Some of the soldiers were sent to go see what was doing in the houses, from which we later heard shots . . . The other soldier divisions remained standing, awaiting further orders. The ghetto was already surrounded by a look-out that had been fortified still from yesterday. Many Christians had assembled far beyond the ghetto, in order to observe this horrible game. Standing still and silent were the 30 thousand Jews at that spot. Occasionally—[there was] a shiver in the crowd, as though an electric current had overtaken everyone . . . The Gestapo began sorting. . . .

With cold, calm, murderous faces, which at times bore sarcastic smiles and expressions, they sent people to their deaths. "Right, left, right, left." We heard the orders from the Gestapo. Whole families were sent to the bad side. Like wolves they tore the children from their parents, divided sisters from brothers, old and young, sick and healthy—all were sent to death! . . .

All day the Gestapo and the Lithuanian forest bandits were out of control. All day we heard the screams of the beaten, the cries of woe of the children for their parents, and of the parents for their children . . . Up until the evening, there were 11,000 people who were "sorted out."

The next day in the morning we found out that all of the 11,000 selected people were taken out in groups to the spot at which they were shot by machine guns.

This is [just] a small chapter of the tragedy of Lithuanian Jewry, and an even smaller one of the general tragedy. Out of the 250,000 Jews [in Lithuania in 1941], [only] about five percent survived . . .

On the 5th yahrzeit of the tragedy, we remember the innocent martyrs of Nazi barbarism; those who died for Kiddush Hashem [i.e., the sanctification of God's name]; those whose memorialization among us survivors must be holy and dear. We remember the survivors who are still languishing in the camps today, in accursed [or cursed, damned] Germany, and are waiting for the correct/proper decision [or ruling] concerning their fate, disappointed with post-war justice.

Image of original Yiddish article in *Der Tog*.

קאָוונער אידען דערמאָנען זייערע קדושים היינט, צו דעם פינפטען יאָרצייט

אין דעם "מארטיראָלאָגישען" מאה פון 28סטן אָקטאָבער, 1941. — 30,000 אידען פון קאָוונער געמאַ אַרױסגעטריבען פון די היימען. — 11,000 קדושים. — װאָס עס איז פאָרגעקומען פון ליטװישען אידענטום.

פון דר. א. ראָבלאָן

בא פרויען זיינען די בעסטע מאַמעס

Appendix E

Cover Page of Collection of Documents Compiled by Eli G. Rochelson to Affirm His Medical Degree and Credentials after Immigrating to the United States

Rochelson, Ilija Gerson,

12 Crown Street,

Brooklyn, N.Y.

Summary of Documents:

While in the concentration camp at Dachau (Germany) - see item 5 below - all original documents including the diploma of Doctor of Medicine were taken away by the Germans and destroyed.

The following documents are submitted as evidence of Dr.Rochelson's ical activities:

1) A certificate issued by the Consul General of Lithuania, stating t Ilija Rochelson has graduated from secondary school, was awarded the ree of Candidate of Medicine and obtained his physician's diploma, issued the University of Vytautas the Great at Kaunas, Lithuania.

2) Photostatic copies of portions of the official medical journal of nas, recording the fact that DR. Rochelson was awarded the degree of tor of Medicine. These copies are certified as true by the Librarian the Academy of Medicine in New York and are accompanied by a statement m the Consulate General of Lithuania in New York vouching for the icial standing of the journal involved.

3) Notarized affidavits from Dr. med. Prof. Jurgis Zilinskas, formerly fessor of the Faculty of Medicine of the University of Vytautas the Great nas, Lithuania, and from Dr.med.Kazys Vileisis testifying to the fact t Dr. Rochelson had obtained the physician's diploma.

4) A statement from the Jewish Medical Association in the American zone ermany, certifying to the fact that Dr. Rochelson was known in Kaunas as ysician, that he was so known in the Kaunas ghetto and in the concen- ion camp of Dachau, Germany, and also certifying to his medical services andsberg (Germany) as noted below.

5) A certificate issued by the American Military Government in Landsberg (Germany), stating that Dr. Ilija Rochelson was in the Dachau concentration camp as prisoner No.81993.

6) A statement, endorsed by the UNRRA, at the hospital for Displaced Persons No.2014 in Landsberg a.L., Bavaria(Germany) , testifying that Dr. Rochelson served as head of the dispensary (Out-Patient Department) and as Assistant Chief of the hospital , and testifying furthermore to his loyal and devoted services.

7) A certificate issued by the American Joint Distribution Committee, Landsberg a.L., endorsed by the Military Government in Landsberg, also testifying to the facts stated under 6.

8) A statement by U.S.Army Medical Officer Lt.Streim, certifying to the fact stated above under 6.

9) A curfew pass, issued by the Military Government in Landsberg, exempting Dr. Rochelson from curfew restrictions because of his duties as a physician in the hospital for former political prisoners.

231

Appendix F

=====

Family Interview Transcript

IN THE MIDDLE 1970s Burt Rochelson tape-recorded more than six hours of interviews with our father, Eli G. Rochelson. Each of us knew there would be a book someday, and this interview, which I transcribed, is the starting point for *Eli's Story*. I quote from it generously in the main text, but I present the full transcript here for those who would like to read all that our father said, in his own words, with Burt's questions included. I use footnotes sparingly, omitting them when the contextualizing or other information is in the main text.—MJR

[BURT: THIS IS for the use of all the generations to come, so they will never forget our history.]

I AM ELI G. Rochelson, dictating my past so far as I can remember. I was born in Kovno, Lithuania[1] August 19, 1907. I had one sister and five brothers. My sister's name was Chaya, and then the brothers were David (who changed his name for Robinson), then Maishe, Mottel, Abraham, and I. Then I had another sister, who died from a childhood infectious disease; as far as I can remember, I was told that she had diphtheria. [*What was her name? I never heard about her.*] My [surviving] sister Chaya had scarlet fever, and she developed rheumatic fever with a severe rheumatic heart

---

1. At that time, Kovno was in the Russian Empire and Lithuania was not independent.

disease. My father, at that time, when I was born, was working, at one time, in a brewery, by letting out the beer and counting, and by, when they came back from selling the beer, counting how many empty bottles they had, and how many they sold. After a while, he opened, we called it in Jewish an "*akhsanye.*" This I don't remember, but I was told it was like a little motel, a hotel; I would say better we'd call it a rooming house. Of course it didn't have the character, at that time, like it has here the motels. Now, then we moved, in a small street in Kovno called Yatkever Gass, where my parents opened a restaurant. I started to remember events, I think, when I was five years old. My brother David, at that time, it was in 1912, he was carrying me, I remember, on his shoulders, and going around all over, the rooms and in the streets; this was vividly remembered by me.

We had, as I said, opened a little restaurant, where we had different type of high-cholesterol food, but very tasty. Every breakfast we had, let's say, the fricassee from chicken, or from geese, boiled in soup with cereal, and then we had piroshkes made from dough with meat. That was our breakfast. There in this *birele*, or we call it restaurant, where we sold liquor, which we didn't have a license to sell, and David had to—the police were coming in often to check if alcohol is sold. And many times my brother when he saw the police he threw away the bottle what he kept, or giving to the customers, and they couldn't do anything because they didn't catch him with alcohol. In 1912—no, in 1912 or in '13, I don't remember, brother David left for America.

The next things I remember, it was before the First World War, when I was going, with other boys, without the knowledge of my parents, riding on the horses. Now, in retrospect, I see how terrible it was.[2] In August 1914, we children were playing near the Nieman River, and we heard news that a war started. Germany and Russia started the war. Of course at that time I didn't know the reason, but that was when a shot was fired in Sarajevo, and the First World War started.

---

2. Here, an overprotective father is speaking to his son.

I will go back, a little back, and I'll tell you what was our relationship with the family. We had there Tante Sarah with her children; her children were Feyge, Leiye, and Taibke. And then Minne had children, it was Uri, Grunye, and Paike. There was another boy, Yankele, who died, who drowned while swimming in the Nieman. Sarah is my father's sister, and Minne is my father's sister. Almost every Saturday, holiday, either we visited them in their house or we were going out, on the Naburus, that means near the river, where we were running around, taking wildflowers, and having a good time, I would say. For some reason or another I remember the flowers which have a very round type of appearance, and when they blew, it flew away. I don't know what the name [probably dandelions]. And after a couple of weeks there were a tiny button-like green fruit which was not edible. But we had the song "run around the beigelach," we called. Then also there were yellow flowers, and different wildflowers, what we enjoyed.

Now, I will return to the event in August 1914. After a week or so, all Jewish population got an order from the tsar.[3] I must say that Lithuania was under regime of the tsar; Lithuanian language was not allowed and was punishable by imprisonment, and they had to teach Lithuanian clandestinely. Within twenty-four hours we had to leave Kovno. This is also very memorable, that we put everything together, our pillows, and blankets and pots, whatever we could, we loaded on a horse and carriage, and we went to our relative. This is another sister of my father, Yente; there were two daughters she had. We went to [a place] called Žežmary. I wouldn't know how many miles it was, but I do remember that the horse got stuck in the deep sand, like dunes, and it was unable to go. We pushed the carriage, we pushed the horse; finally we came there and we stayed there for a short time, and we returned back to our house, to our house in Kovno. But it seems to be there was another order from the tsar that not only from Kovno but they [Jews from many areas] have to leave Lithuania. Because

3. In fact, the expulsion from Kovno began in early May 1915.

they suspected that the Jewish people, by knowing Jewish language which is similar, the derivate from German, may become spies for Germany.

Then we again went through the same ordeal. We went to, all the Jews went to the railroad station, we went to a train, we were traveling a day or two. As a child, at that time I was six years old, I would say already seven. I remember vividly, when the train stopped, and they said, "You can go out now." It was a small town, and the light was visible, the light over the leaves of the trees, and to me it was a fascinating picture. At night, the electrical light and the trees. We slept overnight at the railroad station. And then, the next morning, the Jewish organizations which were there, [*where?*] in Khorol, a little town near Kharkov, and then they helped us out. We stayed for a while in Khorol but we didn't like it. And then we moved to another small town called Izyum. Izyum is a little provincial small town belonging to the county of Kharkov. This town Izyum—the word "Izyum" means a raisin, but that was the name. Now in Khorol, also I remember, we rented a little apartment which was near a river. In the spring it was flooding, and we had to make, erect like little bridges with plain boards over wooden horses to walk out to the streets, because there was water, and in the house was water. [*What were you doing for money?*] For a living, my father opened a grocery store. [*How did he have the capital?*] Now, we were helped by the Jewish organizations, and by the people who supplied these—The money they got is from the local charitable Jewish organization and from the people who were selling. But we didn't like it, we got the letter from Rostov-na-Donu [Rostov-on-Don] in the south of Russia, when we had some friends by the name Pakus [*Eli spells it.*]. These people wrote that we should come to Rostov-na-Donu; it's a big town and more possibilities to make a living, and more, better opportunities for education for the children.

I want to tell you, which I also remember, that my grandmother, maternal grandmother, was with us, and she, may she rest in peace, was very sweet. She always was hiding *kopkes* (it means a penny) and hiding candies, and when we behaved she was giving each child a penny, a *kopke*.

But she got very sick, and she died from pneumonia, and this is very—This I remember clearly.

Then we moved to Rostov-na-Donu. Rostov-na-Donu, a major metropolitan city, beautiful city, and we moved in a suburb called Nakhichevan. And to go to the center of city, we used these so-called trolley-cars, or tramways as they called, with the wires overhead. There we lived in Rostov with a rabbi together, Margolis. And that was already about when the revolution started in Russia.

[*How is it that they kicked you out of Lithuania but they let you live in Russia?*] Before we left for Rostov-na-Donu, the revolution started. There was excitement in the streets. There were parades, going with red flags, and they were singing "Internationale," and saying, "Down with the capitalists, with the murderers, and with the tsar. Let's live the proletariat, let's live Trotsky and Lenin." And we had—we children were watching, the excitement from the people, everybody had a red flag, and slogans about the new regime of the Proletariat [pronounced in the European way, with stress on the last syllable], and the eventual victory of the Communism. [*How did your family feel about the revolution?*] My family's reaction is hard to say, but I think they were stoical, and they saw that nothing can be done, and they didn't probably like too much the tsar, maybe they hoped that with this Communist regime, that's my speculation, there will be better times.

Now we came to Rostov-na-Donu; there, we established in Nakhichevan a little, it is called ice cream parlor, with a candy store and fruit. I remember we children, at night, we had our fruit, and watermelons, and grapes, and all type of tropical food, outside the store and inside, people were coming from all over the city because we did a very good job. We had different type of ice creams, and early in the morning we had by hand, we had to turn metal drums, with the sweet cream and sugar, vanilla or chocolate, and we had also different kinds of pastries, and we made a very nice living. It wasn't near our apartment house, but it was, oh let's say, about, fifteen minutes or a half hour walk to our house.

Then in 1917 or '18, the tsarist army, or the White Guardians, as we call it, the *gladetsy*,[4] occupied Rostov-na-Donu. There was fighting going on, you could see dead people on the streets, dead horses, horses who died and killed by compression the people who were riding, and it was terrible. Then again fighting in a couple of weeks; the Red Army took over, and then again it went to the White. Several times the city changed the hands, till finally of course the Red Army was victorious, and they settled there.

I must say that my brother Maishe, at that time, was mobilized. He was taken by the White Guardians in the military. In spite of the fact they were antisemitic, anticommunist, they took him and he was working for them.

While it was changing, when the Red Army came back, one—early in the morning, we heard a bell, ringing. I came out first, and I saw there was an old-looking man with a beard and I didn't recognize him, till finally it hit me that it was my brother Maishe. Seems to be, he escaped from the White Guardians army, where he was taking care of the telephone lines, and he escaped; he deserted the White Guardian army and [went, later] to the Russian army. He came back to our house. He was with a beard, and completely unshaven, dirty, with plenty of lice. And my mother cried, everybody cried.

And then there was the Red Army. Then again, attack, and this White Army started to attack Rostov-na-Donu. My brother decided, because he was a deserter, he was afraid they may catch him, and that would have been terrible, went to this, our ice cream parlor, in the backyard—in the back room, excuse me, where he was hiding and covered himself with a lot of boxes and cans, they shouldn't find him. And imagine, at that time when the White Guardians came, they were in the backyard of the store, but they didn't open the backyard [the back room]; they were all looting. And what we did at that time, to make appear that it was looted already, we opened the front door, we took out and broke the windows. And he was hiding there, while the door was open, and therefore they didn't touch anything,

---

4. I have been unable to find a definition for this term, and it is possible I misheard it when transcribing.

and they didn't look in the back. Then finally the Red Army took over, and then he was able to go out of the hiding, and he became an ardent Communist. When we came back to Lithuania he didn't want to go back. He wanted to stay in Russia.

[*OK, you are ten years old at this time, you lived in three different cities and two countries. Talk a little bit about what your life as a Jew was like and your education and your customs there.*]

Of course our Jewish education started when I was already five or six years old. I remember clearly the name of the teacher was Mayerson. And usually we started to have in the morning, and come in the winter time, was already dark when I came home, and there we studied. When we came to Izyum—to Khorol—there I studied also with a rabbi, a *melamed*. But we were not staying there, as I mentioned before, too long, and we went to Izyum. Izyum we were a little longer, and there everything is—thanks to my sister Chaya, who talked Russian, and was in a Russian gymnasium, and she was the one who guided us all through the years and even taught me and my brothers Russian, how to write and how to read.

There we went to a national, they called, a tsarist type of school, a public school, where I had to go to quite distances. Now in this school, there were, I would say, 95 percent or 90 percent gentiles, and we the Jews were few. Of course we looked differently, maybe we didn't have a *payah* and yarmulke, but I wore tzitzis, and I was making *tefillin* every day and praying three times a day. But when we came there, there was the icons on the walls, with a big cross, and a pope was coming, and they also had, so-called coaching into the Russian religious topics. And they had, let's say, with special writing in Russian Slavyonic type of script. I had to learn that, and when we tried to say we are Jewish, they said, "never mind, you have to stand up, you have to pray." The only thing, we didn't have to cross ourselves. That they didn't compel us. But what I remember, going home each time, I had to go different streets because we Jews—I personally remember on me they were throwing stones, attacking you, beating you up, but in spite—[*Was it by kids or adults?*] Usually we were attacked by kids the same age, maybe a little older, one or two years. [*Was that Izyum?*] This was Izyum. [*How about in Kovno? Did you see anything like that?*] No, in Kovno we didn't experience anything antisemitism, and I don't remember anything to tell you we were beaten up. But I will come later, when antisemitism started in 1934, 1935.

But the main thing that we experienced as children, they were molesting us, and beating up, and in spite of this difficulty we continued to go and study. When we came in Rostov-na-Donu, as again the charitable organization helped us, and we went to a shul there, in Nakhichevan, and there we [were] meeting children in free time in the backyard. There in the shul, of course where I was going every Saturday, and *yomtavim* [Jewish holidays], and even became a member of the choir, with the *chazzan* [cantor], and I was singing on the Jewish holidays, like Rosh Hashanah and Yom Kippur; I was a member of the choir. I even remember now a certain melodies, which were carrying on and, imagine, at that time I was staying Yom Kippur almost all day and Rosh Hashanah praying with the *chazzan*.

Interestingly enough—I want to mention about the shul which I remember well. When I came I was a newcomer among the Jewish boys. We were playing in the backyard, we call [it] "Yampolke." You know what it means, Yampolke means you take a stick with sharp edges from both sides, you put beneath [it] a little stone, and with another long stick you hit it, and when you hit it, it goes in the air, you hit it again, and it flies. And the more you are able, the more points, then you are the winner. But when I came as a newcomer, they started some, especially a redheaded guy, he was a little older and stronger than me, irritated me, molested me, and called me names and so on. [*A Jew?*] A Jewish fellow, in the backyard, in Rostov; we're talking about Rostov. And he came and he says—and I said to all these boys, "Hey, boys, come into the backyard, I want to show you something." And this fellow with the redheaded, with the freckles, and he was irritating me and made me mad, I said "look boys, I will show you that this guy will never go to me near." And I gave him such a beating that since then I became one of the heroes and became friendly with this guy. Now this is the moral: If a person goes too many times and you're taught, you finally react, "Hey fellow, you stop it!"

That was one part. Now my education, I can tell you, consisted partly with the Jewish religion and mostly, at Rostov already, I was at that time already twelve or thirteen years, going to gymnasium. Gymnasium is equivalent like high school here at that time. And it was a Russian gymnasium, so-called Shershevskovo; Shershevskii, he's a Jewish man, who was the director. There we had also lessons in Hebrew. And I was going there for a couple of years, and I can tell you that I learned a lot of Russian from this school, too.

We had to go with the tramway, or this trolley car. I didn't have open money and sometimes I wanted to save the money for a movie, or the money for ice cream or for some others, and I tried to go like a stowaway. Then we were hanging in the back, were hanging here, and when the conductor came we jumped off from the trolley car. In the beginning I didn't know, I jumped the wrong way, and I fell on the ground. But we managed this, and that's when I continued with the school.

Now in 1918, '19, things became worse, in this respect. Why I continued in this school under Russian domination, I mean the Russian Communist domination. It was difficult with getting food, it was started famine or starvation in all of Russia and in Rostov-na-Donu also. First of all, we didn't have water, in the winter, we had to go to a pump near the house in Nakhichevan, and imagine there is cold like in Alaska, because there is hot summers and very cold winters. You go with a pail, and you go up and there is a hill of ice, you go up, you have your pail and you try to go down, Bingo! Everything spilled out and you go again and you bring it. Now the main thing was to make a living. We had to close our store there. [Why?] Because we couldn't get supplies, number one; number two, the Russians were looking at any people who were enterprising as remnants of capitalism or capitalistic enterprises, and they just, we were afraid and we couldn't get even merchandise. The only thing we could do, there was like a marketplace in Nakhichevan, and we, buying bread, let's say, and selling bread, and we make profit to have for us at least a few slices of bread profit—bread—no money, but bread. Otherwise if you ate it up the bread we didn't have money to buy it the next day. Several times, and then we also had thread, needles, little tiny things which we could sell it. But the Russians made many times, we call it *oblava* [a raid], it means, *oblava* means they surrounded all our, from all streets, and were catching those who were selling. They didn't like even this, they didn't want any enterprise, this already is the beginning of the capitalism. And to make the story short, they have rations, we starved. One day they would have dried fish, salty, the other day they would have salt, the third day we will have sugar, or peas or pea soup. That was all we could have, and we really starved. [*Did they give your father a job?*] No, we didn't have a job, nothing. [*Where did you live then? What was your house like?*] Now our house was heated with a stove, a coal-burning stove, and also wood-burning stove. Now we had to supply these. I and my brothers were going, and I had to carry, let's say, I remember, a whole sack, a canvas sack, with coal I was getting, and bringing home, going for miles bringing home to have some for the coal stove; also wood we were getting, to keep warm.

I got sick; while in gymnasium, I had chills, and I felt very, very sick. There was an epidemic that time in Russia called Espanka [Spanish flu]. It was in 1918, the famous influenza epidemic which we now have still people who went through. When I came home I told my mother I am very, very sick. She put me to bed, and I became delirious. The only thing I remember is seeing rats going over the chest across my bed, and various types of wild pictures, imaginary of course. And I was sick for a long time, and I remember that an Armenian doctor came at that time to our house, and I think, in retrospect, that he gave me an injection intravenous, was Salvarsan. Excuse me, this is a later disease, I have to—yes, mixed up. I had the epidemic of flu and I was sick. Then a couple of months later I got sick similarly. But then we called this Armenian doctor who gave me Salvarsan because I had "typhus recurrentes," recurrent fever, which has two or three attacks between a free period. I think he gave me Salvarsan. Salvarsan is given usually with perhetapaiada [?], when the person has lues [syphilis], but this wasn't lues, but it was a recurrent fever. I had two attacks, I think a third was too. I was very sick, but this Armenian doctor, really, I should say, saved my life. This is a spirochete obermaierikh.[5] (You have a lecture in medicine, Burt.) Typhus recurrentes: I probably have antibodies for that. That was the second time. Then there was also an epidemic of cholera, people were dying within twenty-four hours. But the government then gave us, those who didn't get sick, gave us cholera immunizations. And I got, I still remember the pain, I had sharp pain with swelling in the arm, but this saved me against cholera. [*Did anybody in your family get cholera?*] No; everybody got an injection.

Now, as I mentioned before, we came to Rostov-na-Donu because of Pakus, who told us that it's better. And it really was better; it's a big metropolitan, beautiful city. [*Where is that, in the south?*] This is near the Black Sea, called Azov Sea, and yet Azov goes in the Black Sea.[6] It's a large, nice town. Now they have over two millions. I see sometimes people, I talk to them, who were in Rostov-na-Donu, even in Izyum or Kharkov, and they tell me the changes that took place. There we got letters from Kovno that we should come back; it's no sense, we should come back. Now, we had, as they say, back—It took about ten days or two weeks, from Rostov-na-Donu through Moscow to come to Kovno. We were all starved. [*How did you go? By train?*] Train, yes.

In Rostov we stopped for about two, three days, I even went with some other guys to Sokolniki, at that time I didn't know what part of Moscow it is.[7] But many children I know got lost, because they left the train and the

---

5. According to Stevens's 1898 *Manual of the Practice of Medicine*, spirochæte of Obermäier is a microbe that causes "paroxysms of high fever that last five or six days" (260).

6. The Black Sea, surrounded by Bulgaria, Romania, Ukraine, Russia, Georgia, and Turkey, is a much larger body of water than the Azov Sea, to which it is connected in the northeast by the narrow Strait of Kerch. Rostov-na-Donu (Rostov-on-Don) is in southeastern Russia on the Don River, just northeast of the Azov Sea.

7. Sokolniki is a district in the northeastern part of Moscow. A train from Rostov to Kovno would have passed through the Moscow area, and even today a journey

parents, and the train left, because we never know when the train would leave. We took a chance, and we went. Then we came to Kovno. Again, what stuck in my memory, we were so starved and so hungry. And it came a cousin, Ozhinsky, she was formerly—this is the sister, from Genya and Rivochke. And then, she brought us to the railroad station hot chocolate, bagels, candies, and other stuff. [*In Kovno?*] In Kovno. Imagine what it meant to us. I still remember the taste. It only points, that things in life, everything relative, things you miss, and you don't have it, when you get it, you appreciate. And I will come to this same subject later, about our real values in life, and what is valuable and what's not.

Anyway we come to Kovno. To make a little shorter, in Kovno I was accepted with my education, and my studying (in Rostov-na-Donu, mostly, and my sister Chaya was the tutor), in the third year of Russian gymnasium, a cooperative of former Russian teachers but who were tsarist [and went to Kovno] to escape from Communist Russia. [*What year was this?*] This was in 1921. [*Is Lithuania independent now?*] Lithuania became independent after the [First World] War. It became independent with the capital city Kovno. Historically the capital city was Vilnius.[8] Now there in gymnasium—[*Now you came back without Maishe, right?*] Maishe was left; he wouldn't go back. [*Was he married at this point?*] No, he was not. Then I went to the gymnasium, and we studied there Lithuanian and all the subjects which was required. After four years of studying, before going in the fifth class, you had to take exams. All the subjects you had: arithmetic, geography, history, Lithuanian history. And then, you were permitted to attend the fifth year, the fifth class. There were eight classes. Of course, the other three years we had to study astronomy, algebra, higher algebra, geometry, and trigonometry, and of course Lithuanian language, German

---

by train from Rostov to Moscow would take between seventeen and twenty-eight hours.

8. Kaunas was the temporary capital of Lithuania from 1920 to 1939, when, the result of a complicated series of military actions, the previous (and current) capital, Vilnius, was ceded to Poland.

language. German language I studied in the third year, and they were very strict because we went on the high level six or seven years. We already had to write about Goethe and Schiller, and even had to memorize certain things from Goethe. Heinrich Heine wasn't allowed, but we were reading Heinrich Heine too. And I think we got a very good education and then after eight years in gymnasium, eight classes, we had to take so-called state boards where a member of the education department was present. First we get a written examination, and then we got an oral examination. It was tough. They gave us a month to study and to prepare, but I remember what struck me, our German teacher Pinagel. I was getting a four. The worst is two, three is "satisfactory," four is good, and five is very good. I was getting four in German language. And when it came to the written work, she says to me in German, "look" ([in German so that] even they shouldn't hear, from the members of the educational [board]) "what happened to you? You were so good, and now they mixed up. I made it somehow you got satisfactory. Now I will ask you orally, answer me." Anyway, I made the state board, for receiving, [as] they call it in Europe, a certificate of ripeness; you are ripe, you are certificated, and with this certificate you can apply to schools [*university?*]; any school—university—lawyer, or theology, or medicine, veterinarian, or dentistry, all type of schools.

Now, when we lived in Kovno, we came there from Kovno, we moved to Slobodke; this is a suburb, that is the place where later during the Nazi regime was made a ghetto. We lived in Slobodke for a while, and then we moved, as far as I remember, on [to] another place in Kovno, in a small town, and my father was working again in the brewery, Wolf-Engelmann brewery.

[*How many rooms did your apartment have?*] At that time we didn't have too many rooms in our apartment, I don't know, I don't remember. In Slobodke we lived on the second floor, like in an attic, we had about four rooms I would say, and in Kovno, where we were before Slobodke, we had to make a living for survival, when we had a cow, first one cow, then we had two cows, we had a goat; and I was given every morning goat [milk], because a doctor thought I had tuberculosis, a female doctor thought I am suffering from tuberculosis but was wrong—[*And what did they give you, goat milk?*] Goat milk, as a treatment, and fresh air, and good food, and sweet cream, and cakes, all these carbohydrates. I think it was a good idea, after starvation. And then we had this, and I remember that the cows, were—We took them to the pastures, but at night they were coming themselves, what was amazing. They knew, each cow knew where to come to their stable, or their place. We didn't have to worry. If sometimes they got *farblunget* [lost], a cow, we were looking, but they came there. And we had chicken, and eggs, in other words—we had milk—. [*Did you have land?*] No land, no; a backyard. [*Then where did the cows eat?*] What I tell you, every morning they went to a pasture outside, not far, maybe about ten houses. There was a big pasture near the river. There where the cows were going. And that was the parents' initiative; they had to do something. I don't know where they got the money to buy a cow, but we had plenty of milk, we had cheese, made cheese ourselves with a towel, and we had sour cream from the milk, and we had butter, and we sold part[?], that, we made a living. We didn't starve at all.

Then from Slobodke I was going to school in summer and winter. As I told you, this Russian school. Now this was on the other side of the city, and I would estimate about four or five miles I had to walk every day, through a bridge. Winter and summer. To go to the school. I didn't have money for the buses, or I even didn't have money to pay the toll for walking, they charged, through the bridge. And my brother, *alai v'sholom*, Motteh and I, this guy asked money, [he] said doesn't have it, wouldn't let us go. Then we had a fight and he hit him. We had a fight because he wouldn't let us go, we said we had no money. That was the way, every summer, every spring, in April, the ice was melting, and usually the bridge was washed away, but we had to go to school: what did we do? We had men for a few pennies, *kopkes*, cents, was taking us with a boat, about ten people in a boat, with oars, and the boat had to go between the ice particles from one side to another, at night coming the same thing back. But we never stopped going to school, we were going to school because we had to. Then we moved to Kovno in the center, I believe as I told you, there near the river, and also near the fish mart. A fish market.

My social life in gymnasium was—we had to study but I still had friends, we met each other, we were going to the river in the summer, and the beach, we were taking trips with the boats, down the stream till Kalatove [Kulautuva]. Kalatove was a resort place from pine trees. All Jewish people went there. But coming back we had to ask the steamboat he should take us upstream, we had to pay him something, but finally he didn't like it, he said, "next time I will not take it, I don't want this monkey business. You go here is OK, but the boat you can leave there," but the boat was rented, and we had to return. Sometimes I got wild, went with a canoe too, which I wouldn't allow my children. And this is until I finished the gymnasium.[9]

I was in gymnasium until 1927. (Did I mention about the exams, and everything, did I? [*You did, you came out cum laude.*] But did I dictate that? Probably I did.)[10] Then in 1927 I applied to the University of Vytautas the Great to the veterinarian faculty, because I knew they wouldn't accept a Jew in medicine. In 1928 I switched to medicine, I was accepted. Unfortunately we had to make a living and I had to work, at the same time attend school. There was no limit how many years as long as the tuition was paid, and I took every year a subject, and I made it until 1934 or '35 when I was drafted. And then, from then on, I finished the other three years and in eight months I get my state boards.

---

9. Kulautuva (Kalatove, in Yiddish) is described as a "settlement in the Kaunas district, 19 km west of Kaunas, on the right bank of the Nemunas River, midway between Kaunas and Jurbarkas. Kulautuva served as a popular resort area for the residents of Kaunas due to having 1500 acres of a dense pine forest and being near Kaunas. . . . Hundreds of Jewish families from Kaunas and the surrounding areas used to come to Kulautuva each summer even before WWI." (Levin, "Kulautuva.") When Ida and David Robinson (my father's oldest brother, who lived in New York) visited the family in 1931, they were treated to a picnic in Kulautuva.

10. This is the first mention of cum laude in the audiotapes.

Of course, while in gymnasium, in the same class there was Misha Meerovich and his sister, Serafima. I fell in love with her, I was invited many times to her house because Misha Meerovich was my friend. We were talking together, he was a very—[11] I'm returning now to the activities in the high school or gymnasium. I was admitted in 1921, and my brother-in-law was admitted and his sister Serafima to the school in 1923. And he was admitted with me when I was already in the fourth or the fifth year. He was a very bright young man, a capable man, he was—he never prepared his homework, he knew when he was present at school, he remembered, he memorized, and he was, in all type of science, or literature, philosophy, he was very adept, he finished with high marks. His sister was also in the same class; we had, at that time, a co-ed school. Now, many times we were walking together, he was talking about Schopenhauer, and Nietzsche, and other things, and I would say, partly my education was also through him, and his education, he got from his father who was a pharmacist, a very intelligent, cultural man.

Now, there I had also, there were mostly gentiles, about 30 percent Jewish, 30 percent gentiles.[12] I had a lot of gentile friends, we were going out together, meeting each other, and there, no signs of antisemitism, or any hostility, was present. The teachers also didn't show any hostility towards us, and we—it was a very neat, close group together, the children, the students, and the teachers.

As I mentioned before, in 1927, I received my certificate of ripeness, or, in other words, eligibility to be admitted to any branch of the university. I applied to the veterinarian's faculty, because I knew a Jew wouldn't be there accepted to medicine. There I was one year; I was studying that time certain subjects, and with the credit I had, I was admitted to the Medical Division of University of Vytautas the Great. I must say that we were very poor. My father was working hard, and my brother Abraham, he was working too.

---

11. Here the first side of tape ends, and side two picks up as follows.
12. Eli likely meant 70 percent gentiles.

He didn't want to go to school. And at one time my father suggested to the mother, "why should we go to school, it's hard with money?" and so on. And she said so long as I want to go to the school, I should continue it.[13] My brother Motteh also was in gymnasium, and he finished before [me], he went to the medical school a few years earlier.

Medical school was very tough; there we felt the antisemitism. We had to take oral and written examinations, but the oral was from fassing[?] subjects only, and the written was also, but this was when we had so-called state boards. Mostly was oral examination. We had to face the professor, and whatever he wanted to ask, he asked. He knew your name, he saw you are a Jew, and naturally we had the most, the toughest questions. I was working also part-time as a bookkeeper, and making a living, and my wife after took it over when I was drafted to the army.

When I was drafted in the army, by '34 I already had my two years, main years, to go to the clinical part of the medical school the third year. And that time was this colonel, a very nice man, the doctor in charge of the hospital. And when I told him my story, he says, "Don't worry, after six weeks, the usual training, you will be free, change your, take off your uniform, and go to medical school." And while I was one and [one-] half years in the army, the same time, I only till about 9:30 I was in the hospital, working. [*You said six weeks in the army . . .*] Six weeks was basic training, but the army you had to be more than one and a half years. And from there I was going daily to school, and I made my third and fourth year, and taking concentration in that I spent a number of years; first of all was hard to pass the exams even without working, but I was able to do it and in 1939 I had all my credits, passing all examinations, and I was finished with medical school, I was no [longer a] student, and I received a certificate of a candidate in medicine.

By this opportunity I want to tell you that everybody was getting [the certificate] June fifteenth, but my certificate they delayed because I didn't

---

13. Later in the narrative, Eli retells the story reversing his parents' opinions.

have eight years credit in Latin. I had only four or four and a half years' credit. And they demanded that I give them a certificate of successfully passing the examination in Latin language. I then hired a theologian who was talking and writing in Latin, and all summer I studied. And when I finished, when I took the exams in theological faculty, I passed the examination. And when I came to the office of the dean, [of] the medical school, the man whom I knew well, was very surprised; he said, "Gee, that's terrific!" And then I got the certificate.

I want to return back about the difficulties in the exams. This is a different system in Europe, especially in Lithuania. We had eighteen subjects, and each time you had to pass oral examination, and face the professor. I had an argument with the dean of the medical college, he was the professor of physiology. Each time he failed me, I had to go two or three times; he said, come in a month, come in a month, and in a month. At one time—And the people, usually the students were waiting outside, and [there] were one or two inside he questioned, and the other outside. One time he said, you come in a month; I got mad, and slammed the door, and then he said—they told me after, a girl, a medical student told me—"You know, he made a remark about you, he said you got mad, he almost broke the window, but I will never let him finish the medical school." Of course I got upset and so on, but finally I passed with him the physiology.

Anatomy was a different chapter. The first year of medical school we had one part of anatomy, and the second year we had the second part of anatomy. We had to do all colloquiums, about thirty-six colloquiums, we called otiology, strasnology [?], neurology, and so on. In addition we had brain studies, and so-called, called, the tracks, various tracks going from the brain. But this professor, his name was Yelinski, he was a known antisemite, and people couldn't pass from first year, many times, and to the second year, or from the second year to the third year, because he wouldn't pass the examinations. And the Jewish fellows sometimes go three or four years, studying all anatomy to pass. But he was such a cruel man, that after you answered all questions, he says—gave another question. If you didn't know: come in six months, come in three months. Anyway, one young student, already three or four years, and he didn't pass, he told him to come in three months, he jumped at him with a knife, and he wanted to kill him. But then the assistant Kropotky came out. And I was then in the building there, nearby. He came out and saved his life. But the man was committed to an insane asylum where he committed suicide. And that was only an illustration how hard it was in Lithuania, especially when you are a Jew. I think Lithuanians, the natives, didn't have too much problems, they have their notes in Lithuanian language, whatever they had, and they passed them immediately. It only was trouble with the Jews. [*Did you know the guy that stabbed him?*] I knew him; I don't remember his name. [*Was he crazy?*] This man who attacked the professor was not crazy, he was just mad and he couldn't suffer anymore. That was the story.

Now, I had to overcome many obstacles: Number one, I was poor, I didn't have money; number two, I had to work; and number three, I had to also face the antisemitism in medical school, and the difficulties I had to overcome. But finally I made it, in June 15, 1940. That was the last day, the last exams I took in histology, and I passed it; we heard that the Russians are coming. The Russians moved in their army on the pretext of protecting Lithuanian independence, and the Russians, it still was the so-called [Lithuanian] democracy under the President Smetona, but after a month or two, they concocted elections for their favor, they elected the Communist officials, some from university even, some members, some professors. And the president ran away to United States, and after November, Lithuania became Lithuanian Socialist Republic. They introduced their money. I was that time—1939, I received my candidate of medicine; in 1940 I already got my, I passed the examinations, and I got my diploma as a doctor of medicine. Then I started to work already, and I worked in several places. That was one in the *krankenkasse*.[14] The other was an internship in the university. We

---

14. Josef Griliches explained to me that Lithuania at that time provided health care to all government employees. The *krankenkasse* was where they received these medical services.

didn't have any difficulty under Russian regime, because antisemitism was strictly forbidden, punishable by prison, and everybody was sweet and nice to us. But we knew that there is an underground favorable to Hitler; that was already in 1940, before the war started. The war with Poland started in first of [September] 1939.

But, I want to mention, that the antisemitism started already as soon as Hitler got the power in Germany; that was in 1934, but it was quiet. When the Russians came—I want to mention also, in my social life, we were going out many times, Sundays, or weekends, we were going to café, restaurants, drinking, dancing, having a good time. But in 1937 and '38, it was dangerous to go on the street before we were attacked by the Lithuanians, the boys, and when we went to a cop, he says, "I don't see anybody." He turned his head, and they continued, and it was very dangerous to go out in the street. The policeman, he turned his head and he says, "I don't see anybody." Anyway, once we beat up a few. There was a Jewish man, a boxer, he beat up one Lithuanian and we went into the Monica restaurant, and then came on the whole group looking for us. But because there were so many people, luckily, they couldn't see us. He came with other boys to beat up the fellow, the boxer. Well that was one of the situations and atmosphere we had in Lithuania. [*Did you see any antisemitism in Lithuania before that time?*] Now, I would say, before 1934, I would say we didn't experience; only after 1934, like the Germans started to send in merchants, which were the fifth column, spies for Germany. And they were propagandists who brainwashed the Lithuanians about the Jews, about the beauty of Hitler, victory in the future, and so on; we started to see signs of antisemitism. As a matter of fact, at the beginning when Lithuania was established in 1921, '23, we had Jewish ministers of the cabinet, so-called Seim[as], Parliament. We had even Jews elected.

Now, until—I was working in the hospital in twenty-second of June, 1941, when we were awakened by explosions. When I got up, I was told that the Germans attacked Lithuania, and the airport is on fire, and there is a war. Now here these few days I think will take quite time to tell what transpired from twenty-first till about, oh, I would say the twenty-eighth of June. I immediately left for home, and of course there was panic, and fear, and so on. As a matter of fact, the same day, the twenty-second of June in the morning, about twelve o' clock, I would say, Lithuanians had already put their national flag (we lived near the military museum) with the Lithuanian anthem playing. Now, this was the most frightening picture, they removed the Russian flag. In other words, while the Germans were not there, the Lithuanians already celebrate their independence, supposedly. And when I came home at that time, everybody, the whole people, converged to our apartment, and we didn't know what to do. The whole streets were full with people, carriages, walking with bundles towards the Russians, towards east. And—But I for some reason didn't move, I was afraid to go with the crowd. And I stayed home, and that evening I got a call to come to the suburb of Kovno, Šančiai to work in the *krankenkasse*, and I came there, as I said I should get a car in the Red Cross, of course Red Cross didn't give me any cars, I had to walk some miles and miles. And in middle of the night I called up the chief from the *krankenkasse*, and I asked him, how the condition. He said the condition is bad, all Jewish doctors left and he would advise me to leave, too, because it will be problems. I said, "What can I do?" He says, "You have a car, at your disposal there, in the aid station; take somebody who gets injured and you go home." Luckily a woman was pregnant, and she and her husband came; I didn't have right to do, but I told the chauffeur to go ahead. We took them to the center of Kovno, to the maternity clinic, a private doctor, and then I left and came home, that was already in the, late at night. We came home; of course the whole skies were, the skies were—It was late at night, there were explosions heard, and bright lights like lightning, from the German planes, illuminating, and looking for places to attack.

I came home, there were a lot of people in hysteria, wondering; I know, the day before a lot of people left towards Russia. Anyway. The next day, about ten o'clock, we decided to go out and see what we can do, maybe we can go to the station. And then, at that time, we were surrounded by

Lithuanians. There were quite a few people with us in a group. And they stopped us and they said, "It is enough to spill our blood on the holy land of Lithuania, and we'll take care of you." And they surrounded with guns, with rifles, but they started to search us. There was one man, Becker, an elderly Jew, and they found *tefillin* and a *tallis*. "Oh," they said, "he is not a Communist, let him go." And while they searched others we ran back, it was not far from our house, and we went back in the house. The day before, no, the same day, we tried to go to the airport, my brother-in-law Misha, and his mother, and my wife and I—[*The airport?*] We wanted to go to, to [the] railroad station. We went to the house where her mother lived, and my wife remembered that she has no stockings, she forgot her silk stockings. I says, "What's the importance, without stockings, in such a time?" "No, no, I cannot go." Then we came back, and an hour or two later we got a call from a man, who said, that Mikhail Meerovich left a message that they left with the train that was the last train going to Russia. And of course, everybody was crying and screaming, and we missed everything, and we didn't know what to do. And it was terrible. In exhaustion, I went in the other room and I fell asleep, and then my cousin, Minne's daughter Paike, woke me up and she says, "Look! There is the Russians with the truck, they're going to Russia from the building." On the stairs on the fifth floor, there were living the Russian family, pilot family, and we went down to them to talk; they were taking the luggage. And he says, "No men, only women we'll take." And the women, when they left for the luggage, they said, "don't worry; you will go in the truck, and we will sit over you, they will not see you." That's the way it went, in the truck, there were soldiers with guns, and from both sides there were mounted Chinese soldiers with the guns ready, because the Lithuanians were ready to shoot any Russians.

I want to go a little back, in the situation on the front. This was the twenty-second when we went with the truck—this was the twenty-third; I am sorry—the twenty-second, when the war started—about twelve or one o' clock, the Russian soldiers were coming back from the front, exhausted, starved, and begging for water, and the Lithuanians wouldn't give it to them. And the Lithuanian partisan underground, when they were alone, not too many Russians, they were shooting them, just killing them, on the streets, wherever they saw them.

Now let's return to this truck. Now we went with the truck to, with the highways towards Russian border, and the highways were full with people, trucks, tanks, the soldiers, the Russian soldiers were so exhausted and dirty, and from dust covered, we couldn't recognize their uniforms, the face, they were sleeping on the tanks, and everything was rolling back, many tanks were broken, many trucks were broken, and the German planes were firing from machine guns from the plane, and a lot of people were killed. Anyway, we intended to go to Ukmerge, but we were told there is too late, because the German parachutists are there. Then in the middle of, while riding, the chauffeur and the Russian pilot from the truck came out, and they knew, we already showed up, and they said, "out of here," and we begged them, we said, "look, what will you, leave us in the middle? What is the difference?" He said, "you better go out"; he put the gun, he said, "we'll start shooting if you don't go, that's an order." Anyway, we had to go with the other people walking, and we changed our direction. And wherever we go, there were the Lithuanian underground, where cut off the road and they were surrounding the Jews. Then finally we turned over of the main road, and we saw a small farm, and we stayed there. There we stayed one night, and the man says, look, his son is a partisan, an underground, they will find you, will kill you. You better leave it. Then we went to another town, where we stayed overnight.

Now, there were a lot of Jewish refugees, and then a man came and asked who is a doctor, they need a doctor. They took me to the forest, a man took me with a gun—he had a gun, a rifle—he took me in a carriage and we went through the forest and we came to see his wife. And when I came to see his wife, she had meningitis. I told him she is very seriously ill, you cannot leave her here. She has meningitis. You have to take her to a hospital. And he—Then some of the—in the farm, in the yard, there were a lot of young men with rifles, and they said to him, "What the heck you have to tell him? Let him go alone." He says, "No, I brought him, I will take him back." He gave me bread, eggs, and lard, or bacon, and we went back to the place, there I found out he was one of the chiefs of the underground in that section. We slept overnight in a barn, and then early in the morning he woke up, the owner, he said, "Look, I cannot keep you. You have to go back. You have to go out, because there will be plenty of trouble. I am sorry. I know you are in bad shape, but you have to leave." And we started to go back to Kovno. It took us about two or three days to go back. [*Didn't you know you'd be in trouble in Kovno?*] Now, here comes the story.

First of all, we already knew and felt, before we left with the truck, that the Lithuanians already started to surround the Jews wherever they could and kill them on the streets. In Slobodke and Kovno, and blood was flowing. Before the Germans came, they were just killing the Jews. I want to tell the story, that the night before we left with the truck—this I found out after—the rest of the people in our apartment and from the building went into the superintendent's apartment. The superintendent himself went to the sea resort, Palangen [Palanga] there, and he wasn't home, and she [presumably his wife] kept them. Then they were going in, in our apartment and the other apartments, and then they went finally to her and says, where are all the Jews? She says, all Jews left. But she had the Jews there. [The tape is interrupted by a ringing phone.]

The question is put down, why did we go back to Kovno when we know that they are killing the Jews? Now, where could we go? I was with my wife and child, and there also other people there with their families, we couldn't go no place. Because we were, from one side were the German parachutists, and from the other side, were the Lithuanian underground, the fascists, the Nazis who were looking for Jews and Russian soldiers, and we couldn't help it. We had to go back.

But before I return to the, how do you say, coming back to Kovno, I want to tell you following story. I sent a little note to a doctor, Mishelski, who was not far from the farm, or the barn we were, and asked him if we could go there to him. The messenger brought an answer and he wrote,

"Please don't come back, because all Jews are killed, I am the only one alive, and I am not sure for my life." And we saw that we cannot go there. And we started to go back to Kovno. Going back to Kovno, we saw a lot of tanks broken, dead Russian soldiers, dead civilian people, and the sight was horrible. Now coming near Kovno, some women, Lithuanian, stopped us and they asked where we are going. We tell them "to Kovno." She looked at us, she cried, and she said, "Please don't go." Why? "It is bad, it is bad." But we had no choice, we had to come back because we were surrounded. We didn't have a place where to be. Nobody wanted to take us, and nobody cared, and wanted to help us, because they were afraid of the Lithuanian partisans. A paradoxical situation developed. That we saw that the Lithuanian partisans [were] very hostile to us, and while going there, going back, we were surrounded by Lithuanian partisans, in a little forest, and they told us they will come more people and take us away. And we knew that that's the end. In the meantime they saw two Russian soldiers on bicycles; as soon as one told the other, "Look, there is Russians," they said, "You stay here in the forest and don't move. We go after them." They went after the Russians, to catch them, and we went, immediately ran away from the forest and were hiding, and we heard that they were looking for us that time.

Now, we started to return back to Kovno, and on the way that the Lithuanian women were crying and telling us not to go, but we knew we have no other choice, we had to come back to Kovno. The paradoxical situation developed, in this respect, that we hoped to see the German Wehrmacht, or the German military, because there was a difference. The German soldiers were not involved in politics, they were not involved in killing Jews. They are looking for some Communists, they were fighting men and we were waiting with them. And sure enough, as soon as we saw the German soldiers we had a feeling of relief. As a matter of fact, they gave candies to the children, they talked to us, and I asked him how to Kovno to go, and he said, "everything is free, the road, you can go, nothing to worry." At that time, they gave an order to Lithuanians, wherever they occupied, not to attack the Jews, and not to do their own justice, because they will do it; in other words, the SS will come later.

Coming back, as I mentioned again, the Lithuanian women warned us what's ahead. There we stopped in a suburb of Kovno, quite a distance, called Karmelita, and there we came in; there were a lot of German soldiers with trucks, and cars, and jeeps, and everything, and we asked one of these men from the town, please let us stay overnight. He says, "You know, I know your situation, but not now, while everything is full of Germans, still. And you go ahead and hide somewhere around, and then come at night." Sure enough, we came at night. He brought us food and he stayed with us. And he says, "In the morning, before the sun comes up, start moving." And we start moving, and we were going—[*How many were you?*] We were there, maybe ten people, or twelve people. [*Where did you sleep?*] In a barn. We slept in a barn, with the Germans. The Germans were in the same yard there, like in the lion's mouth. But we stayed there overnight; he was very nice, this man—[*Lithuanian?*] A Lithuanian man. We were going back, towards downhill, towards Kovno.

I want to mention that we going downhill, this street, long street was leading to our house. There some of the people said they want to go through the bridge to Slobodke, and some said to go this way. I said, "Don't go to bridges. In case like this, in a war, there are soldiers watching the bridges, and it's dangerous." But they didn't listen. But we and some group went down, home. I actually heard they had a very bad fate going to the bridge.

When we came home, we found, of course, Germans were all over. My brother was with his wife there and we went to our apartment, and we stayed there. The killings from the Lithuanians stopped while the German army came. And then there was a notice to the people, to the Jewish people, in Kovno, that by August 15, we all have to leave our apartments, and go to the ghetto in Slobodke. And in August 15, by that time, around, we took whatever we could, our belongings, in a horse, carriage, and we went to Slobodke. In Slobodke we had a little tiny room, maybe twelve by ten, or even less, and the tiny hall in the front and that was our quota. [*Were you with your brothers and sister then, or were you with your family?*] The only brother was Abraham, who came also to ghetto but he lived in another place. [*And your parents?*] Going about this fate of my parents; when the war started, my brother Motteh was a doctor in a small town, and the mother was with him, and there was a man who told me after, in concentration camp, that he begged him to come back to Kovno. No, he said, he doesn't want to. It was near Shaktiel, near Shakiai, we call the town, a little town in Lithuania.[15] And, I understand, they had the same fate like all other Jews in the small towns. There they were, they just came, and were killed. And Abraham and his wife and daughter were there in Kovno. [*Were they killed by the Lithuanian partisans or by the Germans?*] By the partisans. They were killed by the Lithuanian partisans.

Then we came by fifteenth of August, the ghetto was of course already had barbed wire, there were soldiers around watching, we shouldn't go away. Then the Germans came, they had a speech, assuring us that nothing would happen to us, and that everything will be fine, and we shouldn't worry, the only thing we should comply with their directives. We should work, and they will get a ration, and all sweet talk. [*Now I want to ask you: What did you know about the Germans or the Nazis or Hitler before the Germans took over Lithuania? What did you expect?*] Now, we in Kovno were realistic, we knew that if Hitler had his way, there will be annihilation of the Jews. Those German nationals, Jewish German nationals, who ran away and came to Kovno, said, "Oh Hitler is not that terrible. It's only a propaganda, he doesn't mean what he said." But I say, "Why did you come to Lithuania?" "Oh, they don't let us work, they took away our business," and so on. But in the beginning they trusted him, and they thought that he doesn't mean what he said.

---

15. In 1981, when I collected information on our family for pages of testimony to be sent to Yad Vashem, Eli indicated that his mother and brother Motteh were living in Plokščiai at the time of the Nazi invasion and were most likely murdered there. Plokščiai is in Shakiai (Šakiai) district or county; the town of Šakiai is the county seat.

In Kovno, in 1934, because of Hitler getting more power, there was a lot of antisemitic manifestations, and the Jews were very uncomfortable. Those who were smart and could, left for America, or outside, even Australia, or China. I couldn't get it because the American consulate told us that there is five persons a year from Lithuania, [and I couldn't go] because I was born there. My wife could, she was born in Leningrad, she said she could go any time to America. That was already under Russian domination. A lot of people went to the NKVD of Russia and got false papers and with false documents, and they got away to China, Japan . . . no, to China. In China they were there of course as prisoners, but the conditions were not too bad at all.[16]

Now let's return to the ghetto. They had a big speech about work, and about food, and about everything, but the first week they said they needed five hundred persons, intellectuals, to work in an archive to prepare the documents. [*When; when was this?*] The end of August, the beginning of September 1941. They took, at that time they took five hundred men; among them was my brother [Abraham]. The police came to my house, and I wasn't there; and somehow happened, I was to Rosenthal, going as a—I knew them, somebody was sick, I went to their house. The Jewish police came and says, "We need your husband, to go to, to work in the archives." She says, "My husband is a doctor," she doesn't know [if] I will be able to come. He says, "He has to, but however he is a doctor, forget about it. We will not touch him." Among them was Abraham, [*What did Abraham do?*] he was working for the supply of food for this ghetto government. [*Was he an intellectual?*] He didn't want to go to any school, he had a very nice, beautiful handwriting, he was intelligent, he finished five years gymnasium, and he says he wants to work and support the family, because I and Mottel

---

16. Although the NKVD now suggests the Stalinist secret police, it also, at that time, included ordinary police functions. Jews in China were prisoners after the Japanese occupation, but because they were foreigners, not because they were Jews. As the narrative suggests, some survivors who have written about this experience have fond memories of the time, despite the restrictions. See, for example, Marcus and Krasno and "The Holocaust: Japan and the Jews."

were studying, and for the father is hard. And as I said before, my mother wanted us to stop, but the father says, "No, let them continue, they want to study."[17] Now Abraham was among them. [*So why did they choose him as an intellectual?*] That was enough for that job; he's not a laborer. When they took all the men and they came there to a certain place and they counted, and there was 502 persons instead of 500. The German punctuality, they said, "We don't need 502, we need 500." My brother and somebody else, [they] said, let them go back together. Among them was my cousin, David, he is Lubovsky, the brother of Genya and Rivochka Lubovsky. And the next day we found out they all were shot, that was the first action from the Germans, we all knew.

At the beginning, the ghetto, I joined the biggest labor force going to the airport of Kovno, rebuilding and building the airport, and doing manual or physical labor, carrying cement back, mixing cement, and doing a lot of heavy work. And we could see in the morning that the Russian prisoners were brought, too, to work, and they were holding each other in a line going to work, and there were also horse carriages where the dead Russians were put there to bury them. They starved terribly. They didn't give them any food, and youngsters, fifteen and sixteen years old from the SS—I saw like a Russian fellow, soldier, went to, stole a cabbage head from a carriage, and he went to him, he took his [rifle] butt and killed this man, and they were killing for every little thing. They were going twelve hours, with almost no food. They were held in a certain barracks outside Kovno, and they usually went miles and miles by foot, and there, they lived there in very miserable conditions.

But I heard the speech while under German domination in ghetto, I heard the speech from Molotov, who said to the Germans, "I know what's going on in the occupied lands, I know your attitude toward the Russian prisoners. It is against the Geneva Convention. But if you don't stop killing our prisoners, I promise you that no German soldier will be taken alive

---

17. Mother and father are reversed in the earlier account.

as a prisoner. You better stop." It seems to be that this helped. They killed, from one hundred thousand Russian prisoners, they say, about ten or five thousand were alive, the others were killed, or starved to death, or heavy work by the Germans. Then, as I said, I worked for a while as a laborer but after, the ghetto got organized, and they appointed me and some other young doctors to work as a physician in the same place, with the working crews in the airport building.

This was till about the twenty-seventh of October. When we came the twenty-seventh of October, 1941, we found that the ghetto was in terrible turmoil, there were all over placards saying that all population, sick, old, and men, and women, and children, should converge in a certain place in ghetto for inspection or some other pretext, and anybody who is found in the house will be killed in his house. And if those who cannot, sick too much, they should take some carriage or carry him to the place. On the twenty-eighth—[*Were you aware that that was a pretext, at that time?*] We suspected it was a pretext. I have it written in a Jewish paper, there, I think, about the twenty-eighth of October selection, the Nazis. We came there, six o'clock in the morning, it was a snowy, wintry day, cold, dark, of course we didn't have any lights, when we came to the place, and we waited about nine or ten o'clock, till the Germans, SS, the Gestapo came, and they started to sort, one goes right, the other goes left. And at that time, my cousin, Shloimke, Minne's son—I forget to mention, she had a son Shloimke, and she has a son Eli, too; Eli left, [he] never came back, we didn't know, before the ghetto was established. But Shloimke became a Jewish policeman and he tried, wanted to make sure that they don't take us the wrong place. We had a feeling, they took the old, and children, and sick people on one side, and the others, more or less healthy looking, they took—[18] And when we came back everybody was crying, and was a panic, and they found out from the Lithuanians over the barbed wires or differently they shot them; they put them on the mass graves which the prisoners had to dig themselves,

---

18. Here the second side of tape ends.

and they were shooting machine guns, and those who was still alive they shoot again even in the grave, and that was the first action. Not only in Lithuania but it was in Latvia, Estonia, and other places of German domination. It was an order from Hitler, and it was the first thing.

Then the ghetto was more or less quiet for a while. Of course before each Jewish holiday they always find a pretext to hang somebody, to kill somebody or some other atrocious act there performed. Every day we went out from ghetto, but we had to have some food. The ration what they gave was very meager; and as a matter of fact, after a time they even stopped giving that also. What we were doing, we were taking some belongings, shirts, ties, or socks, whatever we had, and if we didn't have our own we took from other inhabitants of the ghetto, for commission. [*You stole it?*] Our own belongings! For commission, some people had a lot of good stuff, I would say, and for a certain commission you took it out and went, and we were trading with the gentiles, with the Lithuanians, and getting some food for that, and I had to return whatever we agreed to give to food. Sometimes there were searches at the gates from the German even the Jewish police, and they took away whatever we had, [what] we brought to the ghetto. The conditions were terrible. We starved, we didn't have any food, and always in danger to our life. I tried, some of my friends, Lithuanian friends, doctors, to meet, and I went out despite the fact there was an order if you go out with a Jewish star alone and they catch, the Gestapo, they will shoot you. But I had to go out. I went to Dr. Mayofski who was near the airport. I talked to him, he says he will do something to hide the child, and after a while he said no he cannot; if it would be a girl he would have done, but it's a boy he cannot. [*Why? Because of circumcision?*] Right. He cannot do that, and he doesn't want. In the beginning he was coming to the ghetto trying to help the people, his friends, with food, till the Germans told him if he comes again he will be arrested. [*Was he a Jew?*] No, a gentile. Mayofski. I went with the star to see him. And he went to help to the gates of the ghetto to see some friends and give them food and the guards told him if he comes again he will be delivered to the Stapis[?], stop to come, and he stopped coming.

I also risked once and went to Dr. Wishnievsky who was in the center of the city, but this time I took off my Star of David because in the city, a lot of Gestapo men, they will see a Jew with a star they will definitely catch him. I took it off but I took a risk and went to him and asked what he can do for me. He said no, he cannot do anything, he cannot help me; he was afraid himself, he was a Russian, you know. And that's that.

Then I was assigned to work for a short while in university, the same university where I was an intern. And there in this—while I was working outside I knew the ways in the underground corridors and the connections. I went through and some of these nurses saw me and recognized; they looked at me with such a pity but they didn't say a thing. I went to the pathologist—assistant pathologist—to his place, because Dr. Zacharin, a surgeon in ghetto, wanted to get something, and he was making packages for him, but this Zacharin never gave me a piece, what I risked with my life to go and bring him. And I brought him several times, packages, after I stopped. He also gave me certain things to give it to him to sell, and get for product the gentile pathologist to sell. And that was one part of this way we had to make a living.

[*What did you know about the Jewish police? What was your attitude towards it?*] Now, the Jewish police want to save their skin; the Jewish police had good food, and drinking, and cigarettes, and alcohol, and women, whatever they needed, because when they needed there are thousands of people coming from work; they just either told the Germans to search or they searched themself and took it away for themself, and they used the food, and food was a very important commodity, and for the food they could get anything, anything they wanted for food—liquor, cigarettes, even money. And the Jewish police, some were on the level and some were rotten. [*What was your attitude about them?*] My attitude was indifference. I don't know. I was in a state of shock and fog and I couldn't analyze and think about them because—Of course when they took away from me the food I was enraged, but you couldn't open your mouth. Anyway, you couldn't go again and protest. Because they were the ones who were selecting people going to Estonia and Latvia, to concentration camp, and other places. [*Did you know any of the Jewish police?*] Yes, I knew a few of them. Berman, he was a classmate from the gymnasium, this is the man who recommended me a job in 1927. He was Alonka Berman, very nice fellow, he was on the level. [*Did their attitude toward you change when they became Jewish police?*] No, no. I would say they were not brutal. They supposedly, with the Jewish Ältestenrat and the police, they supposedly were working with the Germans for the benefit of the people. [*Were they ostracized by the Jewish community?*] No, no. Dr. Elkes, he's a good medical man, was also assigned in Ältestenrat and he did a lot of things for the Jews. Now this continued more or less with certain atrocities until 1943 when an order came out that they need certain Jewish people to go to a concentration camp in a north suburb of Kovno, Panemune called. And it was a concentration camp, a lager, with a lot of barracks, but the way we heard they said there is good food, and they have to work, but it's not too bad. [*Had you heard about concentration camps at all at that time?*] There were rumors, yes, there are concentration camps. [*What did the rumors say?*] That it's bad, that's all. [*Were there rumors of extermination?*] About Auschwitz we heard rumors just 1943, '44, but we couldn't be sure.

Now, they wanted us to go to this concentration camp. In the ghetto was the conditions so bad that I have, in December of 1943, I decided with my wife to go to this camp. Here is a picture enlarged, and we are sitting in the truck and going to the concentration camp in Panemune. [*Did you have a choice about going?*] Yes, I had a choice. [*Did people try to talk you out of it, or no?*] No, I decided to go but then I thought I will have a better ration and some relief. [*Did you go with your wife and child, or were you separated?*] Here is my wife, and here is my child, somewhere here. . . . Here is our friend Beirak and she, Beirak, and here on this is looking some of our friends. This is Ginstein, Paula Ginstein from Vilna. Here we are on the truck going there to the ghetto. These are taken clandestinely. This man, he risked his life. He had a hole in the button on his coat. He took plenty of pictures. But this guy, I found out he took this and I got from him.

When we came there in the concentration camp in Panemune, the women, the husbands and wife and children could be in one place. There was a big room with bunks, and then my wife and child were together. And they had bunks. Every morning we had to run to work with speed. And a German was standing at the door and he said, *Los, los!*; make fast, fast. And those who didn't move got hit over the head. And as soon as the bell rang to get up they gave us five or ten minutes to have coffee and we had to run out to work. [*Did the child have to work there, too?*] No, the child did not work. He was staying in the camp. [*What did he do?*] There were other children. Nothing. They didn't touch the children, at that time. But I can tell you when going to work many times in ghetto I took the child with me, because there were rumors that when we are at work they will surround all kids and take them away, or old men; then many times we went to meet you [?] they said you cannot take the child there. But there in Panemune concentration camp from 1943, December, till about the beginning of March—then my wife got sick and she developed diphtheria and again they gave permit to go to the Jewish ghetto, to the ghetto in Kovno, and to admit her to the hospital because she had diphtheria. And we came back by horse and carriage and I didn't have shoes—I had shoes with holes. And while, it took about 3 or 4 hours with the horse and carriage to come, it was cold in the winter, and when I came the same night I developed chills, fever, terrific pain, in the left side, and I developed pneumonia, and Dr. Berman, at that time, was a physician in the ghetto and I was critical, I lost my consciousness, and they gave me some sulfa, I could, when I was awake. And they assigned a nurse to my bed; I was two or three days unconscious, till I woke up and the nurse screamed that I went out of my coma, and the relatives asked Berman what will be, he says God can help him, he is very critically ill.

Anyway, my wife had diphtheria and there was a doctor, a distant relative of my wife's, seems to be, Greenberg, and he was the guy who was going between the ghetto and Kovno city and meeting a lot of people, and he had diphtheria serum and I asked him to bring me some serum to inject for the wife and he says they have to pay me, and I didn't have [anything] to pay, cigarettes or money, or something; I didn't have any valuables, I was a poor church rat. Anyway, somehow he did get it to me, somehow I gave him something, and he gave it to my wife. Then we found out that my son got sick, and they brought him to the ghetto. [*What was he sick with?*] Meningitis. The same story, meningitis antiserum, I think we got some anyway.

Then came the twenty-sixth of March, 1944. There was the famous and infamous children's selections, in all Baltic states, and all children have to be delivered to the Germans. Imagine what it called. My son was sick, still, he was sick for a week already. And I tell to the doctor, Zacharin, look, bring the child here, he says I cannot. Anyway, I got the child without his permission. They were the Germans like wild dogs running all over the ghetto, looking for the children, going in the house. Women were fighting for the children, immediately shut the windows; they were fighting, surrounding the children, took them away, to Auschwitz, or somewhere, I don't know. Anyway, my wife recuperated, my son was feeling better, and while I took the liberty to take him in my room. And I had him under my blanket, with my legs up, and he was laying there. He knew the danger already, it was in '44, he was ten years old, yes, ten years old. I know they were coming, they came to the hospital, they looked in refrigerator, they looked in the basement, they looked in all rooms. Then they went—There was set partitions from cubicles for the patients. I was a patient after recuperating after pneumonia. Then there was a doctor sick on the other side, an elderly doctor, Orbach, and his wife was around, and when they came they took him, and they took him away. And they were taking the children from wherever they could. And it was terrible, terrible tragedy. They took a lot of children, some were able to save. Now, they took this old Dr. Orbach, and they took him away from the bed, and we knew what it is, and his wife knew, too. She asked them, what are you doing? Why are you taking my husband? He is nothing wrong with him. No, we'll take him. No, she says, you cannot take him; he is healthy, and he is a doctor. She says, never mind, and she was fighting. So he says, OK, come with us. We'll give you a good place. And they took her away with the doctor.

Now they were going on inspection, and here is what always in my mind, and I think about. They were going from cubicle to cubicle; in some places they found children, some guys, and they took it away. Now, I was laying there and, supposedly sick, and Dr. Zacharin, the chief of the hospital, introduced me to the Gestapo man. He says, this is a doctor, but he is a young man, he has a little cold, he will recuperate, he will be able to work. He was very nice to me, you know. I was probably white like this sheet of paper. You know, the Gestapo man gave a look under the bed, he didn't pick up the blanket, and he went out and said loudly, no, this room is OK, everything is OK. The other guys would hear, they shouldn't, you know—I have a feeling and suspicion that he intentionally didn't pick up the blanket, and he suspected that somebody is there but he let go, I would think. I mean, it was one of those rare Germans who had some conscience and couldn't see that, but they had to comply with the law and the instructions from Hitler. And that was, I was able to save the child.

And we were in ghetto till about, I would say till the end of June, and beginning of July. [*In the hospital?*] No, no. We went from the hospital but we returned to our previous apartment we had. [*Did you still have to hide your son?*] No, after that I didn't have to hide the son. [*Didn't they realize?*] No, no, that's OK. That is a certain group they send, and after it's OK. They didn't do anything. And we came to our one-room apartment, and there there were—Many times they send out supposedly for searches the White Guard[19] and the prisoners, with lots of soldiers, the Russians who deserted to the German side. And here we had the same trick. We had cut a hole in the ceiling and camouflaged with the papers there; the whole ceiling was with paper. We had a lot of, we put it inside and when they passed by we had the doors open like I did in Rostov-na-Donu; the doors were open, everything was empty, disarray, and when they came in, the Russians, the soldiers, they said, Oh, they cursed, nobody's there. [*The Russians? Or the Germans?*] I told you, there were the Russian deserters who worked for Germany.

19. Eli here mistakenly uses the name of the old tsarist army in referring to Russian soldiers used by the Nazis.

The Germans send the Russians, deserters, to look for the Jews and carry out certain orders. And then we are hiding upstairs and we heard them, came there, "nobody is there." And another time when it was we were hiding beneath the table, they couldn't see us, they came in, they opened and they left. Then they broke the door from a little closet outside, a little place where you keep a lot of supplies, a pantry, they broke this, looked there for the people. [*Was the ghetto disbanded already at that time?*] No, the ghetto was still there. [*So they knew that there were Jews there.*] Yes, but they were looking, certain orders to carry out in the houses, to go. The ghetto of course was still in existence.

[*So were you in the ghetto now or not?*] Of course I was in the ghetto. From the hospital we came to our one-room apartment. [*And the Germans didn't know you were there?*] All Jews were there. I went to Panemune because I wanted to be, then they got sick, then they took us to the ghetto hospital—But we left a lot of Jews in the ghetto. I left in December of '43, but about 70 percent of the ghetto population was there like it was before, only 30 percent maybe left for Panemune. In other words, when I came there was no broken law; and they didn't ask us to come to Panemune; they didn't say so, you see. And we were in this apartment, and staying there in hiding, when certain actions, transactions were carried out, but we were able.

In the beginning of July we heard rumors that the Russians in 1944 [were] doing very well, and they were chasing the Germans all over, going to the Baltic states. The Germans felt it was getting bad and they wanted to have the Jews from the ghettos from the Baltic states deported farther into Germany. And then they decided the time is ripe to liquidate the ghetto. As a matter of fact before that they took from little towns where they still have a few Jews working for the Germans, they brought them all in the ghetto. They thought Jews could be left around in Lithuania there. Most of them, 90 percent, were killed, the Jews in the towns. But this working force, they took people from ghetto working force, they brought them to the ghetto. We knew that something is cooking very bad.

[*Was there any talk at that time, things are getting worse, there's talk of liquidation . . .*] Of resistance. Now, the question of resistance. There is a book from Yellin in Jewish, I got it from Israel. Yellin was a Communist, and his brother. He solicited young fellows, not married, mostly single—or young women and fellows—to go to the woods, the partisans, to have a resistance. And they joined the partisans, the Russian partisans, the Russian, Lithuanian underground to work against Germans. The trouble was that we heard they wouldn't accept anybody, they were afraid for spies and traitors. But with Yellin's recommendation you could go. [*Did you know Yellin?*] I knew him because his father owned a library in Kovno. I knew Meir Yellin and the other Yellin. I have a book here. Anyway, one of the Yellins once went out, and it seems to be somebody told the Germans, they were after him and they killed him; there is a description, how he killed himself, actually, he was surrounded by the Germans, he shot at them—But that's not the whole resistance. The resistance was a passive resistance where the Jews first of all brought a lot of equipment, not militarily but other, food, and chemicals, and so on. Number two, they changed the gates from certain munition factories, instead to have the right side, they sabotaged. Wherever they could and whoever was involved in the underground was doing, not everybody, and I don't know how much trouble they caused. [*Did you know anybody in the resistance?*] Yellin. [*But I mean personal friends—*] No, I didn't. It was very clandestinely, and nobody—. [*Did anyone approach you to join?*] No. [*Never?*] Never. [*Was there any talk among you and your friends about starting a resistance?*] No—People were afraid to talk, and they didn't talk; and they were not in the mood to talk. They were depressed, starved, and in fear. In ghetto was only passive resistance and organizing these people who would go fight against Germany in the woods. And about the resistance in the woods and the trouble the partisans, the anti-Nazi partisans, did to the Germans was known. They derailed trains, there was shooting. They [the Germans] were sending out the native Lithuanians to fight with them in the woods because the Germans were afraid, themself. And that was the story, about that [. . .][20]

While in the ghetto we saw that a lot from Jewish people were passing the gates from the ghetto to the Ninth Fort, and some people were able to talk through the gate and they told them they are going to a new settlement. But the settlement was for—and the Ninth Fort where the Germans killed a lot of French Jews, German Jews, and others, in the Ninth Fort in Lithuania.

[OK, so it's July 1944 . . .] Beginning of July 1944. Before that a certain event happened, a significant event. They took some, before already in December '43, they took some people to the Ninth Fort, Jewish men, who were digging out the dead bodies and burning them on piles. But they gave them food and drinks and everything. And they were living there in the Ninth Fort with the Lithuanian and German soldiers. In December there is the famous escape, where a Russian engineer knew the all things from the all plan of the fort, and he, with the help of the Jews and with contact outside, on December gave their vodka ration to the German and Lithuanian soldiers. They got them drunk on Christmas, and then they escaped, with linen, through the fort down, and trucks were waiting for them and they all escaped, from the Ninth Fort, and the Germans was mad and upset. They searched the ghetto but they were hiding in the ghetto. Some went in the ghetto, some went to the partisans. [The Russians?] This was the Jewish resistance with a Russian engineer prisoner, you know, but they were all Jews. That's the famous escape. Now in the beginning of July [1944], or end of June [actually late March, at the time of the Children's Action], maybe, all police were called, they want an inspection for the Germans. And they all took them to the Ninth Fort and they all shot them.

---

20. This ellipsis indicates the one omission I have made from the transcript. Eli and Burt began discussing the Warsaw Ghetto uprising, but neither one had full factual information. Since it is irrelevant to Eli's own story, I omit the account rather than try to correct it. The subsequent account of resistance in the Ninth Fort is also at second hand and contains a few errors which I correct in the narrative.

[*The Jewish police.*] They shot the Jewish police. We knew that is ominous, and there will be problems. Even my friend Berman, Alonka Berman; one or two policemen were saved.

In the beginning of July there was an order that the Jews will be deported, but we should go voluntarily. And they gave a certain date. At that time people started to dig underground, and tried to save themselves. My [aunt] Minne and her children and Shloimke (Shloimke was still alive; he escaped the Ninth Fort), there was an apartment house in the middle of the ghetto and they dug under the basement. And they told me to come to give a look, maybe I can with my wife and child. I went there, there were thirty and forty people in a small dungeon under, and there was no air, and there was no heat, and no water, and I thought we will die from starvation. I wouldn't do it. And I said, I will not do it. We knew that the Russians are coming, anyway. Then we saw that people were voluntarily going, the Germans surrounded, took them to the train. [*What happened to the people in the tunnel? Did they get out?*] I will come to that. As I told you, we had an opening in the ceiling. And we decided instead to get killed there from suffocation we will go upstairs and hope for the best. The same stair. My brother, and his wife, and I and my wife and child went up. [*Your brother had a wife? Which brother?*] Abraham. [*Did he have any children?*] A daughter. I'll tell you about them later. We went upstairs and took the ladder and covered up, and there, you see, this was a one-room house, the whole house was in one room, and there through the opening of the boards I could see what's going on, and observe; and we were observing. We were there about two or three days. [*Did you have food up there?*] No, nothing. Whatever we had we tried to keep it going on. [*And no water, of course.*] Maybe we had water. We had a well in our backyard; maybe we ran out at night to get water at the well. Then in a few days we saw the ghetto, explosions and fires. We lived near the Catholic cemetery, nearby. And we're going for the—One part of the ghetto nearer to us, more fires, and then loudspeakers went that all those hiding should go out, because we soon will put dynamite, will explode, and put on fire. And I said no, let's wait, maybe they will not.

As a matter of fact, we tried to run through the fence on the Catholic side, which was not too bad, but there were Lithuanian soldiers who said, what do you have? You give me, I'll let you go through. They took away whatever they had, valuables, and they reported to the Germans. And we found out that was no sense to go because they were traitors. They wouldn't let you go through. They took away everything and that's all, and that's the reason we were staying, and couldn't escape.

When they came, the loudspeakers, the next day, near us, we decided to go out. And as soon as we go out we were surrounded by German soldiers. They didn't beat us up, nothing, we go to this point I think near the Jewish hospital, and there they took us when a lot of people were collected, they took us to the train, and in the train we were like cattle, in cattle wagons with no water, with no food, and they locked up the gates and it took us a week till we came. [*Did you know where you were going?*] We thought we are going to be shot. To kill us. That was our feeling. [*What happened to the people in the tunnel?*] Later; it will come. We went for about five, six days, in the train, they said all women should go out. [Now Dad speaks in a soft and tender voice, here to the end of "I'll tell you about that, too."] And we had our child with us, he was ten years old, and I said to my wife, what should we do, should he go with you or with me? She said, let him go with you, better. She gave me what she has, rings, earrings, other valuables, keep it with you; take it. And I took him with me. She was left in Stutthof, near Danzig [now Gdansk]; I'll tell you about that, too. And we went from there. When we came to the concentration camp Dachau, it was a big field, the Germans met us, and they put immediately to work on barracks. There were barracks already erected but they made more barracks. After a while, a couple of weeks, they started to have bunks for us, and there started the ghetto [concentration camp].

Now I will come to the concentration camp life later. But before that, I would like to mention what happened to the people who were hiding. After, the Russians came about five or six days later [to liberate the ghetto] and there is already in ghetto. Now I would say that a lot of people were digging underground holes to hide themselves, and among that killed were also Minne and her children, were killed there, in the bunker, because they exploded the apartment house, and there was only one group who dug enough a passage underground in the middle of the yard where they survived. But the trouble is they didn't have—couldn't go out, because the apartment house was demolished; there were no way [to] escape till one person knew—a Jewish man, I don't know how—he told the Russians, look, there are people hiding in the middle [of the yard], dig 'em out, and they dug them out, and they took them out alive. They were for five or six days. [*Was this the tunnel that you were going to join?*] No, this was in another, farther. Their tunnel [Minne's, was] under the basement of the apartment house directly. That, they [the others, who were later rescued] were smart enough to dig out and make a tunnel outside. There they were trapped by the debris and the cement and the bricks of the apartment, you see. And they couldn't go out. They would have died if not this man, called their attention; there must be people living there, hiding. And they dig it up and they found them—they were alive. Winick and others, a few people. [*You heard about this years later, of course.*] After the liberation we heard the story. [*So the people in the tunnel that you were going to go into—*] Not a tunnel; it's under the basement a hole, a dungeon. They all died, because of the explosion and fire. But you know, I told you, the Germans were going, and ripping up all, house by house.

And then we came, as I told you, by train we came to Germany. We came by train to Dachau, we came there, there was a big speech from the *lagerführer*, it means this man in charge of the concentration camp. And he said, you fellas should remember, you came here to work, and if you don't work we know what to do with you. And if we Germans lose the war, don't be so happy about, because you will lose, too. That was the greeting speech. After that they started to have groups, finding out what profession, what type of things they can do. At that time you should remember there were already not very old people, because the old all were killed. And they were sending to work. I was assigned in the beginning to Moll construction company, about six or seven miles from the concentration camp, where I was doing as a laborer work, as a matter of fact they assigned me once on the scaffolding for underground airport, to work with cement and picking up these pails with cement and letting down by rope, but I couldn't work because I couldn't stand any height, and I told the Jewish supervisor that I can't go. He said, never mind, you'll come the next day. But next day I joined another group, I didn't have to work this way. This was for couple of months, working until they assigned me to a first-aid station for this Moll construction company in the woods where I had wood for the wood stove to burn in the winter, but I didn't have any food; I really was starving. And at one time there were three shifts, there were working about five or six thousand people from different concentration camps, you know. One of, a Jewish supervisor came and he tells me that, hey, he'll give me some food. What does he send in? He sent me the peel of the potatoes. He had food plenty, but he gave me the peels of the potatoes. I had a stove, I boiled it, I ate like a horse, and then I got very, very sick. I remember I had palpitations, I got weak, I couldn't move, and then Dr. Goldstein (he doesn't remember that), Dr. [Lazar] Goldstein came and he says, look, they all come, already ready to go, they're missing the doctor. They cannot know, what happened to you? I said, I got sick. [He said,] You better go, you'll be in serious trouble. We were without guards, you see. Then I went out and came there, everybody was waiting for me. And one of the guards went and gave me *whoosh!* and I fell down, but I stood up because otherwise they would kill. And then the other German guard told him that he was wrong, I am a doctor, he shouldn't have hit me, and that's all. Every day going to work, going back, we were singing Russian songs—Russian—and the Germans loved it. They asked us to sing the Russian songs. [*Why did they love it?*] Because it's a good melody, and hundreds and hundreds of people singing, you know, it fetched them up. And that was the ghetto for a while—the concentration camp.

I worked as a doctor and once they assigned, from the ghetto they assigned me to go with a group of concentration camp inmates to the baths, to *entlausing*, because they're getting lice, to get rid of these, people, and we went there with some German functionary and we were there, and we all had to undress and wash and coming back, and they were waiting and then I asked one of the Jewish *kapos*—a Jewish *kapo* is a Jewish functionary for Germans, who supervise. I said, Look, can I go with them to a concentration camp, why should we stay there. He says, go ahead. I went ahead and a German stopped me, why are you going? I said, the *kapo* said—He said? He has no right to say. We have to say. To make a story short he said, take off your pants, and he gave me twenty—Now, that's one of these episodes.

Then, they assigned me to this—in December, started to appear these flecticles, or typhus exanthimatico, typhus fever, from the lice, and it was the first cases in the camp and they made a quarantine and I was assigned to the intermediary between, but Dr. Zacharin, in spite of his all bad features, gave secretly to me and Dr. Berman, supposedly, immunization against these flective.[21] I know it works, because a lot of people after liberation got sick and I didn't. I had been immunized, and once I said—you shouldn't talk to anybody, and once I talked in front of somebody to doctor Hahn[?] and he said Sssh, because it was secret. And how did he get? He got it from the Germans. He explained to the Germans that we have a few cases, and the doctors should be protected, and, sure enough, the Germans gave it to him. It was a big secret.

In December 1944 I was assigned to a quarantine of people who had typhus fever. Now, I was working there and at the same time they put me on the list of doctors in the *krankenreview*, or so-called little hospitals from the concentration camp. I was going every day to the Moll, back and forth, and I'm getting weaker and sicker, going out from the concentration camp going to work, there was a little hill, and I couldn't make it. And once Dr. Berman saw me and he says, look, you look sick, and *zog ich* [I say],

---

21. At one point Avraham Tory notes, "Dr. Zacharin is a responsible person, but for various reasons he is not popular" (227). Clearly he was kind and helpful to Eli on more than one occasion (including the visit of the SS to Eli's hospital room), while at other times Eli saw him as less than generous.

Look, Dr. Berman, I am sick. I am starved, the legs are swollen, the scrotum is swollen, the belly is swollen, I cannot last anymore. And I knew a lot of people, when they came to this stage, they developed a diarrhea, colitis, and that was the end.[22] I said I will not be able to continue it; I am very bad. He said I will try to make an opening for you in the *krankenreview* and sure enough I was there relieved from the duties going to the construction company, and I ate better, and after a while there, in December, developed the typhus, they assigned me to this place in a separate quarantine within the concentration camp. And as I said before, I was immunized. There was another doctor, Greenberg, I can tell this, who was having a very good job outside the concentration camp, and having food and having everything. He was one of these guys who were able to accommodate to each condition and not to suffer. Anyway, after the quarantine ended, in January or February, he wanted to stay in the hospital, but the Germans had a certain quota, how many doctors. And Dr. Berman told me, you know what, I cannot help it, he gave cigarettes to Dr. Zacharin, you didn't have it, I will put him on the place of you but you can still be in the hospital and when the Germans come for an inspection you will hide in some of the barracks. Anyway, I did it for a while and then we started to go again; I felt better, I started to go to the Moll construction company in the first-aid station. And here certain developments are very interesting.

About end of March or beginning of April—['45?] '45, yes. A German soldier was coming and talking to me, bringing me one day potato, the other day bread, and trying to be friendly. I was frightened with this goodness, here there's something suspicious, probably from Gestapo an agent. He wanted to find out, he asked me questions; What do you think, the Germans will lose, or no? I said, I don't know, I am here a prisoner, I don't know what is. Look, I am telling you, we are losing. And I didn't make any reply. Then he opened, he says, Do you think I am SS man? I have SS man's uniform; here, look, I am Wehrmacht; I am soldier, military. He put that

---

22. Here the third side of tape ends.

on me. I am not the same thing. The reason was he wanted to have some-body to protect him after the war. About the twentieth of April the guards didn't pick us up to take to the concentration camp. We were waiting, and waiting, and they didn't come. We know that something is cooking. And, sure enough, after about five to six hours they came to pick us up and we came to the ghetto, there was the *lagerführer*, the chief of the concentra-tion camp, [who] says, Voluntarily, whoever wants, we will transfer him to another place. And there were a lot of volunteers who agreed to go. I was, agreed, too, and Zacharin says, You go as a doctor with them. I had already everything ready. And I will never forget, a guy from Kovno comes to me and he says, You are so stupid, Why the heck you have to go? Isn't this bet-ter to die in ghetto or going there to the Alps and be shot in the Alps? At least you have two or three days life here in ghetto—in the concentration camp, I mean. You are better off. Don't go. And I listened and I listened, and I think, He is right. Why should I? OK, then, I took off my rucksack and didn't go. Berman found out, he was mad like a dog; I said Look, I don't go, and forget about: I will not go. And I want to mention something, two days before, I exchanged my ration of bread with a Russian prisoner. The Russian prisoners were also, too, but they have a separate part, and theirs a little better. I gave him bread and he gave me potatoes. The potatoes were rotten, but he gave me a whole bag of potatoes and I kept it and then I took from the hospital pharmacy a lot of tablets, Decalcit, called, it is a Swiss vitamin D and calcium tablet, which has a lot of sugar. I took about five hundred pills. Then came the last call and the *lagerführer* says, Look, only the sick and unable people will stay there. The others should leave the concentration camp. There was no choice. If you are the old and left, you will be shot. Then we went. [*Was your son with you at this point?*] Oh, no, this I didn't mention to you; I will tell you.[23] And he said, you have to leave.

I want to mention, that in the beginning, when we were in the concen-tration camp, when we arrived in concentration camp, the Germans said

---

23. This statement, an aside, is said in a very soft voice, the same soft voice Eli often uses in this narrative when referring to his son, "the child."

that all children should be in the morning in a certain place, and they will take them to a child camp where they will have all good conditions and be fine. And there was Dr. Kaufman, he had a child, and I, and a lot of people had children, and the next morning they put all people in the—for counting, the people, and the children, too. While we were waiting for the count or *appel*, I ran out; he was in another column. I said, Burt [Borya], go ahead and take the sweater. And stupidly enough I didn't tell him to stay there. Because they were all going outside, the Germans will come and kill them out. And he went for the sweater; I asked after, this man there, who was the supervisor of the bunk, he says, My son? Yes. Did he take a sweater? Yes. I says, you are lying, he probably wasn't here, he took the sweater for himself. He says, Yes, he came and he took, and he went. And then I got a *geruss* [regards], in November or so, that he is OK, and everything is fine, then he's playing chess with the other boys, and nothing wrong. After the liberation I found out that in spring of '45[24] he developed measles, and the Germans saw measles, and they liquidated. That's the story, and I couldn't believe it, and he told me, and a man, he was a three, four years older told me, that he knows Burt [Boris], and he knew what happened, and that was the story, with him. Then I was very happy when in November the Hungarians came from Auschwitz, and they looked for me, and I said, how do you know to look for me. They said your son sent regards and he asked us to look for you. That he is fine. [*He was in Auschwitz?*] In Auschwitz.

I saw there is no choice, I had to go and we went by train, some type, we didn't know which direction. And there, the next morning, the train was attacked by English planes, or American planes. And they killed the engineer of the locomotive and each time there was an attack the Germans told us to go out, and when the attack subsided they told us to go back. A lot of people were killed at that time and one of these running away for shelter, I and another guy, Baikovich, I saw him, I says, look, there is no sense, let us go back, and the Germans said to go us back. We couldn't go

---

24. Since Auschwitz-Birkenau was liberated on January 27, 1945, Borya would have contracted measles earlier than the spring.

to the left because the railroad station was burning, other places, I heard, with those people who went there, the native Germans shot at them, probably they shot at them, they were afraid, and there was shooting and fire— [*Did you know the war was over at that time?*] I suspected, I didn't know the war was over. But then we went under the train elevation, through a, like a sewer pipe, with him, we went on the other side of the elevation, and there we felt entirely different atmosphere. It was quiet, and peaceful, and we start to walk through the forest—then we went with another few other refugees, I know Dr. Lichtenstein, he lives in the Bronx, and some other people—and we all went together and we slept overnight in the woods. Baikovich was very hungry and he says, I want to go to a German house and get some food. I says, You are crazy, you will be killed and reported, don't do that. And I remember when we are going already to this place we heard a truck coming. And we went down the elevation into a ravine, with boxes, cans, and something to hide, and we saw that there are German soldiers and higher [unintelligible] driving. I get out at night and then we were hiding somewhere and there are two houses, and we saw a German soldier came and his wife came out and she was crying, and crying, and she says don't go, he says, I have to go, and he left and then we saw it is dangerous. So what we did, we went, already started to get—That was the first day, I think. It started to get a little light, and we went, we saw a chapel, we saw a chapel in the road, and we tried to hide in the chapel. And, sure enough, we came up and there was, you know, there, religious artifacts, and pictures and everything, a little tiny room for prayer, what they have it all over Europe. And I went up on the shoulders of another and tried to open the boards to go up and hide. We couldn't, we couldn't open the boards. Then we left to the woods, and the forest, and we slept all night and the rain was raining. We heard shooting all over, from all places, and we knew that the Russians already or Americans are near, and we were sleeping there. Then, middle of the night I saw—one night I slept on [the] outside [of] the other people. The next night I said to Baikovich, Never mind; I froze all night. I will sleep in the middle and you sleep outside. I heard voices, and

I give a look, and then I see, the sun didn't come up yet, the two shadows coming out covered with protecting colors [camouflage], canvas, what they have. Usually the military, the German pilots had it, airplanes. And sure enough we heard them talking in a foreign language. And we got up—and, after, we saw the insignia[?]. And one guy took out cigarettes, the other took out bread, and he said, Here you have it. It was the biggest feast we had for a long time. Then as the day came on more people came, more refugees came in, and then on the third day, I think, it was twenty-ninth of April, a guy, a Polish guy (I have the description about this, too, a whole article) came out and said, the Americans are down the field, in the forest. I said, you are a dirty liar. And he said, you, doctor, are stupid. I am telling you that these are the Americans. And then he says, I will prove it to you. And he comes an hour later with a lot of food. And I said to the other guys, you know, this fellow there, he didn't get it [from the Americans?]. He says, You know what? You want to stay there, stay. To make sure enough, another guy went and we found out the Americans are [there], and he saw the American soldiers, motorcycles—and American motorcycles, and soldiers, we kissed them, and so on. And he went into a German place, and he says, Give us place for these people. And the German, you know, he still didn't want. He put us on the attic. And then on the attic this doctor—Mr. Koton, came, and he started to choke me. [*The Polish guy?*] He was a Lithuanian, I knew him—his father, his son—he got crazy, you know. And I took and I was fighting, till others separated us, and then we went down and they gave us food. [*Why did he do that to you?*] He got out of his mind, just like that. Suddenly he's free, and you know he didn't know what to do. Loss of senses, I don't know. After, he was embarrassed. They separated—He just choked me. Then we went down and they had us meat and pea soup and eggs, of course, and other people got sick, got diarrhea, but I was able. And then we went back, by the thirtieth of April we went to Landsberg-am-Lech, it wasn't far from concentration camp. There Dr. Nabriski came and I made things, and we have to organize a hospital. [*You know, Landsberg-am-Lech is where Hitler wrote* Mein Kampf.] Yes, where Hitler wrote *Mein*

Kampf and where this *lagerführer* Kurtz was hanged after a trial, he was in the prison and hanged after he was convicted.[25] [*The* lagerführer *of what, Dachau?*] Of our concentration camp, number one, where we were, where we had the famous speech telling us that we shouldn't worry; if Germany lives, we will live, too. We organized a hospital. We took from the German places a lot of beds, a lot of other things, and we had obstetrician, a dermatologist, I was the chief of the OPD [outpatient department]. Thousands of people we saw, and a lot of people had lice, typhus, typhoid fever, a lot of [them] died from the consequence. Some had got dysentery, diarrhea from the food, and there we spent our time as doctors, till March 1946 I registered there to go to America.

[*Wait a second. About the family, when you were liberated, how did you go about finding out?*] Now, after I got liberated I found out about the fate of my son. I couldn't believe it. I was hysterical, I was crying. I said, it doesn't matter, give it up. Then I talked to others, they were concerned. I had to face reality; that's that. I said, they told me in November he is alive. He says, look—As a matter of fact he had a brick with him to stand up to look taller. He knew what it is to be a little shorter. He was a tall fellow, anyway, and he was able to escape the fate until he got the measles. Came the measles, came into the doctor, the doctor needs to give an order. That was the terrible tragedy. About my wife, people were coming to Landsberg-am-Lech from all places, and there, women told me that she—my brother's wife and child, Sarah, in different places. My wife got dysentery. [*Your brother's wife and child, what?*] They were also in Stutthof concentration camp. [*They were alive?*] They had a march; the Germans took them to another place, and while this she got dysentery, and weak, and she died from exhaustion, starvation, and disease. My brother's wife had the same fate from Stutthof, in a different section, where they told me that she also got dysentery. And she was on a march with the Germans; she died from starvation, disease, and exhaustion. And when she died, and a witness

25. The prison, in the city of Landsberg-am-Lech, was separate from what became the displaced persons camp.

told me, that her daughter Sarah—she was then thirteen or fourteen years old—so she saw her mother died, she just lost her consciousness and she died at the same time.

[*Abraham, what happened with him?*] My brother Abraham, gave me the full report Marc Rubin—Marc Rubin, you know, from the laboratory. He was with him in the lager number 2. Dachau. There were 3, 4, 5; lager number 2, I was in number 1. I was able to communicate with him, with my brother, and sometimes send him bread. He was very honest. He wouldn't take a thing more than his ration, but he was assigned to give the bread to the prisoners. And once in a while he gave it to me a piece of bread. Then I found out that he was giving bread to some and the agent stopped [?] and he didn't give it to me, but I let him know through another guy in another camp, it was miles and miles away, please don't give because I don't get it. And then I told him that maybe he should come to lager 1; I told him I am starving myself, but he had a good position. Then the liquidation of the lager started, then they liquidate there, and there he could have a choice; he could come to lager 1, or lager 4. Lager 4 was infamous, we call it an elimination camp, where they killed the people by starvation, not by shooting. And to come here, but anyway, I found out, after, that they assigned [him] to go to Czechoslovakia. He had a lot of varicosities, and he had a little infection in the concentration camp. And he went to the mine, Joachimstahl mines, famous with uranium and other things, and there he got an infection, and he died from starvation, infection, and later, not fit to be a miner. That's what happened to him.

Then I went from Landsberg-am-Lech to go to the United States, but before that I also registered to go to Russia. [*What about Mikhail Meerovich, your brother-in-law?*] About Mikhail Meerovich, he went to Russia with his mother, on the train at that time. When after the war he came to Lithuania, he was working as an engineer, he developed a heart disease and he died of heart disease, in Lithuania, some years ago. The same thing as two years later she died, his mother, in Lithuania. Also from hypertension and heart disease. He never had any children.

Now in Landsberg-am-Lech I registered first to go to America and then before that I didn't know where to go, go to Israel or to Russia. I decided to go to Russia, still look for my relatives, because I wasn't sure about the fate of them—my wife, my child. I didn't know yet, till after a while confirmed. But I registered with the Russian major there, and [he] put me on a list to go back to Russia. And trucks with flowers and orchestra, and music, went towards Berlin, to Russia. And then, I knew [my brother] Dave's address, 12 Crown Street, and I saw a man, Poretsky, this is Dr. Perry's brother, a soldier, American soldier. And I gave him, he says he went to the States, I says give a letter to my brother. To Israel I didn't want to go, and I will be frank 100 percent. I had enough in ghetto and I had enough in concentration camp; there was a lot injustices from the Jews against their own Jews and I didn't feel like going there. I had enough suffering and I decided either I go to America or to Russia. But as the time passed, a couple of weeks, there were coming people, who were ardent Communists, crying and begging, not to go to Russia because as they came to there to the points of destination the Russians searched them, questioned them, treat them as criminals, and said if you are alive that means you were collaborating with Hitler; and the younger men they sent either to the army or Siberia, took away all their belongings, whatever they had, little, and they said not to go. Of course, then I changed my mind. And I got a letter from Dave, I should come to America, he would give me money for a plane, and so on, but of course no private people could go by planes, and to make a story short I went to München, to Munich, in March 1946 and there I waited for the calling to the American consulate. Now, there is a little incident where I was registered to go with the first ship, but someone from Lithuania, good friend, took over my place, and I had an argument with the man from the Joint Distribution [Committee], he was responsible for that, and I talked to the American functionary, the military officer, and he says you probably know why it is. I say, I know, why don't you tell me; I'd better not talk about that. I didn't know English; there was a woman who was translating my Yiddish to English. And then

I came June 18, 1946, I came to the United States. [*What happened with your being registered to go to Russia?*] After this Russian colonel or general found out that I don't go to Russia, he was mad; he says, you promised, you registered, you have to go. I says, I changed my mind. He says, you cannot change your mind! Remember, we will never forgive you, if you come to Russia [later] and you didn't go. I says, look, I have a brother in America, I go to America. You're making a mistake; you have to go with us. No, I will not go. That was the story. [*Were you curious at all about where your brother Moshe was now?*] Now, I didn't know about my brother at all, Maishe, until some years after the war. [*But did you suppose that he was in Russia then?*] Oh, he was in Russia, I'm sure he was in Russia. [*So you had a brother in Russia and a brother in America both.*] Right. We were not corresponding too much with my brother in Russia, and I didn't know [in] what town he is, therefore I went better to America.

Now, what I want to point out, several little things, which I think is interesting. I called this, silk stockings. The whole life changed because of silk stockings. Because if my wife wouldn't have insisted about silk stockings I would have gone with my brother-in-law, mother-in-law, my wife to Russia, and the child, and of course the child would have been alive, and I would have been a doctor in Russia in the army like a lot of other people were; that changed the life completely. Now, other things which comes to my mind, is Dr. Berman. I have a lot of respect, have and still have respect for this medical man and as a human being. He was the one responsible who got me a job in the *krankenkasse* in Lithuania when the Russians came, he was responsible for treating me in ghetto, and giving help, and assigning me a nurse, he was also responsible for pulling me out of these consequences of extreme starvation and exhaustion in concentration camp. And Dr. Berman really was a nice man and a friend, which I didn't realize until he showed me these deeds.

While in concentration camp, they looked for a doctor in a Belgian camp, and they wanted to know and somebody gave them my name. And they said that there is plenty of food; there is not a Jewish camp, it is Belgian prisoners, and I would have very well. I said, gee, it is a good idea. Then I went to Dr. Berman and I talked to him; what does he think? He says, Look, in life you stick to your people. Don't go in different places, because here in such a situation, you are going to a different place, you will be the only one with, unable[?] and you'll get into trouble. However, I had an appointment there, and, imagine, I went with the guard outside the concentration camp to the so-called, this *militaristube*, the house where they had the guards. And I went there and I waited for appointment. Then a German doctor, a big shot, came in and he says, who is the doctor, he has an appointment? They says yes, then another went to him, one of these low-echelon military men, and says, you know, he is a Jew, you know that. Oh, he says, if he is a Jew, then forget about. And that was fortunate enough, and lucky. [*Why?*] Because if I had gone there in Belgium, and they found out, after, I am a Jew, they would say you hided your identity, and I would be exposed to mistreatment and a lot of trouble. This way, I went to the—with my people.

While in the camp I also was in danger once, in the beginning, where they lined up a lot of people and they, one of these *kapos*, one of the German prisoners, a German prisoner, selected me to go to Lager 4. And I knew already Lager 4 is no good, somebody told me, and he put me there, in another column. There was another *kapo*, another guy, and I tell him, Look, Erich took me from here; he says, You? You're the doctor; no, no, you need to stay here. *Zog ich* [I say], look, I cannot do it, because he says I should stay there. Then he took a short man, a German Wehrmacht man, an *oberscharchter*[?], he says, Look, he told me the story, you know he is a doctor; he says, Let me see who it is. He came in, he says, that's the doctor? He says, Take him out! He took me out, and that was a terrible time to go. [*He knew who you were?*] The other *kapo* told him I am a doctor, then he put me back to the column I was, to stay in the concentration camp lager number 1. You know, you never know. But to go into unknown places in a camp is dangerous.

What I want to point out, Dr. Berman after the war made a remark; he says to me, Look, I have everything in America, he says, food galore, anything I want, and life is good, he says, but you remember when we got the watery soup in concentration camp, and we found a little potato, don't you think that was the best treasure you ever had? And that was the most fascinating remark, and truthful, because there were [it was only] water! In the morning you got a slice of bread with black coffee, and in five minutes you had to run out to go to line in the columns and they counted you ten times, for hours sometimes, because each time they count was a different count, to make sure nobody escaped. Who could escape, the stupid Germans? Who were, escape from the concentration—? In Germany? In ghetto, maybe, not in Germany. Anyway, then you got, you went to work. You came back 5:00, you didn't have anything to eat; maybe, I don't remember, in the lunchtime maybe they gave you a piece of bread; then you were, your supper, and they gave you the piece of soup, and that's all. And several times I want to be smart—and the Jewish concentration camp inmates worked in the kitchen, I had one like aluminum military can and the other is a plate. What I did, The plate I was hiding under my shirt, and the aluminum can I took it out first to get soup. I got the soup, I put it in my belt like this, with a hook, across my prisoner uniform, it was blue and white, the prisoner jacket, and then I went with the plate. And one of these *chikhak*[?] says, look, I notice you do it every day, several times; I will fix you up, I will report you. This bastard. After, he was sick, and I took care of him. After liberation, he broke an ankle, and before liberation in the concentration camp I give him a medication, Kuprex called, like now you use Kwell, for delousing—you were full of lice, after liberation—but he didn't allow me. [*Why did you take care of him, after the liberation?*] An order. [*After the liberation, you didn't have any order.*] After the liberation, yes. But he knows, he was avoiding me. But these guys, you see what [was] happening: they were taking the food from the prisoners, whatever there, they had all day, trading for other goodies, and taking away from the concentration camp people, and he's telling me, You're taking too much, there will not be left for the others, and we had water, two [unintelligible], no fat, nothing. That was the story of concentration camp.

Now, I came to the United States in June 18, 1946. [*What was the boat trip like?*] The boat trip was good, we were happy, we were having two or three tiers bunk, that was military ship. [*All Jews?*] All former inmates of concentration camps. [*Was it crowded?*] Yes, it was crowded. [*The food?*] On the boat there was plenty of food. The Jewish organization from New York gave $10 to each and we bought cigarettes and all other things, and we were very, very happy. We came in about five or six days,[26] in the morning, and we were awakened by screams; we see the Statue of Liberty. But they didn't go in, into the port, into the pier, until the sun came out. [*Do you remember seeing the Statue of Liberty?*] Yes. [*What were your thoughts?*] Oh, I was very excited. Then we saw a lot of people going to work, on little boats, going to work—I don't know: they do it now, too? There are a lot of people going to work and they were waving to us. Then we came in when the sun came out already; we came back, we saw this Statue of Liberty again, excited, happy, and then I was met by my brother Dave, and I stayed with Dave for about one month, and then I, without knowledge of English, I took a job as an intern, and [*What happened? You got off on Ellis Island?*[27]] Dave was in America, I was corresponding with him, and I was very happy, of course he recognized me, and I recognized him. As a matter of fact, he went into the ship to meet me, because he was working for the merchant marine, and after they bawled him out; he has no right to go in, even if he is working in that way. Anyway, I was with Dave for over a month and then went to the Maimonides Hospital; I got several offers as an intern.[28] I went to Maimonides Hospital for a year internship, $35 a month, with a lousy room with bats at night. [*How did you get it? I thought there was trouble in verifying your MD degree?*]

---

26. In fact it was twelve days.

27. Eli, in fact, disembarked elsewhere. After the Immigration Act of 1924, Ellis Island was no longer the main entry point for immigrants, serving only as a detention site for would-be immigrants whose status was questioned (www.ellisisland.org).

28. Maimonides Hospital (now Maimonides Medical Center) is located in the Borough Park neighborhood of Brooklyn. At the time Eli started his internship it was called the Israel Zion Hospital; it became Maimonides Hospital in 1947.

Oh, this is another story. Then I was working at the Maimonides Hospital, $35 a month, as I said, food was OK, but the room was terrible, with bats, and I worked all year; at the same time I studied English, I went to a tutor, I had to pass my examination in English and then pass my—after I passed the examination in English I was permitted to take the State Boards. [*Now you came back without Maishe, right*] The first of July, 1948 I got my license to practice medicine, after it took me eight months to take the State Boards.

After Maimonides, I took a job in Washington in the Casualty Hospital; I worked for a few months from seven in the morning, [to] seven at night. They put me in a room in the attic. At that time there were no air conditioning and I was simply suffocating, in spite of the fan. They asked me to stay, they said they would give me every week to go to New York, for the money, for the railroad, but I said no because I had commitments with the Swedish Hospital. I went as a resident to the Swedish Hospital and after that I decided to have some experience in lung diseases and I went for a year in Brooklyn Thoracic Hospital, where I worked the whole year in pulmonary tuberculosis doing pneumotology, pneumo-peritoneum, and treating—at that time they had streptomycin—and INH-PAS.[29]

While there I got acquainted with my present wife, Pearl, and this is interesting, too. While working in the Swedish Hospital they brought on Yom Kippur night, while I was listening over the radio in Temple Emanu-El, the Yom Kippur services. They told me to come down, and there is an old lady who fell down and busted her head. I came down, was an old, nice Jewish lady, and I talked to her in Jewish; Oh, she says, wonderful, you talk in Jewish. I want to give her a needle for anesthesia, she says, No, if you talk to me in Jewish, I don't need anything, and sure enough I put in about sixteen stitches, did a good plastic job, and then she was admitted in the hospital for further observation, skull X-rays, and observation. And then I met Pearl, a young healthy wholesome-looking farmer's daughter,

29. Two antitubercular drugs.

that's my usual taste, but I didn't talk to her. At first I mixed up her with [her older sister] Betty. Then I talked to my patient, Mrs. Friedman, I says, Look, Who is this nice lady? I would like to go out with her. She says, Oh, no, she is married, she has children, and I say, That's so? She says, Don't worry, I have another daughter for you. OK, I would like to see her. And then I said to Mommy, I got in touch with her; I saw her once in an elevator in a beret, I saw her in an elevator and I liked her: the pink cheeks with the nice hat, and I wanted. Then, she says, No, I have a date; I cannot go out with you. And I got so mad, I says, OK—I didn't tell it to her, but, so you want to go out with somebody else, OK with me. And I didn't intend to even to talk to her because she couldn't break a date with another fellow, you know. To make the story short, somehow we were talking, talking, till she got me in her net and I said, OK, we'll get married, what's the sense. I don't regret. She's a nice girl when she wants to be and when she doesn't want to be you have to watch out. But otherwise in general it's OK; I am grateful and thankful. I have two nice, good children, Meri-Jane is wonderful, and Burt, too, and I think they somehow, protesting and disagreeing, took the parents' advice and they are going on the right track. I hope so, and everything will be dandy.

In conclusion, make a résumé of all this what I said. Life was tough. I had a lot of odds against me. I was stubborn and decided to finish medicine, and to go through with that. I think the fact that I was a doctor saved my life several times, and I pursued in spite of antisemitism, in spite of the difficulties, and demands which we had. I thank God I was able to finish, I'm able to continue in the medical profession, and I'm really in this respect happy.

That is the story of my life, in short, with not too many details. The life in ghetto and concentration camp, it is one package of events which pertains to myself. I want to say that a lot of other people suffered much more than I, and a lot of people went through with more horrors, with more tragedies, and sicknesses they developed as a consequence of the persecution. I can tell you that the Germans is a very covert people, they were—if you kept your hands in the pocket they thought you have a gun, and they told you immediately, pick up the hands up. The whole Nazi movement was led by a maniac, psychopath, who somehow was able to hypnotize masses, promising them a lot of things, and his idea was, as he said in *Mein Kampf*, not only [to] conquer territories; he wanted to get rid, not only of the Jews, he wanted to get rid of a lot of other nations and rule, and the Germans, as he said, would work two or three hours and the others will be slaves for him. We should be grateful to the wisdom of Roosevelt and the valor and the perseverance of the Russian people and Russian army, who were able in spite of the odds against them, with the help of the terrible winter in Russia, to reel the army of the Germans backwards, and to establish a relative peace.[30] I only hope and pray that in spite of the fact, [that] there is liberty in America, Americans would understand there is limit to the liberty, there is a limit to hate propaganda, one part of the population against another. I am talking here about the

---

30. In the NYPL interview Eli is more critical of Roosevelt and the Allies, as appears in a part of the transcript he had not yet edited (although he placed brief editorial revisions on the previous page): "After coming to America and there were a few articles in the press pointing out to the fact that Jews could have been saved to a certain degree, if Roosevelt wasn't stubborn about—and there was a history about people who were going from port to port and they came to America and they wouldn't let them in [. . .]. I feel the Second World War, the end, in the beginning of 1945, and even I would say the end of '44 when the Russians pushed out quite a lot of Germans from the territories—they were more concerned with political advantages and strategic considerations than with saving the Jews from destruction. Auschwitz could have been liberated in 1944 . . . Dachau, the (whole) concentration camps—Buchenwald and others [. . .] could have been saved if they would decide to push out the Germans as soon as possible and after that come to some political consideration or—what would we say? . . . or dividing the European continent among themselves, to do it after. I think the procrastination, the slowness, the complete callous disregard for human life is to blame on the Allies. But they had to go according to the book, according to the previously arranged plan, and occupy Europe. A lot of people could have been saved" (Rochelson, NYPL 42–43).

Nazi movement, and neo-Nazi, not only in Europe but also in America, and I still hope that the Civil Liberties Union[31] will have the sense and the guts and the brains to distinguish where freedom ends and where freedom starts, and not to allow to poison people against other populations. Thank you very much.

---

31. "In 1978, the American Civil Liberties Union (ACLU) took a controversial stand for free speech by defending a neo-Nazi group that wanted to march through the Chicago suburb of Skokie, where many Holocaust survivors lived. [. . .] Although the ACLU prevailed in its free speech arguments, the neo-Nazi group never marched through Skokie, instead agreeing to stage a rally at Federal Plaza in downtown Chicago" ("ACLU History"). These events were prominent in the minds of Holocaust survivors in the late 1970s.

Bibliography

"The 131 Boys of Kovno." *Kovno Stories.* www.eilatgordinlevitan.com/kovno/kovno_pages/kovno_stories_131.html.

"ACLU History: Taking a Stand for Free Speech in Skokie." American Civil Liberties Union. www.aclu.org/free-speech/aclu-history-taking-stand-free-speech-skokie.

Aderet, Ofer. "Glorifying a Nazi Collaborator in Lithuania." *Haaretz*, English edition. May 15, 2012. www.haaretz.com/news/features/glorifying-a-nazi-collaborator-in-lithuania-1.430508.

Aleksiun, Natalia. "Christian Corpses for Christians! Dissecting the Anti-Semitism behind the Cadaver Affair of the Second Polish Republic." *Eastern European Politics and Societies.* Sage Publications 10.1177/0888325411398913, http://eeps.sagepub.com hosted at http://online.sagepub.com. 2011.

———. Conversation with author. Tel Aviv, Israel. June 17, 2013.

———. "Jewish Students and Christian Corpses in Interwar Poland: Playing with the language of Blood Libel." *Jewish History* 26, no. 3/4 (2012): 327–42. Accessed online through *JStor.*

"Annexation of the Baltic States." *World War II Database.* http://ww2db.com/battle_spec.php?battle_id=283.

Bankier, David. *Expulsion and Extermination: Holocaust Testimonials from Provincial Lithuania.* Jerusalem: Yad Vashem, 2011.

Beizer, Michael. "OZE." *YIVO Encyclopedia of Jews in Eastern Europe.* www.yivoencyclopedia.org/article.aspx/OZE.

Berkowits, Laszlo, with Robert W. Kenny. *The Boy Who Lost his Birthday: A Memoir of Loss, Survival, and Triumph.* Ed. Jody I. Franklin. Lanham, MD: Hamilton Books, 2008.

Berger, Frances "Fruma" Gulkowich, and Murray "Motke" Berger. *With Courage Shall We Fight: The Memoirs and Poetry of Holocaust Resistance Fighters*. Ed. Ralph S. Berger and Albert S. Berger. Margate, NJ: ComteQ, 2010.

Bernstein, Israel. Report to HIAS, New York, and HICEM, Paris, from Vilnius, March 22, 1940. YIVO MKM 16.7, RG 245.5, folder 92. Archival typescript. YIVO Institute for Jewish Research, New York.

Bloch, Eric M. "Rochelson Family History." Unpublished. 194 pp. Family document, circulated by Eric M. Bloch, Milwaukee.

Boder, David P., PhD. *Topical Autobiographies of Displaced People: Recorded Verbatim in Displaced Persons Camps with a psychological and anthropological analysis*. 1951. Typescripts of English translations accessed at Yad Vashem, June 2013. Also available via *Voices of the Holocaust Project*. http://voices.iit.edu/david_boder.

Boehling, Rebecca, and Uta Larkey. *Life and Loss in the Shadow of the Holocaust: A Jewish Family's Untold Story*. Cambridge, UK: Cambridge University Press, 2011.

Brent, Jonathan, and Vladimir P. Naumov. *Stalin's Last Crime: The Plot Against the Jewish Doctors 1948–1953*. New York: Harper Collins, 2003.

Budnitskii, Oleg. "The Jews in Rostov-on-Don in 1918–1919." *Jews and Jewish Topics in the Soviet Union and Eastern Europe* 19 (1992): 16–29.

The Clandestine History of the Kovno Jewish Ghetto Police. By anonymous members of the Kovno Ghetto Jewish Police. Trans. and ed. Samuel Schalkowsky. Introduction by Samuel D. Kassow. Bloomington: Indiana University Press, in association with the United States Holocaust Memorial Museum, Washington, DC. 2014.

Clevs, Arnold. Interview 1202. Visual History Archive. USC Shoah Foundation Institute. Accessed online at the United States Holocaust Memorial Museum on January 24, 2017.

Codikow, Ralph. Oral History interview. United States Holocaust Memorial Museum. Accession Number: 1990.416.1. RG Number: RG-50.030*0055. collections.ushmm.org.

Cohen, Beth B. "Face to Face: American Jews and Holocaust Survivors," 1946–54. Patt and Berkowitz, 136–66.

Cohen, Sharon Kangisser. *Testimony and Time: Holocaust Survivors Remember*. Jerusalem: Yad Vashem, 2014.

Czech, Danuta. *Auschwitz Chronicle, 1939–1945*. Translated from the Polish. New York: Holt, 1990.

"DP Camps in Germany." Archival documents in the YIVO archives, YIVO Institute for Jewish Research, Center for Jewish History, New York. File IDs RG 294.2 and MK 483. Individual files are indicated in footnotes.

Eilati, Shalom. Conversations, 2009–2013.

———. *Crossing the River*. Translated from the Hebrew by Vern Lenz. Tuscaloosa: University of Alabama Press, 2008.

Elkes, Joel. *Dr. Elkhanan Elkes of the Kovno Ghetto: A Son's Holocaust Memoir*. London: Vale, 1997; Brewster, MA: Paraclete Press, 1999.

Epstein, Helen. *Children of the Holocaust: Conversations with Sons and Daughters of Survivors*. New York: Putnam, 1979.

"Evidence of Jewish Escapees From the Ninth Fort in Kovno on the Burning of the Bodies." Shoah Resource Center, http://www.yadvashem.org. Accessed June 24, 2015.

Faitelson, Alex. *The Truth and Nothing but the Truth: Jewish Resistance in Lithuania*. Trans. Ethel Broido. Jerusalem: Gefen, 2006. Accessed online at Google Books.

"Fun Unzer Bilder-Galerje." *Landsberger Lager-Cajtung*, 1.12 (December 31, 1945): 6. Accessed online via Leo Baeck Institute digitized holdings, https://archive.org/details/landsbergerlager1220unse_ead.

Gartner, Lloyd P. "The Great Jewish Migration 1881–1914: Myths and Realities." Kaplan Centre Papers. Cape Town: University of Cape Town, 1984. Rpt. in Gartner, *American and British Jews in the Age of the Great Migration*. London: Vallentine Mitchell, 2009.

Gay, Ruth. *Safe Among the Germans: Liberated Jews After World War II*. New Haven: Yale University Press, 2002.

Germany: A Memorial. List of National Socialist Camps and Detention Sites, 1933–1945. "List of places: Concentration camps and outlying camps: Concentration camp Kaunas." www.deutschland-ein-denkmal.de/.

Gilbert, Martin. *The Holocaust: A History of the Jews of Europe During the Second World War*. New York: Henry Holt, 1985. Accessed online at Google Books.

Ginaite-Rubinson, Sara. *Resistance and Survival: The Jewish Community in Kaunas 1941–1944*. Trans. from the Lithuanian by Karla Gruodyte and Darius Ross. Oakville, ON: Mosaic Press, 2011.

Godin, Nesse. Interview 7072. Visual History Archive. USC Shoah Foundation Institute. Accessed online at the United States Holocaust Memorial Museum, March 2017.

Goldstein-Golden, Lazar. *From Ghetto Kovno to Dachau.* Ed. Berl Kagan. New York: Esther Goldstein, 1985.

Gordon, Rachel. Oral History interview. Accession Number: 1999.A.0122.764. RG Number: RG-50.477*0764. The United States Holocaust Memorial Museum, acquired from Jewish Family and Children's Services of San Francisco, the Peninsula, Marin and Sonoma Counties, and used with their permission. Accessed online at the USHMM, January 24, 2017.

Greenbaum, Masha. *The Jews of Lithuania: A History of a Remarkable Community, 1316–1945.* Jerusalem: Gefen, 1995.

Greene, Joshua M., and Shiva Kumar, eds., in consultation with Joanne Weiner Rudof. *Witness: Voices from the Holocaust.* In association with the Fortunoff Video Archive for Holocaust Testimonies, Yale University. New York: Free Press, 2000.

Griliches, Josef. Interviews: May 31, 2011, October 2012, and conversations with author on other occasions.

Grossmann, Atina. *Jews, Germans, and Allies: Close Encounters in Occupied Germany.* Princeton: Princeton University Press, 2007.

Gutman, Ephraim. Interview translated from German and Yiddish into English, in Boder, *Topical Autobiographies.* Chapter IX. Spools 124, 125-A. Second Typing. The entire translated interview is also available in *Voices of the Holocaust,* http://voices.iit.edu/interview?doc=gutmanE&display=gutmanE_en.

Heymont, Major Irving. *Among the Survivors of the Holocaust—1945: The Landsberg DP Camp Letters of Major Irving Heymont, United States Army.* Cincinnati: American Jewish Archives, 1982.

"HIAS: Welcome the Stranger. Protect the Refugee." https://www.hias.org/.

HIAS-HICEM Archives, Series II, France I. YIVO Institute for Jewish Research, Center for Jewish History, New York. Individual files are indicated in footnotes, and larger files elsewhere in this list.

"HICEM." Shoah Resource Center, http://www.yadvashem.org.

Hilliard, Robert L., PhD. *Surviving the Americans: The Continued Struggle of the Jews After Liberation.* New York: Seven Stories Press, 1997.

Hirsch, Marianne. *The Generation of Postmemory: Writing and Visual Culture After the Holocaust.* New York: Columbia University Press, 2012.

"The History of ORT: Jacob Oleiski, 1901–1981." http://old.ort.spb.ru/history/emg/olei.htm.

Hoffman, Eva. *After Such Knowledge: Memory, History, and the Legacy of the Holocaust.* New York: Public Affairs, 2004.

"The Holocaust Timeline." *About.com 20th Century History*. http://history1900s .about.com/library/holocaust/bltimeline3.htm.

"The Holocaust: Japan & the Jews." *Jewish Virtual Library*. http://www .jewishvirtuallibrary.org/japan-and-the-jews-during-the-holocaust.

"The Influenza Pandemic of 1918." https://virus.stanford.edu/uda.

Kassow, Samuel D. "Inside the Kovno Ghetto." Introduction to *The Clandestine History of the Kovno Jewish Ghetto Police*. By anonymous members of the Kovno Ghetto Jewish Police. Trans. and ed. Samuel Schalkowsky. Blooming- ton: Indiana University Press, in association with the United States Holocaust Memorial Museum, Washington, DC, 2014.

"Kaunas/Kovno." *The Yad Vashem Encyclopedia of the Ghettos During the Holo- caust*. Editor-in-chief Guy Miron, co-editor Shlomit Shulhani. Vol. 1, A–M. 290–99.

Kobrin, Rebecca. "Beyond the Myths of Mobility and Altruism: Jewish Immi- grant Professionals and Jewish Social Welfare Agencies in New York City, 1945–1954." *A Jewish Feminine Mystique?: Jewish Women in Postwar America*. Ed. Hasia R. Diner, Shira Kohn, and Rachel Kranson. New Brunswick: Rut- gers University Press, 2010. 105–25.

Krakinowski, Nissan. Interviews and conversations with the author. New York, NY, October 24, 2010; Port Washington, NY, June 1, 2011.

———. Interview 12197. Visual History Archive. USC Shoah Foundation Insti- tute. Accessed online at the United States Holocaust Memorial Museum on January 25, 2017.

Kravetz Moshe. "Moshe Kravetz Story." *Kovno Stories*. www.eilatgordinlevitan .com/kovno/kovno_pages/kovno_stories_m_kravetz.html.

———. Personal interview with the author, Nurit Nahmani serving as translator. Haifa, Israel. June 11, 2013.

Langer, Lawrence L. *Holocaust Testimonies: The Ruins of Memory*. New Haven: Yale University Press, 1991.

Levin, Dov. "Kaunas." YIVO Encyclopedia of Jews in Eastern Europe. www .yivoencyclopedia.org/article.aspx/Kaunas.

———. "Kulautuva." *Pinkas Hakehillot Lita: Encyclopedia of Jewish Communities, Lithuania*, Ed. Dov Levin. Asst. ed., Josef Rosin. Jerusalem: Yad Vashem. Translation by Shimon Joffe. www.jewishgen.org/yizkor/pinkas_lita/lit _00595b.html.

———. *The Litvaks: A Short History of the Jews of Lithuania*. Jerusalem: Yad Vashem, 2000.

Levitan, Eilat Gordon. "The 131 Boys from Kovno." http://www
.eilatgordinlevitan.com/kovno/kovno_pages/kovno_stories_131.html.

Lewin, Jacob. Interview 30148. Visual History Archive. USC Shoah Foundation
Institute. Accessed online at the United States Holocaust Memorial Museum
on January 24, 2017.

Lichtblau, Eric. "Surviving the Nazis, Only to Be Jailed by America." *New York Times.*
Sunday Review. February 7, 2015. https://www.nytimes.com/2015/02/08/sunday
-review/surviving-the-nazis-only-to-be-jailed-by-america.html?mcubz=1.

Liekis, Šarūnas. *1939: The Year that Changed Everything in Lithuania's History.*
On the Boundary of Two Worlds: Identity, Freedom, and the Moral Imagina-
tion in the Baltics, 20. Amsterdam and New York: Rodopi, 2010.

"Lost Capitol Hill: Casualty Hospital." *The Hill is Home.* www.thehillishome
.com/2010/09/lost-capitol-hill-casualty-hospital.

Lowe, Keith. *Savage Continent: Europe in the Aftermath of World War II.* New
York: St. Martin's, 2012.

Lubinski, Kurt. "*Sie haben es mitangesehen*" ["You Have Witnessed It"]. *Aufbau/
Reconstruction: An American Weekly Published in New York.* December 27,
1946: 1–2.

Lurie, Sol (Shaya). Oral History interview. United States Holocaust Memorial
Museum. Accession Number: 1999.A.0039. RG Number: RG-50.030*0141.
collections.ushmm.org.

———. Telephone conversation with author, October 4, 2013.

Marcus, Audrey Friedman, and Rena Krasno. "Holocaust Refugee in Shanghai."
The Jewish Magazine. January 2010. www.jewishmag.com/140mag/holocaust
_refugee_shanghai/holocaust_refugee_shanghai.htm.

Mendelsohn, Daniel. *The Lost: A Search for Six of Six Million.* New York: Harper-
Collins. 2006.

"Messages scrawled by Jewish prisoners on a wall inside Fort IX, shortly before
their execution." Explanatory caption for photo #81146. Photo Archives,
United States Holocaust Memorial Museum. https://collections.ushmm.org/
search/catalog/pa11922.

Mishell, William M. *Kaddish for Kovno: Life and Death in a Lithuanian Ghetto,
1941–44.* Jerusalem: Gefen, 1998.

Oleiski, Jacob. Interview translated from Yiddish into English, in Boder, *Topical
Autobiographies.* Chapter XXX. Spools 54, 209. Second Typing. The English
translation is also available in *Voices of the Holocaust,* http://voices.iit.edu/
interview?doc=oleiskiJ&display=oleiskiJ_en.

"OTASCO." *Oklahoma Historical Society's Encyclopedia of Oklahoma History and Culture*. http://digital.library.okstate.edu/encyclopedia/entries/O/OT004.html.

Patt, Avinoam, and Michael Berkowitz, eds. *"We Are Here": New Approaches to Jewish Displaced Persons in Postwar Germany*. Detroit: Wayne State University Press. 2010.

Prichep, Deena. "The Gefilte Fish Line: A Sweet and Salty History of Jewish Identity." *Food History & Culture*, National Public Radio (NPR). September 24, 2014. http://www.npr.org/sections/thesalt/2014/09/24/351185646/the-gefilte-fish-line-a-sweet-and-salty-history-of-jewish-identity.

Rifkind, Simon H. Report to the Chief of Staff, Headquarters, U.S. Forces, European Theater, Office of Military Government (U. S. Zone). UNRRA file S-0402-2-7. Archival typescript. UNRRA archives, New York.

Rochelson, Burton. "An Old Fashioned Doctor." *Narrateur: Reflections on Caring*. Hofstra Northwell School of Medicine Art & Literary Review 5 (2016): 66–68.

Rochelson, Dr. E. "Kovner Yidn dermonen zeyere kedoshim haynt, tzu dem finften yortseit" ["Kovner Jews remember their Kedoshim today, on the fifth yahrzeit"]. *Der Tog* [*The Day*]. October 28, 1946: 1.

Rochelson, Eli G. "Family Interview." Recording of an interview with Eli G. Rochelson, conducted by Burton L. Rochelson, mid-1970s, transcribed by Meri-Jane Rochelson. Family collection.

———. Letter to International Tracing Service, Arolsen, Germany. June 10, 1950. Copy of typescript. Family collection. [Order of listing changed.]

———. NYPL. Recording of an interview with Eli G. Rochelson, conducted by Marsha Rozenblit, July 28, 1974, transcribed by the American Jewish Committee [NYPL interview]. New York: American Jewish Committee, 1974. Audio cassettes, Jewish Division, New York Public Library. Typescript of transcript, with revisions by Eli G. Rochelson, in personal library of author.

———. Tape 1. Recording of an interview with Eli G. Rochelson, conducted by Burton L. Rochelson, mid-1970s. Family collection.

Rochelson, Eli. Recording of an interview with Eli G. Rochelson, conducted by Marsha Rozenblit, July 28, 1974, transcribed by the American Jewish Committee [NYPL interview]. New York: American Jewish Committee, 1974. Audio cassettes, Jewish Division, New York Public Library. Typescript of transcript, with revisions by Eli G. Rochelson, in personal library of author.

———. Letter to International Tracing Service, Arolsen, Germany. June 10, 1950. Copy of typescript. Family collection.

Rosenfeld, Alvin H. *A Double Dying: Reflections on Holocaust Literature*. Bloomington: Indiana University Press, 1980; paperback edition 1988.

Rosin, Josef. "Kaunas (cont.)." *Pinkas Hakehillot Lita: Encyclopedia of Jewish Communities, Lithuania*. Ed. Prof. Dov Levin. Asst. ed. Josef Rosin. Jerusalem: Yad Vashem. Translation at www.jewishgen.org/yizkor/pinkas_lita/lit_00542.html.

——. "Naishtot (Kudirkos Naumiestis)." English edited by Fania Hilelson-Jivotovsky. http://kehilalinks.jewishgen.org/naishtot/naishtot1.html.

——. "Shaki (Sakiai)." English edited by Sarah and Mordechai Kopfstein. http://kehilalinks.jewishgen.org/shaki/shaki1.html.

Rothstein, Edward. "Playing Cat and Mouse with Searing History." Exhibition Review of the Anne Frank permanent exhibit at the Museum of Tolerance, Los Angeles. *New York Times* October 14, 2013: C1, C5.

Silber, Sharon Mary. "Joseph Silber (1915–2007)." Unpublished biographical essay by Dr. Joseph Silber's daughter. Sent to author via e-mail attachment, September 14, 2017.

Smith, W. B. Report on Conditions at Displaced Person Center in Lansberg [*sic*] to Lt. Gen. Frederick E. Morgan, Chief, European Regional Office, UNRRA. December 7, 1945. UNRRA file S-0425-43-6. Archival typescript. UNRRA archives, New York.

"Soviet Seizes Jewish-owned Brewery." *Jewish Telegraphic Agency* October 20, 1940. http://www.jta.org/1940/10/20/archive/soviet-seizes-jewish-owned-brewery.

Spiegelman, Art. *Maus*. Vols. 1 and 2. New York: Pantheon, 1986, 1991.

Srole, Dr. Lee. Letter of resignation in protest against unhealthy conditions in Landsberg DP Camp. December 5, 1945. UNRRA file S-0425-43-6. Archival typescript. UNRRA Archives, New York.

Stevens, Arthur Albert. *A Manual of the Practice of Medicine*. Philadelphia: W. B. Saunders, 1898. Accessed online at Google Books.

"The Story of the S. S. Marine Flasher." http://thekesslers.com/family/tibor/Marine_Flasher.html.

Teirstein, Alvin S., MD. "In Memoriam: Coleman B. Rabin, MD." *American Journal of Industrial Medicine* 22 (1992): 1–31. Accessed online.

Tory, Avraham. *Surviving the Holocaust: The Kovno Ghetto Diary*. Ed. Martin Gilbert. Textual and historical notes by Dina Porat. Trans. Jerzy Michalowicz. Cambridge, MA: Harvard University Press, 1990. Print.

Trachtenberg, Martin, and Minna Davis. "Breaking Silence: Serving Children of Holocaust Survivors." *Journal of Jewish Communal Service* 54.4

(1978). Accessed online via the Berman Jewish Policy Archive, Stanford University.

United States Holocaust Memorial Museum (USHMM). Digital assets and archives. www.ushmm.org.

———. "Einsatzgruppen." *Holocaust Encyclopedia*. www.ushmm.org/wlc/en/article.php?ModuleId=10005130.

———. *Hidden History of the Kovno Ghetto*. Boston: Bulfinch, 1997.

———. "Kovno." *Holocaust Encyclopedia*. www.ushmm.org/wlc/en/article.php?ModuleId=10005174.

———. "Stutthof." *Holocaust Encyclopedia*. www.ushmm.org/wlc/en/article.php?ModuleId=10005197.

VICTORIA discussion list archives, post of November 19, 2013. https://list.indiana.edu/sympa/arc/victoria/2013–11/msg00096.

"Volfas Engelman." Wikipedia.

Waltzer, Kenneth. "Kovno Boys: A Story of Survival at Auschwitz, Buchenwald, and Mauthausen." Paper prepared for 37th Annual Scholars Conference on the Holocaust hosted by the Samuel Rosenthal Center for Judaic Studies, March 11–13, 2007. Case Western Reserve University, Cleveland, Ohio. Typescript provided to author by Kenneth Waltzer.

"Who Was Shut Out?: Immigration Quotas," 1925–1927. *History Matters: The U. S. Survey Course on the Web*. http://historymatters.gmu.edu/d/5078/.

Wise, Rachel. Interview 36122. Visual History Archive. USC Shoah Foundation Institute. Accessed online at the United States Holocaust Memorial Museum, March 2017.

Yelin, Meir, and D. Gelpernas [Gelpern]. *Partizaner fun Kaunaser geto* [*Partisans of the Kovno Ghetto*]. Moscow: Emes, 1948.

Young, James E. "Toward a Received History of the Holocaust." *History and Theory* 36, no. 4 (1997): 21–43. Accessed online through *JStor*.

Zalkin, Mordechai. "Antisemitism in Lithuania." *Antisemitism in Eastern Europe: History and Present in Comparison*. Ed. Hans-Christian Petersen and Samuel Salzborn. Frankfurt am Main: Peter Lang, 2010. 135–70.

Zisman, Leo. Interview 11929. Visual History Archive. USC Shoah Foundation Institute. Accessed online at the United States Holocaust Memorial Museum, January 25, 2017.

Index

THIS INDEX COVERS the main narrative from the introduction to the epilogue, as well as appendix F, the family interview transcript. It does not cover any other appendices or the preface and acknowledgments, or the chronology. I index the names of authors and translators when they appear in the narrative or explanatory notes, but not when only in citations or parentheses. City and town names are identified by the state or country in which they are currently located. The title "Dr." appears with a name when it is used in the narrative. Italicized page numbers indicate images. Finally, I index the names—often only the surnames—of people Eli Rochelson mentions in his interviews. These may be of interest to families searching for information.—MJR

Meri-Jane Rochelson and Burton L. Rochelson, January 2015. Family collection.

Meri-Jane Rochelson, PhD, is professor emerita of English at Florida International University. She is the author of *A Jew in the Public Arena: The Career of Israel Zangwill* (Wayne State University Press, 2008), editor of Zangwill's 1908 play *The Melting-Pot* (Broadview, 2018) and his 1892 novel *Children of the Ghetto* (Wayne State University Press, 1998), and co-editor of *Transforming Genres: New Approaches to British Fiction of the 1890s* (Palgrave-St. Martin's, 1994).

Burton L. Rochelson, MD, is professor of Obstetrics and Gynecology at the Donald and Barbara Zucker School of Medicine at Hofstra-Northwell. He has published many articles on high risk pregnancies, as well as the reflective essay "An Old-Fashioned Doctor." He is the author of a book and lyrics for a musical play, *The Rule of Disorder*.